THE ANCESTRAL ROOF

CLARKE, IRWIN & COMPANY LIMITED

TORONTO

VANCOUVER

THE ANCESTRAL ROOF

DOMESTIC ARCHITECTURE OF UPPER CANADA

BY MARION MACRAE IN CONSTANT CONSULTATION WITH, AND SOMETIMES
IN SPITE OF ANTHONY ADAMSON, WHO WROTE THE FIRST WORD AND THE
LAST WORD AND MADE THE DRAWINGS. PHOTOGRAPHS ARE BY PAGE TOLES

*To the gentlewomen of Upper Canada in the person of
a descendant, Augusta Bonnycastle Adamson*

by CLARKE, IRWIN & COMPANY LIMITED
ISBN 0-7720-0023-9
5 6 7 8 RCS 76 75 74 73 72
Printed in Canada

The first word

Except for very sparse settlement adjacent to old French and British forts and trading-posts and for the occasional isolated cabin of a voyageur or independent fur-trader, that part of Canada which is now Ontario was still complete wilderness in 1784. In this year began the organized settlement of the displaced Empire Loyalists who had remained faithful to the British Crown during the American Revolution. The story told here is of the ancestry of the domestic buildings of Ontario during the eighty-three years from that momentous date until 1867 when four colonies of British North America confederated to become the Dominion of Canada. This ancestry may not exhibit to the world great examples of domestic architecture but, considered either in the light of history or in the forest surroundings of their time, the fact that so many houses of some worth came to be built at all in those first eighty-three years is a great achievement.

On May 16, 1823, the residents of Kingston petitioned the Government of Upper Canada to preserve the ancient, presumably French, buildings of that city. Nothing was done. The French heritage has vanished. There may be walls of houses in the Windsor area from pre-Loyalist times but any evidence of French influence on the design of Ontario houses is curiously lacking except in the Ottawa area. Style in domestic architecture in Ontario remains a product of competing British and American influences. Then, the rapid urbanization of the great centres of population in this century, and the frequent devastating fires of fifty and a hundred years ago have left very few early buildings in Toronto and in a number of other cities which are now important twentieth-century centres. During the writing of this book, approximately one house in eleven which we found interesting or of architectural merit has been either pulled down, burned or so altered as now to lack interest or merit. Our architectural heritage is vanishing, and not slowly. It is in need of understanding and of protection.

For protecting our building heritage, credit must be given to the Ontario Government and to the Ontario Conservation Authorities, particularly for their work of restoration at Upper Canada Village, Morrisburg, and at Pioneer Village, Toronto. The Historic Sites Branch of the Ontario Department of Travel and Publicity under Mr. Donald McOuat has also shown a growing interest in architecture. Of immense importance is the federal government's somewhat tardy beginning of an inventory of Canadian buildings. One of its three pilot projects is at Niagara-on-the-Lake under the direction of Mr. Jack Herbert and his assistant Mr. J. E. H. Richardson of the Historic Sites and Monuments Branch of the Canadian Department of Northern Affairs. Credit is also due to the City of Kingston for its own architectural inventory and to many small municipalities and historical societies which have saved and maintain good local buildings. Finally, respect is due to the Architectural Conservancy of Ontario, a private society which for thirty years has been trying to prod the public conscience to recognize that buildings can of themselves be notable even though General Brock, Sir John A. Macdonald or the Minister of Fisheries under LaFontaine never slept there.

This book may have received its first inspiration in the offices of Dr. Weller and Dr. Roos of the University of Illinois when they encouraged Miss Marion MacRae to begin a degree thesis on the social and architectural history of the early settled area of the upper St. Lawrence. Instead of a thesis, a book for publication came to be written. It is the product of an association formed during the assembling and restoration of the buildings which now form Upper Canada Village on the St. Lawrence near Morrisburg.

We both wish to acknowledge with respect the work of a number of persons, in particular of Colonel Meredith of Ottawa for the collection of his own early photographs now in the Public Archives of Canada, of Mr. C. S. Buck for his thesis on early buildings now in the Library of the University of Western Ontario, and most especially we want to acknowledge the work of Dr. Eric Ross Arthur, the author of the only published monographs on early Ontario buildings which include: *The Early Buildings of Ontario* and *Small Houses of the Eighteenth and Nineteenth Centuries in Ontario.* The history sections in the Ontario Conservation Reports by Mr. Verschoyle Blake have been of value to us. The measured drawings made by students in architecture at the University of Toronto and now in the Public Archives of Ontario, though often inaccurate, are a massive repository of information.

Others have contributed by their work to the sum of knowledge on the province's architectural history. It is impossible to enumerate them all but Mrs. William Angus of Kingston, Mr. Allan Douglas of Windsor, Mr. Peter Aykroyd, Mr. Courtney Bond, Mr. Edward Fancott, all of Ottawa, Professor William Goulding, Mr. Albert Colucci, Miss Ruth Home, Mr. John I. Rempel, Colonel John McInnes, Mr. B. N. Simpson, Jr., Mr. Peter Stokes, all of Toronto, Mrs. Jeanne Minhinnick of Picton, Mr. Richard Dumbrille of Maitland, Mrs. R. H. Neil of Thornhill, Mrs. Gwen Metcalfe and Mrs. Robert Simmons of Hamilton, Mr. Allan Gowans of the University of Delaware and Mr. and Mrs. Ronald Way of Kingston have all made important contributions in the special field of architectural history or in historic restoration.

The authors and the photographer wish to express their personal thanks to all the householders, their families and their dogs who have borne with intrusion and inquisition, who have had their chairs stood on, their meals interrupted and have been startled by flashbulbs. They are far too numerous to name, but we should like particularly to express our gratitude for the kindnesses extended to us by the late Miss Barbara Jones of Prescott, the late Mr. Cyril Inderwick of Perth, and the late Major Drew

Thompson of Cayuga. We should like personally to thank Miss Marjorie Ball of Niagara-on-the-Lake, Mr. W. E. Elliot of Goderich, Miss Mary Mack of Cornwall and Mr. Orlo Miller of London for particular local assistance. We also wish to express our thanks to Their Excellencies, General and Mrs. Georges Vanier for allowing us to examine Rideau Hall.

The Canada Council has given the publishers a grant of two thousand dollars toward the cost of publication. For this we are very grateful.

A book on early Ontario architecture is long overdue. The authors of this book make claim neither for originality nor for genius. They hope that others will come, fill in the gaps, specialize and correct the errors. They have naturally tried to avoid errors but the history of Ontario architecture lacks documentation. Long hours have been spent in libraries, museums and public archives, usually with negative results. Not a few hours have been spent listening to oral tradition which the buildings themselves show to be patently false. In a first book on any subject, certain matters have to be neglected. We have chosen to ignore methods of construction and not to spend time in the research necessary to illustrate the works of particular architects. Nor have we been able to give equal geographic representation of the buildings but have used the ones which seemed to us to be the most appropriate architecturally for the story told. We regret that some cities, such as London, may therefore seem to be ignored.

The scale of plans and elevations in the first six chapters is 1 inch to 20 feet. The scale for these in the Last Word is 1 inch to 30 feet. The numbers interspersed throughout the text refer to the accompanying illustrations of the buildings.

People search libraries, not streets and roads, for local history. The purpose of this book is to encourage our readers to see, and having seen, to understand.

Toronto
October 15, 1963   ANTHONY ADAMSON

Contents

1. The Georgian entrance door, six sturdy fielded panels in a strong frame, carried a brass knocker and hinges but no other exterior hardware, since the entrance door of a Georgian gentleman's home was always opened from within. When the door-knob on this house was installed later, the trim had to be cut away. The White House, Williamstown, 1805.

2

1
The last Georgians

"All houses wherein men have lived and died are haunted houses." Longfellow's romantic statement conjures up visions of a band of guardian spirits, the shades of the owners and builders. An architectural survey raises spectres of another kind.

The early houses of Ontario appear to be haunted by several curious myths. Should you approach the owner of an "old" house and, after expressing interest in its beauty or its age, ask for further information, you are likely to hear about one or all of these myths. The most pervasive is that of bricks imported from England. The second is that the granary or barn which has narrow air vents in its heavy masonry was used as a fort against "the Indians." The third concerns the aperture in the cellar wall, now possibly blocked, which gave access to an outside cellarway. One is solemnly assured, for reasons which it is difficult to fathom, that this was the way "they brought in the horses." The peculiar pioneer activity which gave rise to this legend is veiled in the mists of time. The door in question is not infrequently located close to the vast cooking fireplace and oven which mark the pioneer cellar kitchen. The vision of a busy housewife happily surrounded by cooking-pots, small children and horses is astonishing. Doubtless research will provide the answer.

All of these myths are interesting in themselves but they pale to insignificance before the spectre of the date. Do not infer that a date will not be supplied you. It will be given gladly. It will be given in all sincerity and innocence. It will be wrong. In eight out of ten cases, the date when land was acquired by Crown deed is pronounced to be the year in which the house, Georgian, Loyalist or Greek Revival, was built.

What then are the reliable sources of information? What is known of the Georgian houses of Upper Canada and of those who built them? Why were the last expressions of the Georgian style built along the north shore of the St. Lawrence River and Lakes Ontario and Erie? Archives, public libraries and private collections supply some contemporary documen-

3

tary evidence. Not all plans and building contracts were used for grocery lists or to stop the holes in broken windows. But by far the greatest amount of indisputable evidence is to be found in the houses themselves.

The reasons for the appearance of Georgian houses on the soil of Upper Canada at the close of the eighteenth century and the beginning of the nineteenth are not to be found by confining one's attention to Ontario. The Georgian style was not indigenous to this area nor was it an organic growth, a universal human response to the basic need for shelter. It was a physical expression of the cultural mental climate of the first settlers of Upper Canada and was present with them, in a wishful state, while they were still living in rude shelters and simple log houses. The settlers did not regard log dwellings as being in any sense architectural. Log construction remained in their eyes a temporary expedient, borrowed from the Scandinavian settlers of the Delaware. That anyone would ever consider log houses admirable to the point of wishing to preserve them was inconceivable to the eighteenth-century mind. So the old log house became a piggery or a cow byre, and a dwelling deemed more suitable to their aesthetic needs rose in its place.

At this point we must rejoin one of our myths — the date on the Crown land deed. Upper Canada was first settled to all intents and purposes in 1783 by the United Empire Loyalists. They came in from the refugee camps of Sorel and Oswego to the dense forests of the upper St. Lawrence and the lower Great Lakes regions with a few treasured family possessions salvaged from the wreckage of their lives. It is very doubtful if they would have been much comforted to know that the conflict through which they had just come was only the beginning of an upheaval which was to devastate Europe and which was to change for all time social and economic life as they had known it.

The Loyalists had lost all their worldly goods. And they had lost a war. But we must not fall into the error of supposing that they had accepted defeat or that they viewed the coming struggle for existence with dismay. Migration was in their blood. All Loyalists were but one or two generations removed from sturdy, adventurous, contentious souls whose convictions — religious, political or social — had moved them to cross the Atlantic. Some of those who had settled in the Thirteen Colonies had found life in the Old World too narrow for their expansive humanitarian views; some had found the same conditions too lax and worldly; others had been simply too crowded. One and all, they sought space and freedom

4

to indulge their aspirations. This led them to found other colonies as the old familiar pattern was established again along the Atlantic seaboard. Many of the Loyalists coming into Upper Canada were from the areas of second settlement in Vermont, western Pennsylvania and Upper New York State. Reared amidst stirring tales of such recent pioneering exploits, encouraged from childhood to believe in the inherent right to freedom of thought and convinced that the moral victory had been theirs, they crossed the barrier of the St. Lawrence and the Great Lakes with confidence in themselves and in the British Government.

The Loyalists have been the subject of a great quantity of writing, not all of which champions their cause. They have been hailed as paragons of all the virtues inherent in the word "loyalty." They have been decried as land-grabbing opportunists and reactionaries who saw place and privilege slipping from their grasp. It is quite likely that such a large group of people was not entirely composed of starry-eyed idealists. There were bound to be some who were selfish and proud and grasping. The same thing could be said of an equal number of their adversaries. The land-grabbing charge may, however, be dismissed as ridiculous. A brief glance at the Loyalist claims indicates that many lost more land than they acquired and that land already cleared and more conveniently situated and consequently much more valuable. The reasons which lead people to join a cause or to refrain from doing so are many, and seldom are they very clearly defined. This seems to have been the case with the Loyalists. All, save one group, were of Western European ancestry. The notable exception was a part of the Iroquoian Confederacy under Chief Joseph Brant which was to settle on the shores of the Grand and the St. Lawrence rivers.

The camps at Sorel and Oswego sheltered displaced North Americans whose ancestors had been English, Irish, Scots, Dutch, Palatine German and Huguenot French. In religion the Loyalists subscribed to all the various established episcopal churches, to Calvinism in all its forms or were Hebrews or agnostics. They obviously believed that freedom of religious choice was possible only under British rule. In the case of the Palatines this conviction was strengthened by the fact that the ruling house was, like themselves, German. The White Horse of Hanover they knew. The Eagle was a strange bird. Descendants of the Royalist Cavaliers, believing in the divine right of kings, saw in the head of the British state the lineal descendant of Alfred the Great, Edward I, Henry Tudor or Robert the Bruce. Distance probably enhanced this view, but it served to bring many useful people into Upper

Canada. Loyalists of Puritan inheritance, apprehensive of the anarchy latent in revolutions, followed the star of parliamentary government through the mud to little York.

All the Loyalists had enjoyed some measure of prosperity which made their way of life worth putting to the test of battle. It is also safe to assume that the migratory Loyalists had been the most outspoken of the conservative elements in the Thirteen Colonies. Whatever they were or were not, they were the last people who built in the continuity of the Georgian style of architecture.

Architecture is by definition the art or science of building. As an art form it is the one most fitted to express the totality of the aesthetic ideal of the age which produced it, representing as it does the creative talent of the architect, the contemporary requirements of society, and the personal preference of the individual client.

The Georgian style which entered Upper Canada in the mind's eye of the Loyalist was the cumulative style of Western European architecture as employed in Great Britain in the reigns of the first three Georges. In the British colonies of North America the style had varied a little as far as methods of construction were concerned. It had altered not at all in concept.

The Georgians were the heirs of the Renaissance. Never from the dawn of the nineteenth century would it again be possible for a truly Renaissance man, one who was completely conversant with all aspects of his world, to exist. The philosopher, the poet, the painter, the soldier, the man of business, each was now to have a separate profession. The age of specialization and piece work was at hand.

In 1453 the Eastern Roman Empire fell and the Renaissance officially began in Italy to replace the Gothic style. The Gothic world suffered from a split personality: it was at once functional and spiritual. In keeping with the spiritual emphasis ecclesiastical architecture was exciting, ceremonious and lovely. Great cathedrals soared heavenward, poem-prayers of faith and stone and stained glass. Convinced that life was but a trial and a preparation for the life to come, Western man was prepared to find his present habitation cheerless and to build beauty for the glory of God.

Secular Gothic architecture was starkly functional. Its greatest patrons were war lords who counted their wealth in men-at-arms. The master builder most to their taste was the one who could choose the best site for defence and erect the largest castle which would exploit the natural advantages of the land. Once these considerations were satisfied, it was

6

necessary to organize within the defensive walls the most efficient method of housing and maintaining a garrison. The yeoman and the serf engaged in unremitting toil or warfare from sunrise to sunset had neither the inclination nor the incentive to build anything other than a shelter in which to live. Lord and yeoman alike added rooms as they felt the need and were not distressed by the visual result. Until the time when the most important client placed the need for an efficient fireplace above that for an efficient drawbridge, domestic architecture lagged. The change in thought had to precede the change in design.

Just such a change took place as Western Europe rediscovered the wonders of antiquity. The change began in Italy, but the greatest influence on English style came through France. Therefore the descriptive term adopted was French (the Renaissance). The most startling revelation to the Gothic world was that the Greeks and Romans based all their thought, art and architecture on the surprising premise that the world was made for man's enjoyment. Another novel idea followed in its wake, that it might be more interesting to live in a Neo-Roman world of law, logic and aesthetics than to die gloriously and futilely for an obscure case in a feudal quarrel. Mohammedans were hammering at the gates of Europe with the sword and the Koran in one hand, carpets and fine glass in the other. The carpets won where the sword failed.

The lord of the "château sur la rivière" returning from a pilgrimage to Rome, which had also unaccountably taken him to Florence and Venice, now stepped with considerable distaste over rotting rushes and old bones on the great hall floor. He was likely to demand that the whole wretched mess be cleared away immediately, that the new turkey-work might be laid on the dais. Next, a pettish question as to how anyone might be expected to sleep in the same apartment with such an ill-favoured crew as the men-at-arms sent someone scurrying for the master builder. Artisans responded to the need. The castle fort became the great country house but a house yet defensive and amorphous in form. It was still a progression in functionalism.

The nascence of domestic architecture as such seems to be closely related to peace, trade and window glass. It rose phoenix-like from the breakup of the feudal system. As Western Europe became less and less a collection of heavily armed fortresses loosely bound into groups by loyalty to petty rulers and became national in outlook, trade and those engaged in it became more influential. It was often these people who employed a master builder, as he was still known, to plan a house for them. The wealthy merchants as a class were accustomed to innovations. Their fortunes were built on having sufficient vision and courage to lead the way. Those, and there were many, who had been brought up under the influence of the new addiction to classical learning were quite prepared to have a master builder compose with space in the Roman way, with solids and voids, as the painter composed with colour.

Human taste in the arts is capricious, wilful and very easily bored. Hardly had the Renaissance style penetrated to the fringes of Europe before it was outmoded at the source. The feeling of being the centre of the universe by now thoroughly assimilated, it seemed to the intelligentsia of the seventeenth century that the universe itself stood in need of a little improvement. If one were to think of social usage in terms of its mirror, the stage, the various ages assume a logical sequence. The Gothic period was a mystery play, the Renaissance a pageant. They were to be followed by the full-blown drama of the Baroque and its sophisticated refinement, the Rococo style.

Baroque is an encompassing term. It spans a great length of time and a vast sector of the earth's surface. It is the splendours of Versailles and the riotous golden scrollwork of an Austrian palace, whose walls dissolve with a fine flourish in the painted vapours of an Olympian ceiling. It is candlelight reflected in the polished serenity of walnut panelling in a Wren dining-room. It is the easy flight of a handsome stair in an old house in Virginia.

While the Baroque was burgeoning gloriously in France at the court of the Sun King, Louis XIV, its development in England had been delayed by such minor nuisances as the Plague, the Great Fire of London and the reign of James II. The high Baroque style became established in England in the hey-day of James' ample daughter and is known by that tolerant monarch's name as the Queen Anne style. Louis XIV enriched Versailles at the cultural expense of the land of France and reduced his nobles to the position of satellites, given immense privilege and denied responsibility. At the same time he unwittingly concentrated the Baroque style in one spot. The position across the Channel was very, very different. Steadily and quietly, all this time, more wealth had been accumulating in the hands of a greater number of people. But the Queen, either from lack of funds, lethargy, or common sense, made no attempt to add to the building programme of William III. It was the peers of England who built palaces and they were scattered over the length and breadth of the land. This did not mean that the landed gentry of England employed Vanbrugh nor did they aspire

8

to the palatial grandeur of Blenheim. It did mean that they had before their eyes examples of the latest style, and in their own area, workmen sufficiently skilled to have built such dwellings. Architects still studied in Italy when they could, but they were at all times conscious that they would design for their own national taste and character.

Younger sons fading, in the English manner, into the comfortable obscurity of the Church, the army or the colonial service, carried with them to the outposts of an expanding empire a liking for commodious, comfortable houses in the style of Wren. They built them in stone or in brick, at home or abroad, and as the eighteenth century wore on, they had them designed in the light Rococo style. As with the preceding fashion, mid-eighteenth-century building takes its English name from the kings in whose reigns it flourished. We have arrived at the Georgian style. The third George was still on the throne when the Loyalist came into Upper Canada with his empty hands and his dream.

He was no rootless visionary, but a man of responsible thought, fearlessly determined to re-establish in the tractless forest the rudely interrupted pattern of his orderly existence. The first goal which the Loyalist set for himself was that of building "the house." This was not a shelter for immediate physical need but a house "like the one at home," the simple dignified epitome of centuries of British experience. The knowledge that he would build it again in his own lifetime made all other titanic struggles possible. There is ample evidence that the Loyalists had faith in their ability to put their dreams into practice. The few personal possessions brought with them at so great an inconvenience were not items likely to be found in the practical equipment of a nomad: heirloom plate, fine china, small pieces of handsome furniture — fragile bridges, but they carried the mind across the years of toil and at every sign of flagging bore their mute witness that order, grace and repose were yet in the world. The spiritual survival of many a Loyalist may have hinged on just such silver spoons as those which roused the British traveller, the Reverend William Bell, to comment scornfully on pretention in a miserable cabin. In the hallway of Homewood, Dr. Solomon Jones' house (2), stands a clock which made the journey from the Mohawk to the St. Lawrence, packed with a precious china tea set, carefully wrapped in two feather beds and slung with ropes between two horses which were ridden by members of the Jones family.

The first Loyalist holding was chosen for him by lot, but a kind fate decreed that it was likely to be on, or very close to, a river or lake. This happy chance does not presuppose

9

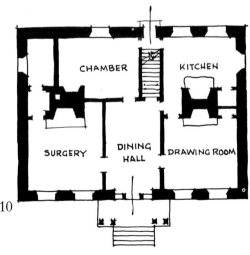

2. *A war party of the Six Nations or an afternoon tea-party — the width of the Georgian hall could accommodate either with ease. The hall of Homewood at Maitland is known to have welcomed both. The floor plan shows the room use at Homewood in 1800.*

CHAMBER

KITCHEN

SURGERY

DINING HALL

DRAWING ROOM

10

an especially enlightened group of surveyors in government employ in 1783. It simply means that the river systems provided the only means of transport in a country devoid of roads. Once settled on his lot, the Loyalist had ample time in which to select the site for his home. It is easy to believe that the site for the ultimate house was chosen soon after the first shelter was built. The eighteenth century was an age devoted to order and reason. The Georgian man of taste and moderate means, purposing to build a house, would choose the site with great care. Some portion of his acreage, fortuitously situated with regard to the possible on-slaughts of foul weather, would be selected. It would also command a pleasing prospect, a pretty expanse of countryside. Clearing the land was exhausting manual labour but once it became automatic in execution it left the mind free to build, discard, rebuild, to indulge in the intellectual exercise of planning a Georgian house. For the Georgian was first and last an intellectual style. Harmony was far more important than self-expression.

Yet oddly enough and all unsought, self-expression is inherent in the Georgian houses of Upper Canada. The homes of the Loyalists were built from memory — the com-bined memories of the patron and the master builder, and memory is treacherously selective. We remember the things we like, just as we believe what we wish to be true. A fortunate few could supplement their recollections by referring to the *Architectural Assistant* or *The American Builder's Companion*, the useful books by Battey Langley and Asher Benjamin. These gentle-men set forth the Classical orders in all correctness and provided plans and elevations for houses of moderate aspiration.

Even more fortunate and far fewer were the dignitaries of the new government, such as the Honourable D. W. Smith, who could call on the services of the versatile Captain Pilkington of the Royal Engineers to design his house (3) or on William Chewett Esq., the Assistant Surveyor General. A few beautifully executed plans and elevations, delicately tinted in water-colour, repose in the manuscript collections of various archives. Such a plan by Chewett for Maryville Lodge, York, to be found in the Toronto Public Library, is illus-trated in a later chapter. One can assume that these few houses were built according to specifications but of tangible evidence in three dimensions there is none. The story of their fate is to be found in some thirty boxes of documents in the Archives of Canada, called "The War Losses Claims of 1812-1814." William Dickson, who had lost two houses, kindly illustrated his claim (4). Inconclusive as this war was in other respects, it marked the end of

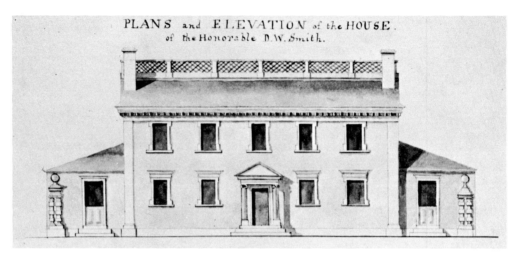

3. The Georgian town house. The residence of the Honourable D. W. Smith, built when Niagara-on-the-Lake was Newark, was burned in 1813. The original plan is in the Public Archives of Canada.

4. William Dickson lost two houses and a law library at Niagara in 1813, but seems to have saved his paint-box. His claim for war losses is one of the few, in the Public Archives of Canada, to be substantiated with water-colours. The preamble reads: "Abstract of William Dickson of Niagara His Claim on the Bounty and liberality of the British Government for contingent Remuneration, for his Real and personal Estate, wantonly and without any Plausable cause, burnt, and Destroyed by the Americans, during the Invasion of the Province, by the Troops of the United States."

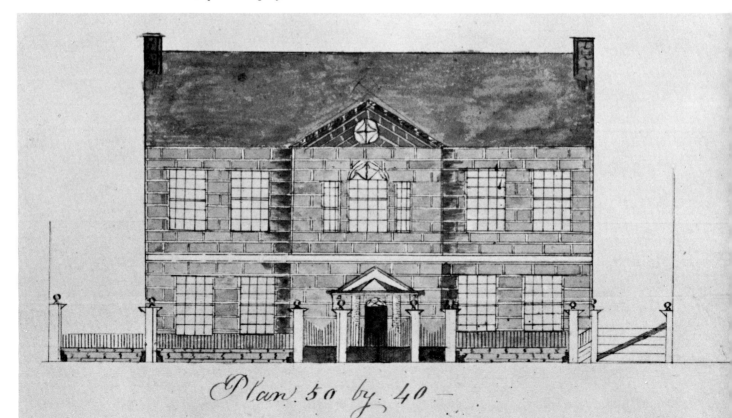

Abstract of William Dickson of Niagara His Claim on the Bounty and liberality of the British Government for Contingent Remuneration, for his Real and Personal Estate, wantonly and without any Plausable cause, burnt, and Destroyed by the Americans, during the Invasion of the Province, by the Troops of the United States —— N° 4 —

For a Brick House, on Claimants farm adjoining the Military Reserve, built the year preceding the War and burnt on the night of the 10th December 1813, when Newark was burnt, which the annexed View represents whilst claimant was a prisoner to the Enemy.

Integer Value ———— £1560

The Walls and cellar remain which are Supposed to be Worth   £200

Deduct also a charge made in account for Dowst charge N° 1 for the Soldiery in Spring 1815, Knocking down Brick Wall, for Chimneys, said to have been done under orders from Captain Romilly of Engineers —— 50 " " "

———— 250

———— 1310 " ..

For a Compleat Law Library, and some Historical & Miscellaneous Works, consisting of more than one Thousand Volumes, Statutes at Large & State Trials, burnt in the House, 500 Guineas ——— 583 6 8

This charge may appear high, neverthless the same Books

the building period in the pure Georgian style of domestic architecture in the Ontario region.

The few Georgian houses of Upper Canada which survive to the present day were not the mansions of colonial governors but were rather the handsome, comfortable houses of respected members of smaller communities scattered over the length of the province from Essex County to the Quebec border. They are houses which were built for a naturally conservative element — legislators, clergymen, physicians, magistrates and landowners — largely designed by them, and highly reminiscent of the Thirteen Colonies whence they came.

Skilled craftsmen were in short supply and those available, having been trained in the apprentice system, could be depended upon for careful workmanship but not usually for innovation. The burden of design lay on the client. In Georgian times this was thought to be a stimulating situation. The gentleman-architect in the manner of Lord Burlington was an accepted fact.

A document exists, dated in 1800, according to which the master mason Louis Brillière agreed to build a stone house of given dimensions in Upper Canada for Dr. Solomon Jones. But let us not seek to find French-Canadian characteristics in Homewood. Dr. Jones was building the house, Monsieur Brillière was laying up the stonework, and the resulting building speaks more of Albany than of Montreal. At the same time, if not a trifle earlier, there was being built in Sandwich on the Detroit River the most decidedly British colonial of the Georgian houses of Upper Canada for Jacques Bâby, Detroit Loyalist, legislative councillor and fur trader with the North West Company. Born in Detroit in 1762 and educated in Quebec, Bâby had completed the Grand Tour in 1783. The domestic architecture of Georgian England was fresh in his mind when he built this house. On one point all these gentlemen would have been in complete accord — the necessity for a beautifully balanced, symmetrical façade. The Georgian was quite prepared, where necessary, to install and glaze windows which were to remain forever blocked and blind in order to preserve the symmetry of the exterior.

Considered either in plan or elevation, the smaller Georgian house is basically a long rectangle. It may vary from a single storey to two and a half storeys in height. In its façade the elements of composition converge on the entrance doorway centred in its length. In plan it is oriented to a central hall. Both situations arise from the Georgian conception of hospitality. Within the unquestioned framework of a class society, that hospitality was open-handed and generous. In even the simplest, smallest Georgian house, some extra embellishment or careful refinement of proportion adorns the entrance doorway, as it does in the Reverend John Bethune's house at Williamstown (1). It was designed to confer dignity on

5. The Jacques Bâby house at Sandwich, 1790.

the visitor as well as on the inhabitant, to make the guest instantly aware of welcome and repose. The front door of the finer Georgian house does more: it is an outward expression of the life within, gracious living made tangible in wood. The weary Loyalist traveller suffering from an assortment of pioneer woes — black flies, mud and corduroy roads — was greatly cheered by a sight such as the entrance door of the Bâby house (5). The tall, graceful frame, the simple beauty of a well-painted, six-panelled door, the inviting glow of polished brass acanthus leaves on the knocker and over all the semi-circular fan transom restored his faith in the world in which he lived. He was as sure that behind that door lay a noble hall with a drawing-room on the left and a dining parlour on the right as he was that constitutional monarchy was the best system of government and port the proper thing to drink after dinner. Though his convictions were not always sustained (sometimes the port was not good and sometimes the room on the right proved to be the kitchen) in the Bâby house, at least, his beliefs were justified. A hall of noble width, even if that means only nine feet, requires more light than can be reasonably expected of a transom however lovely. Several wilderness Georgians surmounted this difficulty by placing narrow double-hung windows of eight panes on either side of the front door and actually framed with it, as in the Bâby house at Sandwich and the White House built by the Fairfields at Collins Bay in 1793 (6). Or they set the windows slightly apart from it as in the Butler house at Niagara (7).

The arrangement of two narrow windows on either side of the entrance door with a fan or straight transom set above the door is a normal late Georgian procedure in Britain and is to be found in many American examples also. In this type of façade the large windows on the ground floor, usually four in number, are equally disposed in the remaining space. The corresponding windows of the bedroom storey are set above them with a fifth window, sometimes more elaborately treated, centred over the entrance door. The width of both

6. Left: The White House, Millhaven, built by William Fairfield, Vermont Loyalist, in 1793, has the early Georgian steep snow roof. The French doors, which open onto the balcony, are an alteration of some thirty years later.

7. The Butler house, Niagara-on-the-Lake.

upper and lower halls makes for a wide space on either side of the entrance complex and the central window above it. If a house is encountered in Ontario which has these character- istics, and in addition, a roof of steep pitch with two regularly placed, blocky chimneys, it should prove to be early. There are instances, however, of houses of this type being built much later by someone who was inimical to change. The Georgian cornice was narrow, projected little and was boldly moulded and embellished with small modillions. These small bracket blocks, employed in every Classical cornice since Andrea Palladio introduced them in sixteenth-century Italy can still be seen on the Jacques Bâby house.

Steepness of roof in the Georgian house, sometimes relieved by dormers, may be explained as a survival of the Queen Anne house, as reminiscent of the Hudson Valley Dutch houses or as a measure to relieve the accumulation of snow. It matters very little. The Queen Anne house was heir to the Dutch tradition of brick construction, double-hung windows and steep snow roof.

With the subject of brick construction we have picked up the trail of our second myth — the bricks which "were made in England." If the scene had been laid in New York State the tradition would have read "brought out from Holland." All the confusion seems to have arisen from the late eighteenth-century bricklayer's habit of referring to the English bond or method of laying brick in a wall as "English brick" and to Flemish bond as "Dutch

16

brick." The truth is that in all small communities where clay was available, co-operative brickyards were set up. Brick is not difficult to make and there is no basis for visualizing the Loyalists toiling like the Children of Israel under the lash. There were two main ways of using brick in exterior walls: it might be exposed in solid brick retaining walls laid in mortar in various bonds showing different surface patterns or concealed behind weather-boarding as fill between the uprights of a structural wood frame. Behind the present asbestos shingle surface of the Bâby house is hidden brick fill. The fill concealed behind the weather-boarding of the Fairfield house is grout, blocks of unburned brick and pebbles.

Stone is the most permanent and the least tractable of the materials employed by the Loyalists. Fiske Kimball, the American architectural historian, tells us that rubble stone was the favourite building material of the Hudson Valley Dutch. They were thrifty people and it was close at hand. For much the same reasons it has appealed to the English, the French, the Highland Scot and the Irish. Where stone masons could be found, stone houses were built. Two of the finest early rubble-stone houses in Ontario face the St. Lawrence near Maitland. Homewood was built in 1800 by Dr. Solomon Jones. The other is the Heck house (8) which tradition claims to have been the scene of the death in 1804 of Barbara von Ruckle Heck, mother of North American Methodism. Be that as it may, Samuel Heck's two-storey stone house did not appear on the assessor's records until 1808.

While the Heck house had a certain historic interest, it had more than a passing claim to architectural consideration. The façade was austere: five evenly spaced windows above, four evenly spaced below and a centre door with a plain transom of five panes. Lest this austerity be attributed to Methodism, it should be noted that identical arrangements of the ground-floor openings are to be found in many early houses. In every case, the architrave trim of the doorway is quietly elegant, the six-panelled door of fielded or moulded panels, of dignified proportion and the early hardware, excellent. The special attraction of the Heck house lay in its plank-panelled halls (9).

Wood panelling as a treatment of wall surfaces came into general use in the Renaissance and continued its supremacy all through the Georgian period. Latterly, it was reduced to the lower section of the wall as a panelled dado (2) and finally, the last vestige, to the chair rail. All partitions in the Heck house were built of vertical planks overlapping each other and moulded at their edges. This form of construction produced a series of vertical

8. *The Samuel Heck house, built near Maitland between 1804 and 1808, was a fine example of sturdy colonial Georgian in its simplest form. It was destroyed in 1963.*

18

panels from a narrow baseboard at the floor to a small wood cornice at the ceiling. The ceilings and exposed undersides of the stairs were plank panelled in the manner of the partitions.

The stair itself was a straight flight of steps with a finely moulded handrail of which only a vestige remains. The balusters were slim, seven-eighths of an inch square in cross-section, with pencil-post newels, square at the base and chamfered from the height of six inches up to a small octagon where they met the underside of the handrail. The upper and lower halls were identical in form, the moulded plank panelling and fine open handrail being repeated on the attic stair, since, alas, boarded in and hidden. Concession to the rigours of Ontario winters has enclosed the fine attic stair-rails in both the Bâby and Fairfield houses as well.

Were the Loyalists who built with small box-like entrance halls more prudent and weather-wise than those who chose the centre stair-hall running through the house, or were they recalling an earlier type of house? The box-hall, as its name implies, does not extend the full width of the house but stops short part way. From it may open a stair-hall, as in Maryville Lodge, or more simply, as in the Jones house, a stair enclosed in walls. If the stair rises within the box-hall, as it does in the Bethune house, it usually does so in a series of short straight flights with landings and a multiplicity of newel posts, highly reminiscent of the Jacobean stairs so prevalent in New England. The box-hall, being wide for its length, assumes the character of

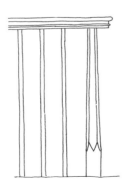

9. The high quality of Georgian joinery was evident in the beautiful treatment of the plank-panelled halls and stairwells of the Heck house. The stair-rail had straight pine balusters and pencil-post newels.

a small reception room. It is often lighted by one or more full-size windows and sometimes contains a fireplace. In every house that has come down to us from Georgian Upper Canada the stair-rail is light in scale with straight squared balusters and a small, simple newel post, beyond which the handrail projects slightly without turning or undue emphasis. The only turned newels are to be found in the Bethune house, an elementary double vase turning. The Fairfield stairway has winders, because it is constructed in the medieval tradition around a post, which extends the height of the house and is relieved by shallow fluting (10).

Welcome was extended in the Georgian hall but the guest was not expected to remain there in a state of suspended animation. Let us move through the Georgian house and consider the plan. In its elementary form, the ground floor consisted of four principal rooms disposed equally, two and two, on either side of the central hall. The drawing-room was on the left, the dining parlour on the right. A bedroom or bedrooms usually opened off the drawing-room and the kitchen occupied a space behind the dining parlour. If a house boasted wings, the kitchen was usually banished to one of these, or it might be relegated to the cellar. In either of the latter situations, small rooms scarcely larger than cupboards were attached to the kitchen. These were "slip" bedrooms for servants. It was not always considered necessary to provide them with windows. The remote location of the kitchen was not designed solely to plague the cook with many steps. Its subterranean or semi-detached situation allowed for cross-ventilation, a most important factor in summer. The Georgian kitchen fireplace in full blast was a fearsome thing.

The plan of the upper floor is similar — two principal bedrooms, usually with fireplaces, and two smaller rooms toward the rear of the house, without direct heating. The secondary bed chambers may have access to the central hall, or may open off the larger bedrooms. When the upper hall was wide, it was often furnished as a sitting-room and was the scene of such domestic activities as spinning and sewing. Weaving, which required more space, was practised in either the kitchen loft or the attic, apartments comfortable only in spring and fall. The attic of the Bâby house seems to have been an exception. The walls were finished with plaster and there is evidence that stoves were used at some time.

The fireplace was Georgian Ontario's only source of heat. Chimneys and flues received great care and attention. Ingenuity was expended in the matter of the bake oven and the disposal of the cranes. Succeeding generations have come to consider the crane as the sole prerogative of the cooking fire and have been led astray on room use. It was not always so. The small fireplace of fine mantel containing a crane and having cupboards close by does not indicate a kitchen. Let the Georgian past seep in and murmur of steaming tea in thin china cups, of hot toddy on a blighting winter's day. Why would anyone of even rudimentary common sense hie all the way to the kitchen and back with a tea kettle when there was a fire blazing merrily at his elbow?

The Georgian might thus make conscious provision for little snacks in hall or bedroom, but the principal reception rooms of his house were designed for formal living. He did not pour libations to the Goddess of the Hearth as did the Roman of old, but he did express his veneration for the household fire by giving the mantelpiece pre-eminent place in both drawing-room and dining parlour. In Britain, this expression would take the form of a fine marble mantelpiece where happy cupids sport with garlands, above which the vast over-mantel of ormolu and mirrors soars at last to the fine cornice uniting the whole composition to the panelled wall of which it is the centre and the crowning glory. In the majority of the Thirteen Colonies a similar, if more restrained, treatment was provided. The over-mantel, in North America, was likely to be surmounted by a broken pediment. Until well after 1750, it was still flanked by a panelled wall. In many cases, as the over-mantel panelling had been designed as a part of the entire wall surface, it was not given a mantel shelf and the

10. The Jacobean stair form is composed of a series of short flights with landings and winders. Common in early New England houses, it is to be found in a few houses of Upper Canada. One of these is the White House, Millhaven, built in 1793.

21

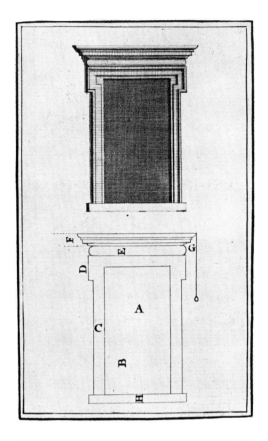

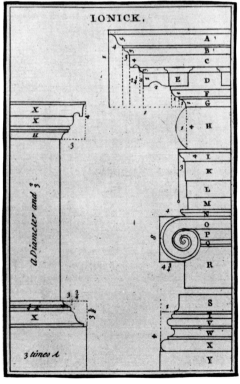

12. A small Georgian mantelpiece with eared trim and original brickwork in the dining parlour of the White House, Millhaven.

13. Left: Two pages from an early pattern-book.

11. Opposite page: The finest Georgian mantelpiece in the province graces the White House, Williamstown. The brickwork has been altered recently.

fire opening below it was surrounded by a simple mitred moulding of Classic architrave trim.

The surviving Georgian mantelpieces of Ontario are as fine in quality as they are few in number. The handsomest (11) is to be found in the small parlour-study of the White House in Williamstown, built in 1805 by the Reverend John Bethune, a North Carolina Loyalist, former chaplain of the Eighty-fourth Regiment or Royal Highland Emigrants, and the first Presbyterian clergyman in Upper Canada. In this pleasant little room the traditional divisions of the panelled wall are represented by a fine wood cornice, a well-proportioned chair rail at one-third of the wall height and a starkly simple baseboard. The only panel is in the centre of the over-mantel, a plastered surface surrounded by a wooden frame moulded on the inner edge. It is flanked on either side by short fluted pilasters whose capitals are formed by a break forward of the cornice. The pilaster bases rest on a narrow mantel shelf. This shelf, moulded according to Classic examples made available to Upper Canadians in many pattern-books, is supported by an Ionic frieze with bulbous torus moulding. The trim around the fire opening, now rebricked, is also Ionic, having the three bands common to the Ionic architrave. The mantel in the Fairfield house (12) has the "eared" architrave recommended for door surrounds (13) by William Halfpenny in his *Practical Architecture*, published in 1736, with assurance that the design is direct from the sixteenth-century Palladio. Dr. Solomon Jones, at Homewood (14), used a simple architrave moulding around his fire opening but eared or projected his mantel shelf in plan to form a more suitable location for candlesticks.

Cupboards with panelled doors were often built beside or above fireplaces in Georgian times. This was especially true of bedrooms where warm, dry cupboards with doors could be made to produce a decorative wall surface. The sides of projecting chimney breasts were often finished with beaded flush panelling, excellent examples of which remain in the Fairfield and Bâby houses. Fireplace cupboards were also to be found in many dining parlours as shown in the Fairfield house (12) and more rarely in the halls, where the hall served in that capacity.

It is not to be expected that the chimney wall of the kitchen would present an elaborately panelled face to the world; this was a functional department. On the other hand, the Loyalist did not cease to be a Georgian at the kitchen door. The door itself would be like the other doors of the house and be surrounded by identical architrave trim, and so

24

14. Opposite page: The drawing-room mantelpiece, Homewood, Maitland.

also the windows. The walls would be plastered down to the chair rail and here the first difference appeared. The chair rail is very simple in form and the dado below it is of beaded random plank of astonishing width set either horizontally or vertically. Such cupboards as may be associated with the fireplace are finished with the same beaded plank and the mantelpiece itself is usually of related construction having a beaded edge next to the brick. Early examples may or may not have a mantel shelf. They usually have an oven on one side and sometimes a stone sink on the other. Whether or not the kitchen fireplace is set in the side or end wall depends on the location of the kitchen. It is nearly always centred in the wall space.

The hearths of fireplaces may be of brick or stone, those in the reception rooms and bedrooms being frequently quite narrow. The kitchen hearth is much deeper for the excellent reason that red-hot iron pots cannot be transported very far. All the characteristic features of the Georgian kitchen (15) are well displayed in the schoolmaster's house in Upper Canada Village.

Sometimes a small circular depression is to be found at one side of the kitchen hearth. In this, sand was pounded to refine it for scrubbing the floors. The flooring of the settler's house was always of thick random-width plank, pegged to the beams below it with oak dowels. The kitchen floor, which received most of the traffic stress, remained in its natural state and was scrubbed vigorously and frequently with water, sand and a stiff brush. Floors in other rooms were painted as soon as the Loyalists could import the ingredients needed to mix the colours.

Oil paint seems to have been available quite early. The colour range was restricted and the quantity not great, so it was reserved for the treatment of wood surfaces. Floors, stair treads, mantelpieces and all interior wood trim were painted. The Loyalist built with pine but he did not admire its appearance and painted it generously. Plaster walls might be covered with the flat paint resulting from a judicious mixture of buttermilk with indigo, red or yellow ochre. The only wood which received lavish polishing and remained on view was the cherry or walnut handrail of the stair. The Loyalist was accustomed to paint out his woodwork to form a pleasant background colour for fine furniture in cherry, maple or walnut. The colours beloved of the late Georgians were all well above midtone — light greens, blue-greens, blue, yellow, ivory and occasionally white. We know that in the colonies whence they came, stencilled walls to imitate very expensive imported wallpapers

26

15. *The schoolmaster's house, Upper Canada Village. The working heart of the pioneer home was the living-kitchen where activity centred around the cooking fireplace. It was flanked by an oven and a stone sink and surrounded by warm, dry storage cupboards.*

were in favour. Only one indication has yet come to us that this may have been done in Upper Canada in its early days, but stencilling may lie undiscovered under paint and paper in many other old houses. Fragments of a rosette repeat pattern, stencilled in celadon green on ivory, survived under layers of plaster on the ceiling of the upper hall of a much altered house in Sandwich.

When the interior appearance of the Ontario Georgian house is conjured up from its long rest, let it be divested of an excess of "homespun." We are looking at fine houses, built for people of taste and some means at the beginning of the nineteenth century. The tractless wilderness might be close at hand but so was the port of Montreal with its cabinet-

16. The solid Georgian shutter made a valiant barrier against extremes of heat and cold.

makers and its silversmiths. To it, under billowing canvas in the tall ships of England and France, came textiles and tea sets, tobacco and spices, fine crystal and dinner wines. We know that toiles (fine printed cottons) were used as trade goods with the Indians in Upper Canada: a piece of one exists in the Royal Ontario Museum. They must surely have been available to Mary Tunnicliffe Jones, Barbara von Ruckle Heck and Veronica Bethune for window curtains and bed furniture.

Sometimes the Georgian window was curtained and sometimes a species of blind made of linen and operated on the Venetian principle was used. The latter left the fine wood trim of the window in full view but must have posed a hazard to closing the inside shutters. Where the thickness of a masonry wall permitted its installation, the panelled Georgian inside shutter presented a handsome window treatment. The double-hung window was set close to the outer surface of the splayed window opening. The resulting deep reveals could then be sheathed with fixed panels or recessed for folding interior shutters. The soffit of the window was usually panelled to match. In houses whose wall construction was frame, the shutters were hung, perforce, outside. Inside or out, they were of solid panelled construction (16). At this time the louvered shutter had not yet reached Upper Canada.

Window glass came ready cut in panes, seldom above seven and a half by eight and a half inches in size during this period and of varying clarity. Windows in most houses of 1800 were composed of two sashes of twelve panes each, as in Homewood (17). The glass was held in place by moulded wooden muntin bars. In some houses, windows of twelve panes to the upper sash and eight panes to the lower were used in the upper storey where less height was required. Attic windows were usually of the casement type, that is, the sash was hinged at one side to swing either in or out as opposed to the double-hung

28

17. *The tail begins. Homewood, Maitland, showing the kitchen wing added in 1810. The tail will grow.*

type of window construction in which the sash was arranged to slide either up or down.

Possibly one instance survives of folding doors used to divide a room before 1800. On the second floor of the Fairfield's White House is a large room lying across the end of the house. It could be divided into two bedrooms by the folding doors, or used as a ballroom or upstairs drawing-room on state occasions. Too many Canadians scoff at the idea of the last Georgians building ballrooms in Upper Canada. Yet, we know from contemporary account that "elegant" ladies journeyed long distances, presumably by bateau or on horseback, to attend Assemblies. Prowess with a logger's axe by day did not exclude proficiency on the dance floor at night, and the proceeds of potash could purchase dancing pumps and pianos as well as door latches.

Fine hardware had to be imported. The local smith could cope with H-hinges or strap hinges and could fashion useful and often surprisingly lovely iron latches for bedroom or closet doors, but all the vast door-locks with the beautiful elliptical brass knobs and the fine brass knockers were beyond his skill. One of the finest Georgian brass knockers of Upper Canada may be seen on the front door of the Bâby house in Sandwich.

A little legend has grown up concerning the design most common to Georgian doors in Upper Canada. The type of door in question has six panels (1). This, you will be told, is a "cross and Bible" door. Certainly the stiles of the upper panelling assume a cross shape. It is inevitable when straight lines intersect at right angles. The wide stile which transverses the door at grasping height seems much more likely to have been designed to take the extra stress which can be expected at this point than to divide the New Testament from the Old. How else would one explain the disposition of the panels in the Jones' entrance door, where the width had made nine seem a reasonable number?

Georgian doorways are usually quite wide and are often rather low, sometimes as low as six feet. Interior doors are thin in cross-section but exterior doors are very substantial. The front door of the Bâby house and the back door of the Bethune house are composed of three layers of plank. Messrs. Bâby and Bethune had just lived through a revolution and they saw little enough evidence of any change in human nature to warrant the belief that such things might not happen again.

Leaving Mr. Bethune's house by either the front door or the back, one finds oneself under a narrow verandah roof. The front verandah is floored, but the back is not. Its

30

posts rest on piers imbedded in the ground. All problems of authenticity having to do with Georgian houses of Upper Canada are as naught compared with the problems of porch and verandah. The wooden porches of North America, exposed alternately to wind, snow, sleet, strong sun and changing fashion, stand in need of frequent renewal of many of their members. Are any of the porches or verandahs of our prime examples original? The porch at Home-wood is not. The handsome door and porch of the Nelles manor-house at Grimsby, built in the 1790's, is admittedly of the 1820's. Quite a number of the houses evade this issue by never having had such a thing. This appears to be true of the Heck and Butler houses. The age and authenticity of the Fairfield double verandah rests on very secure evidence indeed, no less than that of the timbers which support it and which are an extension of the frame of the house itself. The railing is open to question. Similar in construction and contemporary in time are the double verandahs of the Gage house on the battlefield of Stoney Creek. The gable raking cornice is swept two feet front and back, which would seem to indicate the presence of both verandahs in the original plan.

The first settlers, the last Georgians, had transplanted little islands of eighteenth-century grace and rooted them in the wilderness that was Upper Canada. Their houses, handsome and sturdily built, had been designed to be an inheritance for their children, yet many Georgian houses of Upper Canada were destined to be destroyed in their builders' lifetime. The clouds were gathering for the war which was to sweep them away and, when the storm had passed, the houses which would rise from the ruins would be built to the Neo-classic taste.

18. *The hall-mark of North American Neo-classicism is the semi-elliptical fan transom set above a wider door with sidelights. Pine Grove, Maitland, 1822.*

2
Potash and paterae

The second phase of domestic building in Upper Canada followed hard on the heels of the War of 1812. Students of world history are wont to dismiss the North American portion of this war as being of little consequence, a nuisance squabble instigated by France to force Britain to garrison the Canadas. As a delaying tactic it was most successful. The Napoleonic Wars were prolonged thereby. So also was the cultural development of Upper Canada whose beleaguered citizenry was forced to abandon temporarily the struggle with the wilderness in order to resume the feud with its neighbour.

Some by-products of the war merit consideration including as they do Laura Secord, the Rideau Canal, the basic right of Canada to peaceful co-existence in North America, and a peculiarly fine type of whitewash. The war had been waged at the architectural expense of both contestants. Much had been destroyed, more damaged. The aforementioned whitewash, erasing the smoke of war from its walls, gave the name White House to the presidential residence in Washington, burned in 1814 in retaliation for the firing of the public buildings of York, capital of Upper Canada.

In Upper Canada the destruction had been more wide-spread in area and more thorough in concentration. When peace came again to the colony's first capital, Niagara-on-the-Lake, two lonely houses stood intact amid the ashes. A good deal of York had been burned, and all along Lake Ontario and the St. Lawrence the homeward turning militia was met with ruins. Whether the occupying troops had been foe or friend the result, structurally, was the same: the house had to be rebuilt. It would often be more accurate to say that another and different house was built. For this was a realm in which the text of the thanksgiving sermon delivered at Stamford, Upper Canada, on June 3, 1814 —"My son, fear thou the Lord and the king: and meddle not with them that are given to change"— did not apply. However much he might subscribe to the first part of the injunction, the well-to-do

Upper Canadian of 1815 had every intention of indulging in change. He set about building with enthusiasm and dispatch. So much so that John MacTaggart, a Boswell of the 1820's, was to write in Volume One of his *Three Years in Canada:*

The orders of architecture baffle all description; everyone builds his house or cottage according to his fancy; and it is not a difficult thing, in passing through the country, to tell what nation the natives of the house hail from, if we are aware of the whims and conceits that characterize them. Thus a plain rectangular house of brick or stone, with five windows and a door in front, and a window perhaps in either gable; the barns, sheds, stables and offices at a respectable distance behind: a kitchen garden off at one end, full of turnips, mellons, onions, cabbages, etc., and at the other end an orchard full of fruit trees with a range of bee-hives in a corner: is the dwelling of an honest English farmer. The wealthy Lowland Scotsman follows the same plan nearly: there is not such an air of neatness and uniformity but there is more livestock about the doors; the pool or river is full of geese and ducks, while round the barn are numerous flocks of hens and turkeys; a favorite cow perhaps, hangs on for friendship about the gate, a sow comes forth with her litter and cur dogs seem not to be scarce.

A house larger than either of these, chiefly built of wood, and painted white with nine windows and a door in front, seven windows in either gable, and a semi-circular one above all, almost at the top angle of the roof, the blinds painted green, the chimney stocks highly ornamented, and also the fan-light at the door; the barns, stables, etc., off at a great distance; the arches of all the shed doors turned of wood in eccentric ellipses, livestock not very plentiful about the place; a disposition to be showy and clean, without neatness, proportion or substantiality . . . it is almost needless for me to say that this is the mansion of Jonathan or the U. E. Loyalist from the United States.

A house nearly as large as the American's but built of stone and high roofed, having two tall chimney stocks growing out of either gable; an attempt to be showy and substantial, without rhyme or reason: an air of great miscalculation and of woeful sacrifice made with the intention to gain something, which something does not seem to have been properly defined; a disposition evidently for a house like no other persons — beyond the reach of architecture, generally met with in a state of dilapidation and decay, the window panes sadly mutilated, old straw hats stuck in to keep out the wind and so forth — this (for there are many such places) was intended for the abode of a person who had made a few thousand pounds in

34

the fur trade — a wild, pushing, Highland-man who had often seen the remotest regions of the North-west.

Unfortunately, MacTaggart did not confide his views on what, in his opinion, constituted architecture. As a civil engineer employed in the construction of the Rideau Canal, it would seem that his theatre of observation must have been the Ottawa valley with excursions to Kingston and York — the areas most likely to abound with honest English farmers and wealthy Lowland Scots in 1826.

The salient fact which escaped John MacTaggart was that, familiar as the pushing Highland fur trader and United Empire Loyalist (often one and the same person) might be with the remotest northwest, not a few of these worthies were equally acquainted with Albany, New York and London. Men of enterprise in international commerce and with a curiosity of a magnitude sufficient to add a third of a continent to the known geography of the world were unlikely to have remained in utter ignorance of the fashion prevailing in these centres. The very diversity of their previous experience rendered them as receptive to experiment in architecture as in other fields.

The passing of the old order and the light-hearted gaiety of the new style must have been greatly deplored by the few surviving builders of the Georgian houses of Ontario. They had been the older members of the Loyalist communities, who had been able through influential friends in both camps to save part of their means from the American Revolution or who had early acquired prominent positions in the new country. By 1820 most of them had passed from the scene and it was their sons or younger friends who now enjoyed affluence sufficient to their architectural ambitions.

Of the style which superseded the sturdy Georgian in Upper Canada, it may be said with some truth that it has no name and that it has many. In Britain it is usually called Adam in honour of its leading exponent, the Scottish architect Robert Adam. In France buildings and furniture of the day commemorate in their designation the unhappy King Louis XVI, whose reign saw the flowering of this cumulative style and its close. The comprehensive international name is the Neo-classic style.

Architectural historians writing about the buildings of the young republic and about those put up in the uneasy decade before the American Revolution have applied the term Federal. They have, with equal facility, ascribed the change from the Georgian style to the Federal style as illustrative of the passiveness of a subject burgeoning into the freedom of a republican, and in its limited context this was true. Obviously both the name and the explanation are not applicable to Upper Canada. The change was international and its roots must be sought in the changing attitudes of Western civilization. The trend towards lightness of colour and to stucco surfaces made the calcimining of the White House permissible, not the other way about.

The economic and social structure of the golden days of the eighteenth century was based on the ownership and profitable use of land. Architectural taste had matured slowly in the leisurely atmosphere of the eighteenth century. It spread perceptibly from the great house to the cottage, and architectural harmony prevailed. By the last quarter of the century, however, its immemorial solidarity was to be visibly shaken.

The plateau of comparative peace and security which existed in the middle years of the eighteenth century had produced two new species of beings in Western Europe, the tourist, and the collector. Admittedly, the interests of English gentlemen on the Grand Tour were antiquarian rather than scientific; it was left for their sons to build the museums. The true dilettanti amassed collections of beautiful things for themselves. Collecting leans naturally toward the decorative rather than the monumental, and when, by a happy accident, the long-buried cities of Pompeii and Herculaneum were rediscovered, the collectors found a style of building with which they were in complete accord. The mid-eighteenth-century gentleman was enchanted with the Classical world but to him the Classical world was a Hellenistic Greco-Roman one.

Whenever anyone considers art forms which are alien to his particular culture pattern, he prefers the expression most intellectually akin to his own. Hence the eighteenth-century tourist, enjoying a similar economic position, chose, like the Imperial Roman, the late over-refined style of the crumbling Greek states. Both ignored the sturdy simplicity of the Greek Golden Age, the Roman consciously, the Briton from lack of evidence. In the topsy-turvy manner of architectural remains, the last style built is usually rediscovered first. It was possible to amble around Herculaneum and Spalato long before one could safely visit Greece. When Messrs. Stuart and Revett did publish their *Antiquities of Athens* the monumental vitality of the Parthenon came as a distinct shock and polite society was inclined to consider it rather vulgarly robust.

36

Impartial examination of the true Georgian style demonstrates that it was harmonious, pleasing and comfortable. It was the modified survival of the Renaissance style. In other words, it was designed for human habitation in the unbroken tradition of antiquity, altered by perceptible degrees over the ages and in each country to suit the requirements of temperament and climate. But mankind, like Louis XV, is easily bored. Something new was required.

Sceptical, sophisticated, on the verge of an era of great social, political and economic experiment, Western Europe sought architectural security in symmetry and the astringent mathematical precision of a Hellenistic Revival to which later architectural historians have given the name Neo-classic. Pompeii and Herculaneum were a great comfort to them. One could actually paint well-disciplined festoons on a flat plaster surface and be *avant-garde* as well as economical. Delicate, spidery plaster ornament lent a pleasing texture to the walls and ceilings without greatly disturbing the tranquillity of the surfaces.

The immediate effect of the new taste on exteriors was toward reduction in the scale of the trim and in a general lessening of the appearance of weight. The strong columns shrank back against the wall to become docile, gently fluted pilasters. Stucco gained in popularity, providing a delicate eggshell background for airy, decorated cornices. Window trim and glazing bars were reduced in size as the panes and the apertures themselves increased. The larger window then led to greater preoccupation with the garden.

If the Neo-classicist was elegant, he was also orderly and exacting. No better example of the type can be found than Josiah Wedgwood. Museum collections abound in examples of his Hellenistic basalt wares. Many of his cameo plaques adorn the mantelpieces for which they were designed. The duality of the Neo-classic appeared in his Queensware, a porcelain with a hard, smooth surface, which was designed to be washed easily and to be within the purchasing power of many. This was because Wedgwood felt that improperly cleansed tableware was a menace to health. The sauceboats should be both satisfactorily Greek and truly clean.

That colonial surgeons concurred with Wedgwood's views on Classicism and cleanliness is evident. A set of Queensware was listed by Robert Kerr, Esq. of Niagara along with forty-six volumes of medical books, medicines, a set of surgeon's instruments and a loving catalogue of fruit trees in claim number one hundred and twenty-five of the 1812 war losses. Mr. Kerr also lost a "two-storey wooden framed house filled with brick,

19. The Grange, Toronto, built by D'Arcy Boulton in 1818. "Some of the residences of the gentry are handsome brick structures," Sir Richard Bonnycastle wrote of Toronto.

forty-eight feet by twenty-four feet with two wings twenty-four by twenty feet (one of the wings finished with black walnut,)" valued at eight hundred pounds. Having made his claim Mr. Kerr could then begin to peruse the handbooks and decide how his new house should be built.

In some respects the survivors of 1814 found themselves in a situation similar to that which had confronted their Loyalist parents: the end of a war found them homeless and not infrequently penniless. But there were substantial differences. The Upper Canadians were on their own acreage, largely cleared. There were skilled craftsmen available and mills, quarries, and brickyards close by; and there were the handbooks for correct detail. Gone was the day when employer and master builder put their combined recollections together and drew up a haphazard plan on a shingle. All Upper Canada that was building in the 1820's was using the Neo-classic style but the colony was vast in area and the small population took its architectural inspiration from diverse sources. Regional differences were early and inevitable. The upper St. Lawrence and eastern Lake Ontario regions seem to have had a marked preference for delicate detail and attenuated proportion: the style in its English and New England phase. Western Lake Ontario and the Niagara area displayed much greater exuberance, giving evidence of a Baroque approach to the Neo-classic which it shared with the Finger Lakes region of New York State. Unfortunately all conclusions have to be based on what remains. In the capital itself, various waves of private enterprise and civic expansions have been devastatingly thorough. The economically profitable but scenically ruinous attempt to make a commercial Zuider Zee of Toronto harbour left stranded, out of sight of the bay they were built to view, the City's two remaining Neo-classic houses, 54 Duke Street and the Grange (19), whose lawn became the city park of the same name.

20. A nineteenth-century vista. The house of Chief Justice Campbell at the top of Frederick Street, Toronto.

Number 54 Duke Street (20), once the home of a Chief Justice of Upper Canada and of an alligator, now houses a number of offices. Thanks to Chief Justice Campbell, who built it in 1822, it was a handsome late Neo-classic house in brick and thanks to the enlightened policy of successive commercial owners the façade retains much of its original character. The alligator was a pet of the Campbell clan. It was permitted to live in the garden and sometimes took the occasional stroll along Duke Street to the apprehension of the neighbours. Leisure, grace and the sparkling waters of Lake Ontario have all beaten a forced retreat from Duke Street but the old house remains as a monument to the Neo-classicists who, whether they were building a province or a house, built it well.

One can scarcely say that grace has departed from the Grange since the large wing to its rear contains, not the usual domestic offices, but the Art Gallery of Toronto. With the Campbell residence and Bishop Strachan's palace, the Grange shared the honour of being one of the truly important houses built in York in the first quarter of the nineteenth century. They had a great deal in common besides the forceful character of their inhabitants. All were brick houses of late Neo-classic style with overtones of the dawning Classical Revival. One, the Bishop's palace, long since demolished, was built by John Strachan, first Bishop of Toronto, and was an emolument not of his ecclesiastical rank, but of his personal acumen in marrying a fur-trade fortune with the lovely widow, Ann Wood McGill. The Bishop's house is no more and the Campbell house is a beautiful shell. One might hope to find the arch-type of the Ontario Neo-classic house in the heart of York and in the residence of D'Arcy Boulton (19) but it proves to be impossible. The Grange had neither an alligator nor a Bishop. It had Goldwin Smith. That eminent English Victorian, who was never a respecter of tradition, could hardly be expected to leave intact the heritage of his wife's first husband. It is, however, a pity that here, as in front of other buildings, the Historic Sites and Monuments Board have so placed their marker that it makes it difficult to appreciate the Grange without its big blue label. Fortunately the powers that reign in the Gallery behind place their labels on the picture's frame and not on the canvas.

A study of the Loyalist architecture of York proving a slightly fruitless task, let us abandon the remnants to the guardian mercies of the Toronto Civic Historical Advisory Board and the Architectural Conservancy of Ontario and seek the Neo-classic where it is still to be found. Amherstburg, Ridgeway, Niagara-on-the-Lake, Grimsby, Grafton, Picton,

21. A country seat in Upper Canada on a summer's day in 1820. Belle Vue, Amherstburg, from the water-colour by Catherine Reynolds in the Detroit Institute of Arts.

Bath, Kingston, the Carrying Place, Maitland, L'Orignal — lovely names, old town sites — each and every one has excellent, and frequently numerous, examples. It is an enlightening experience to tour southern Ontario using as a road guide a map which was published in 1834. Cornwall, Cataraqui, Dundas and Vittoria loomed as large as York in the days when the fur trading economy had just been displaced by the timber industry and the problems of agriculture still preoccupied the minds of financiers. The economic supremacy of central Ontario was yet to come.

Seemingly the initial step towards building a fine Neo-classic house in Upper Canada in 1818 was to marry a fur trader's widow. Bishop Strachan set the example; Robert Reynolds of Amherstburg followed suit. He even married into the same fortune when Thérèse Bouchette des Rivières, widow of the step-son of James McGill, became his wife. Perhaps Thérèse provided the name as well as the money. At any rate Belle Vue, a brick house of imposing size, still looks out over the Detroit at Amherstburg, surviving but much altered since that day in 1820 when Catherine Reynolds painted the water-colour of it (21) which now reposes in the Detroit Institute of Arts.

Belle Vue in 1820 had the Neo-classic plan beloved in Virginia: a large central hip-roofed block with gabled dependencies attached by covered passages to the main unit. In Miss Reynolds' water-colour the large windows, their lintels ornamented with keystones on the façade and sides of the house, were glazed with double-hung sashes of equal size, six panes to a sash, making a total of twelve panes per window.

The water-colour shows a small-scale repeat pattern in the roof cornice such as would be produced by the application of the Neo-classic Doric Order. Belle Vue in its hey-day was Neo-classic in the true Adamesque sense: all principal reception rooms enjoyed fine proportions and delicate detail. The mantelpieces, now perhaps over-restored, boasted the reeding, the paterae (flat, formal rosettes), the swags of fruit and flowers which graced the best buildings of Robert Adam or Samuel McIntire of Salem, the wood carver-cum-architect who was his most ardent follower in New England. If there were a skilled carver at hand, one had the wood of one's mantelpiece, door and window trim elaborately enriched. If such skill was not available, then metal or composition mounts could be, and often were, purchased and applied. Such a combination of materials for the desired effect was quite in keeping with the taste of a generation that enjoyed rosewood furniture with brass inlay or ormolu mounts. It appears that the composition mounts for interior trim were to be had in Montreal whence Mrs. Reynolds herself had come. They most certainly found their way up the St. Lawrence to the Cornwall area and formed a part of the trove of Adamesque on the upper St. Lawrence.

The Neo-classic mantel from which a detail is shown (22) exists in a fascinating stock-pile of Upper Canadiana. The collection was salvaged by the Ontario-St. Lawrence Development Commission from the villages and farmsteads submerged by the damming of the St. Lawrence in 1960. The mantel in question came from the drawing-room of a house which stood on the river bank of the St. Lawrence at Moulinette. Built of salmon-buff brick in the Neo-classic style by Adam Dixson, first man to build a power dam and canal on the upper St. Lawrence, it was noted with surprise and pleasure by Philip Stansbury in his *Pedestrian Tour in North America* in 1821. He described the mills at Moulinette and the mill-

42

22. The complexity of Neo-classic enrichment, Moulinette, 1821.

owner's house, "a fine brick building with wings." Alas, since Phillip Stansbury was not a water-colourist, no record remains of the fine house at the peak of its fortunes. When the Crown, its authority vested in the Province of Ontario, arrived to salvage what was left of Neo-classic Moulinette, that peak was long since past. However, there is an early photograph in the United Counties Museum in which Adam Dixson's house appears, the wings clearly apparent and the decorative roof balustrade still in place. When the photograph was taken in the seventies, the verandah of the house had already gone and its lawns and trees been shorn away by the new canal of 1843.

When the Dixson house was new, it was one of a number of large houses similar in scale to Belle Vue but differing in plan. Some had wings rather than dependencies, wings extending laterally as in Alwington and Fraserfield, or parallel to the main portion of the house as in the Dixson house.

The Dixson kitchen, which occupied the east wing, did not have the normal Upper Canadian cooking fireplace, but a brick and iron stove built out from the flue and having a large horizontal cooking surface. The door which gave access to the kitchen wing from the dining-room retained to the day of demolition its painted graining, the mellow sherry-brown of eighteenth-century undyed mahogany. Remnants of beautiful painted grainings such as this are to be found here and there in the province — substitutes intended in the late eighteenth century to replace rare imported woods. Painted grainings were literally portraits of the fine figures peculiar to mahogany, rosewood or satinwood, and were originally drawn from actual examples. Even when endlessly reproduced, they were still painted individually by a master craftsman with a good brush and fine colours at his disposal. These grainings should never be confused with the late nineteenth- and early twentieth-century mechanical graining produced with opaque paint and rubber combs.

Upper Canada had fine wood at hand, cherry, curly and birdseye maple, black walnut, and the ubiquitous butter-nut sometimes called white walnut. Used for handrails and furniture in Georgian times, these woods now made their appearance in the interior trim and the entrance doors of the Neo-classic house.

The Neo-classic was an international style. The very controversy on the question of origin, Great Britain versus France, underlines the lack of regional influence on its conception. The terms Adam and Louis XVI are almost interchangeable. No such reciprocity existed between Georgian and Louis XV. The Neo-classic was also an intellectual style, mannered, correct and emotionally chilly. Consequently international unanimity on so high-flown a plane was destined to be short-lived. Only in areas removed by the formidable barrier of the Atlantic from the political hubbub rocking Europe at the beginning of the nineteenth century had the Neo-classic a chance of survival. Successful survival being directly related to the ability to adapt with speed to changing conditions the Neo-classic was altered and it endured in North America. In some areas of Upper Canada it was in use as late as 1840. By that advanced date the deviations were more pronounced than the Neo-classicism.

The Neo-classic was an expression of gracious space, both real and apparent. The excessive rigidity of plan inspired by Georgian ideas of balance had been modified; whereas the Georgians frequently employed cubes, double cubes, circles, semi-circles and quadrants in their architectural composition, the typical Neo-classic motif was the ellipse. Restrictions of near-pioneer existence in Upper Canada precluded the building of many elliptical rooms, but once the mind had admitted the idea as being desirable, if unattainable, certain design shackles had been shed.

Ceilings were higher in the new conception of space and as the ceilings rose so perforce did the walls. If the building material were amenable, a favourite device was to break the surface of the exterior wall visually with a blind arcade, the applied non-structural arches sprung from slender pilasters or piers. Structural arches of masonry were best left in the semi-circular Roman form for strength. No such consideration hampered the worker in wood whose arcading was an applied decoration. He was free to describe a line which proceeded in slow, beautiful elliptical curves from cap to cap of the moulded pilasters. The normal sheeting for wooden walls was clapboard, excellent as a weather repellent but busy as a surface. To the purist with a fine composition to display, it was as irritating as a line drawing on ruled paper. The difficulty was overcome by finishing the façade with a carefully fitted flush siding. The resulting quiet surface is a part of the timeless charm of the Neo-

44

23. *The Poplars, Grafton, built by Eliakim Barnum, 1817, has the timeless charm of Neo-classicism in wood.*

classic houses of Upper Canada — those tall, white houses with nine windows in front — the homes of the Loyalists which so disturbed MacTaggart.

There is, fortunately, no need to employ the past tense when considering the design of these houses. The best example stands by the Queen's Highway near Grafton (23). Once known as The Poplars, it has been preserved since 1937 by the unceasing efforts of the Architectural Conservancy of Ontario, and is now a museum. It was built in 1817 by Eliakim Barnum to replace his home which was accidentally burned during the War of 1812 by British soldiers billeted there during the retreat from York. Colonel Barnum was a Vermont Loyalist. It is possible that his architect was also. In the immediate area of Grafton and Colborne there are several houses whose similarity of plan or use of decorative motif indicates the presence of an architect or master builder and his apprentices building over a considerable period of time in the style of Samuel McIntire and his follower, Asher Benjamin. The houses in question ring all the changes from the excellent to the clumsy, the endless variations possible between an inspired architect and a stubborn client or conversely between an enlightened patron and an incompetent craftsman. Where inspiration met with understanding, architectural harmony remains. In the Grafton area, the earliest is the best.

The Barnum house is a large timber-framed house, a two-storey centre block with one-storey lateral wings, the back and sides clapboarded, the flushboarded façade relieved by blind arcades, and the whole painted white. The roofs of block and wings are all of the gabled type. Unlike any other remaining Neo-classic houses of Ontario, save one, the centre block is oriented in the manner of the Classic temple, its gable forming a pediment above the façade arcade, the cornice and raking cornice enriched.

Axial change in the main block of the house made alteration in the plan necessary. The centre hall had to go. It was all very well to enter the cella of a pagan temple by a door centred in the narrow façade. It was not practical in a nineteenth-century house. Fortunately the Neo-classic was an antiquarian rather than an archaeological style: no searchings of artistic conscience were required. The entrance doorway was moved to one side and as it was, even when set in a pilastered frame no wider than the window above it with its opened louvered shutters, it fitted quite pleasantly between the two end pilasters of the main arcade.

The pilasters of the Barnum door are smaller replicas of those which support the

24. Maple Grove was begun in 1787 by Jeremiah French and completed in 1820 by George Robertson. It was relocated in Upper Canada Village. The gay vase-topped fence has been reconstructed from a daguerreotype of its contemporary, the Brouse house in Iroquois.

arcade. This order is a species of carpenters' Tuscan, the column not unlike Roman Doric, but without fluting. The orders employed in the design of Neo-classic houses in Upper Canada were almost invariably Roman in origin. They were used with enthusiasm rather than with scholarship. The Doric Order has an entablature whose frieze is decorated with a band of alternating triglyphs and metopes. The triglyph, as its name implies, is a type of grooving in groups of threes. The metope of the Doric was invariably a square block. Not so the metope of Upper Canada in the 1820's which was usually a rectangle whose proportions varied all the way from extremely long, as in the Grange porch, to classically accurate in the Nelles house at Grimsby. The Barnum metope occupies a happy position in the middle. Above the Barnum frieze, under the eaves, can be seen the decoration of evenly spaced blocks found in many early houses of this province. The blocks are components of the Doric Order, and are known as mutules.

Decorative windows were used to light the attic storey of many early houses in Upper Canada. These might be circular, elliptical or segmental in shape, sometimes appearing as a pair of quadrants separated by the width of an enormous chimney. Where the

25. The entrance door, Maple Grove, Upper Canada Village.

depth of space did not warrant glazing, sham fans were sometimes constructed, moulded and painted to represent muntins and glass. One such fan can be seen clearly in the Barnum house, centred in the tympanum of the pediment. Similar fans were placed, one in either end gable of Maple Grove in Upper Canada Village near Morrisburg.

Not all the timber-framed houses of Upper Canada were painted white as one might be led to suppose by reading MacTaggart. In some houses the white trim was set to advantage against a background of cane-yellow or stone-blue. The stronger colour combined with underscaled garland trim on the entrance door and the elegance of sham fans made of Maple Grove (24) a composition of Wedgwood Classicism. The name Maple Grove, which was originally associated with the house and mills of Jeremiah French, U.E., was later transferred to the small farming community which grew up around them, and now reverts, by default, to the house. The community was removed to make way for the St. Lawrence Seaway. The Ontario-St. Lawrence Development Commission rescued the house, one of the few of its era which still has a room whose walls are hung with the original paper. Begun in 1787 by Jeremiah French, late of Manchester, Vermont, its Neo-classic façade

48

was added *circa* 1820 to the order of George Robertson, merchant, who had recently married Colonel French's daughter. The double swag and pendants of husk moulding applied to the entrance door at that time can be seen in the accompanying photograph (25). This particular motif, direct from Pompeii, is far better suited to interiors, but was used externally *ad infinitum* in the Windsor area of Vermont at the same time that it was being perpetrated in eastern Upper Canada.

In 1820 Upper Canada was a thriving, enterprising entity. The original nucleus of stubborn, energetic North Americans had been augmented by a steadily increasing volume of colonists — investors, craftsmen and labourers. With the passage of thirty-seven years the melting-pot had developed a personality of its own. As the apprentice became the master craftsman so the buildings which he produced grew less faithful to the impersonal international style. The citizens of Upper Canada had assimilated the Neo-classic and made a part of it their own; that part shall, henceforward in this study, be called the Loyalist style. At its best the Loyalist style is both functional and beautiful; at its worst it has that horrid fascination known to all followers of the arts as "interesting."

Houses of the Loyalist style in Upper Canada retained many of the features of the larger Ontario Georgian centre-hall plan. There was still an equal balance of the room divisions on either side of the hall. The major difference seems to have been in an increased inclination to relegate the kitchen to the cellar or to a rear wing. As the majority of houses still had a vast cooking fireplace, the earlier considerations of heat and ventilation were still in effect. The designer of the Loyalist house had as an additional reason the emergence of the dining-room. The dining parlour of the North American Georgian house doubled, on occasion, as a sitting-room, and its furniture was capable of being arranged in a very flexible manner. The Loyalist house was designed at a time when a more formal existence was possible. The dining-room occupied a fixed position and was designed accordingly. In some houses the elaborate mantelpiece formed the central focus of one internal wall and, flanked in formal balance by arched recesses of varying depth containing shallow cupboards or the doors giving access to the kitchen, made an elegant composition. In other dining-rooms there was a single arched recess large enough to hold the sideboard and often constructed to accommodate snugly a fine piece of furniture already in the family's possession. The remaining wall space was occupied by a pair of matching doors, one leading to a hall or kitchen,

26. *The dining-room had replaced the dining parlour by the first quarter of the nineteenth century. The Clench house, Niagara-on-the-Lake, 1816.*

the other concealing a wine or dish cupboard. Of the former type one of the most pleasing has been illustrated (26). It forms one of a pair of reception rooms in the Clench house, Niagara-on-the-Lake. There is some dispute concerning the use of this room. At one time it served as an office to Colonel Ralfe Clench, late of Butler's Rangers, for whom it was built. Had this house possessed the dumb waiter often incorporated in Loyalist houses with subterranean kitchens it would establish the location of the dining-room beyond any doubt.

When Niagara-on-the-Lake was fired by American troops, the Clench residence ignited with the rest. The Clench family in all its ramifications, having fled its various other establishments before the enemy, was en-camped by the stream which runs through the garden of the ancestral home. As it was wash day, the fire was put out by the homely ex-pedient of emptying the contents of the wash tubs on the blaze. Unfortunately smouldering timber and relaxed vigilance allowed the house to be destroyed completely three days later.

The present Clench house was in the process of being built from 1816 on and was not actually completed until 1831, a fact which accounts for stylistic variation in mantelpieces

27. *Drawing-room door, Poplar Hall, Maitland.*

28. Chaste simplicity marks the drawing-room of the Neo-classic rectory, Pine Grove. The darker paterae on the mantelpiece are of cherrywood with birdseye maple centres.

and trim. The Clench mantelpiece shown is a fine example of the boldness and vigour which was achieved, without sacrifice of taste, when the elliptical fan and fluted column became the design idiom of the southern and western Lake Ontario region. Variations on this theme are to be found in many houses of similar antecedents, in Niagara-on-the-Lake, in Queenston and as far down the St. Lawrence as Maitland and Poplar Hall, which was built by William Wells after the War of 1812. With the elaboration of fans and fluting went a strongly restless line. The mantel shelf, hitherto a slightly shaped board of modest proportions, was enlarged in order to be cut back and to break forward again above the central and terminating panels of the frieze. Frequently the frieze and shelf combination was repeated in decorative over-doors in drawing- and dining-rooms. The drawing-room door at Poplar Hall (27) was related in just this manner to the mantelpiece. On either side of the door may be seen portions of a richly patterned chair rail.

A few miles down river from Poplar Hall there was being built, at approximately the same time, a house with some similarities and with marked differences of style. This was Pine Grove rectory, built near the Blue Church above Prescott in 1822 by Dr. Robert Blaikie, a clergyman-physician from Ecclesfield in Yorkshire. The corner of Dr. Blaikie's drawing-room (28) clearly indicates the high degree of personal taste which inspired the design of the whole house. Many of the moulding profiles are identical with those of Poplar Hall but they are used in Pine Grove with restraint. Paterae on the trim of door and window openings are small, circular and restricted to the corner-boxes. The mantel shelf is of the early type, its straight edge relieved by reeding. The elliptical paterae of the mantel, left unpainted by the present owners to show the fine figure and colour of Ontario hardwoods in appealing juxtaposition, are of cherry with birdseye maple centres. Graceful Regency furniture, similar to the chair in the photograph, was brought out by Dr. Blaikie in 1822 to furnish his home.

The front door of Pine Grove is such a fine example of the arch-type entrance door-way of the Loyalist style that it has been selected to head the chapter (18). The Loyalist door has six or eight moulded panels and fine hardware from the imposing knocker to the ulti-mate refinement of an elliptical door-knob set at hand level. It was of greater importance in 1822 to have the door-knob under one's hand than to have the keyhole under one's nose. The only knob on Dr. Blaikie's door is on the inside. Loyalist entrance doors were opened from within in response to the knock. On either side of the door and framed with it are

29. Opposite: A client of taste and a stair builder of no mean skill collaborated to produce one of the finest spiral staircases in Upper Canada at 42 Prideaux Street, Niagara-on-the-Lake.

sidelights, the glazing held by muntin bars, whose patterns repeat to some degree the composition of the fan transom above. This doorway occurs again and again with seemingly endless variety in houses from Windsor to the Quebec border. It seems so typical of the style that to see such a doorway is to say automatically Loyalist style house. Be careful, remember the wave of enthusiasm for the Colonial house which swept North America in the twentieth century. The fanlighted door was much copied at that time, but superficially. It was thicker and less refined.

Early fanlights such as the Barnum one have wooden muntins (thin, beautifully moulded wooden bars) radiating from a curved block, often carved, set over the centre of the door. At the peak of the Loyalist style, white metal glazing bars were introduced, trimmed with cast paterae and swags as set forth in Mr. Benjamin's admirable work and still following the radiation lines of the ellipse. The transom at Pine Grove is an example of one of these. Other fine transoms not shown are to be found in the Thompson-Rochester house in Ottawa, the Cartwright house in Kingston and Woodburn Cottage, Beamsville. By the time the MacMartin house was built in Perth the

30. Above: Skill without fanfare. A stair with straight flights of steps, slightly turned newels and a handrail which projects beyond the bottom newel is frequently found in the Neo-classic houses in the Counties of Northumberland, Prince Edward, Grenville and Lennox and Addington.

31. Right: Herring-bone reeding forms a decorative pattern on the drawing-room mantelpiece in the Weller-Morrison house at the Carrying Place.

54

metal designs were getting out of hand, and worse was to follow. The impression left by the later transoms in the Niagara area, with their multiple geometric confusion, is of a designer who had been given a compass and told never to lay it down. Such designs indicate a dying confidence in an outworn style, a dissatisfaction which was soon to lead most designers along diverse new paths of more probable Classicism or improbable romance.

A Loyalist style element of durability far greater even than the fan transom was the spiral or semi-spiral stair. The stair illustrated (29) is to be found in Niagara-on-the-Lake in a mellow red brick house at 42 Prideaux Street. Great skill in joining was required to produce a stair of this order. Countless lesser builders achieved pleasing results by combining a straight flight of some height with a few winders as the upper regions were approached and by reserving the spiral for the bottom step and the newel cage. Later stairways, still gracefully spiralled, acquired turned balusters increasing in complexity and in bulk as the century wore on. Many Loyalist stairways have turned newel posts encircled by the "cage" of balusters. Fine newels in polished brass are still to be seen in Niagara-on-the-Lake, Queenston and Prescott. In other houses of approximately the same age iron newels were installed and painted to match the balusters of the surrounding cage. Houses of this period often have a marked division of hall space. The stair or after portion is separated from the entrance section by a wide elliptical arch, sometimes centred with a keystone, and supported as shown by moulded pilasters. The moulding in this house, as can be seen, is of the sharply linear type.

In that area of Upper Canada dominated architecturally by the Barnum house and embracing parts of Northumberland, Prince Edward, Grenville, Lennox and Addington counties, the same division of the centre hall sometimes occurs. The moulding in this area is most likely to be reeded or gouged. The Neo-classic staircase in favour in these counties expressed the Loyalist refinement already seen in the spiral stair but with greater simplicity. Straight flights of steps, slightly turned newels, tapered balusters, and a handrail which projects slightly beyond the bottom newel and rises with a graceful swan curve to meet the rail surrounding the well are common to the Blaikie house (30) and to many of its contemporaries. Many people seem to imagine that early stair-rails were heavy. This is not true. It was the late Victorian rail which was ponderous. Georgian and Loyalist alike inclined toward elegance and had light handrails and thin balusters whose strength depended on selected wood and fine craftsmanship.

One of the finest reeded mantelpieces (31) remaining is in the Weller-Morrison house built in 1829 at the Carrying Place. It is one of the three houses erected for the children of Asa Weller. Here continuous ownership by Weller descendants, fortunately inheriting the discretion which presided over the building, has preserved the trim of the house in mint condition. The reeding has been carefully painted, moulding profiles are clear cut and the brick surround of the fireplace retains the muted patina of many years. The fine scale of Loyalist trim suffers most grievously when mistaken zeal picks out the mortar with contrasting paint.

The Carrying Place is, as its name implies, the narrow neck of land which prevents Prince Edward County from being an island. Here in years past all bateau cargoes had to be unloaded, carried across, and reloaded on waiting boats, a tiresome, time-consuming operation. Asa Weller, Vermont Loyalist and shipowner, decided to eliminate the shipping difficulty. He conveyed the bateaux across on rollers. The Weller family continued to be interested in the transportation of Upper Canada. With Loyalist friends and family connections keeping inns along the St. Lawrence and Lake Ontario it seemed almost inevitable that it should have been a Weller who established the Toronto to Montreal stage coach line. William Weller's yellow coaches sped along the narrow tortuous roads of Ontario until the coming of the railway.

The existence of Loyalist houses was too often dependent on a transitory prosperity. Some of the most imposing were built when the owner was on the brink of unforeseen financial difficulty and their very size has rendered preservation troublesome. Belle Vue at Amherstburg and Fraserfield near Williamstown are surviving monuments to the mistaken belief that extensive country estates in the European manner were economically sound in Upper Canada. Belle Vue faces a precarious future surrounded by a town. Fraserfield, retaining many of its Loyalist manor-house characteristics, is an unwieldy size for an Ontario farm in a depressed agricultural area. Many houses in the Loyalist style were built with money given in compensation for 1812 war losses. Fraserfield and Belle Vue enjoy the distinction of having been financed to some extent with 1812 war profits. Robert Reynolds and Alexander Fraser were both quartermasters, apparently efficient, and suitably rewarded. Dr. Thomas Rolph recounts on page 139 of his *Brief Account of a Tour of the West Indies, U.S. and Upper Canada* that "Colonel Fraser of Fraserfield has a fine farm, well cultivated,

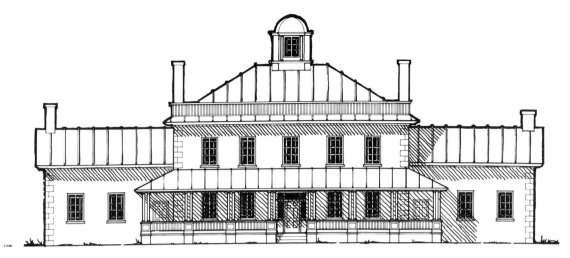

32. *"Colonel Fraser of Fraserfield has a fine farm, well cultivated, with a handsome residence on it."*

with a handsome residence on it." The fine farm contained one thousand acres of land and the handsomeness of the residence can be verified by the accompanying drawing (32). In the drawing the verandah, with its paired Tuscan columns, and the roof balustrade have been restored. Built on a height of rolling land with a wide lawn and a walled formal garden of the kind still flourishing at Duldregan near Hawkesbury (33), Fraserfield presented a dignified façade to the visitor approaching by any one of the three avenues. The avenues and the last vestiges of the formal garden have almost disappeared but the crowning touch of Loyalist magnificence, the cupola, can be studied in the detail photograph.

Belle Vue is brick. Fraserfield is built of rubble stone, stuccoed and grooved in

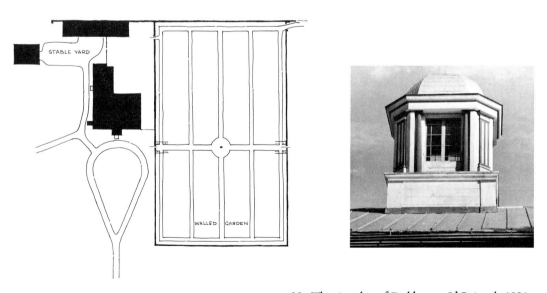

33. *The site plan of Duldregan, L'Orignal, 1821, shows the walled formal garden, one acre in extent.*

34. *Stone Acres, Brockville. A fine mantelpiece in which reeding and colonnettes were composed to form the focal point of a handsome drawing-room.*

imitation of ashlar, with cut stone quoins. The interior executed in the Classical Revival manner presents a puzzle the answer to which is to be found either in a later change of taste on Colonel Fraser's part or in the necessity of repairing fire damage, suggested by the charred structural members in the cellar.

Fire was, and still is, a constant depleting menace to our architectural heritage. It explains the scarcity of large wood-framed houses of early date. Brick and stone had a fighting chance but were by no means immune. As recently as 1958, a disastrous fire destroyed Kingston's most impressive stone house in the late Loyalist style. Alwington, built by Charles and Caroline Coffin Grant in 1834, seemed destined from the beginning to have been both important and unlucky.

In 1841 Kingston began its brief, meteoric period of prominence as the alternate capital of the United Canadas. The Governor required an official residence in Kingston, Canada West. The most desirable house was Alwington, an eminently suitable choice. Charles Grant, Baron de Longueuil, builder of Alwington was descended on one side from a British Colonist and on the other from the noble and interesting family of Le Moyne. The Grants seem to have possessed their home in tranquillity but misfortune dogged the lessees. Two governors, Sir Charles Bagot and Lord Sydenham, died there as a result of accidents. The latter expired, we are told, supported both physically and spiritually by his chaplain, the Reverend William Agar Adamson. We learn further that Dr. Adamson recited a psalm chosen for the thoroughness with which it denounces all those misdeeds of which the Governor was flagrantly guilty. Lord Sydenham was dying of lock-jaw. Truly a touching scene played with Regency gestures against a background designed in the late Loyalist style.

The mature Loyalist style was capable of producing houses of ornate, formal charm in the style of Alwington but in its waning years it fell into repetitious lethargy. Mouldings tended to be extremely linear, knife-edged and complex. The corner-box of door and window trim, which in the high Loyalist style held fluted paterae as at Pine Grove or a formal grouping of four slightly agitated acanthus leaves, degenerated to a series of razor-sharp concentric circles, reducing visual satisfaction at no gain to maintenance.

Multiplicity of detail was practised internally with varying degrees of success. The mantelpiece of the drawing-room at Stone Acres (34) near Brockville has elegant little colonnettes to support the terminal panels of its architrave. The whole composition is a delicate and restrained balance, an excellent Neo-classic design executed with great skill. Four colonnettes are relatively safe, ten verge on the foolhardy, although the drawing-room mantelpiece (35) in the Davey house in Bath continues to express both order and elegance. The upper range of the Davey colonnettes, just a trifle bulbous on close

35. The Davey house, Bath. Detail of the drawing-room mantelpiece with more colonnettes.

36. Harrison house, Niagara-on-the-Lake. Too many colonnettes.

37. A ballet of light and shade. The Harrison house, 157 Queen Street, Niagara-on-the-Lake.

examination, seem wispy and emaciated in comparison with those of the Harrison mantel-piece (36).

One of the beautiful legends of Niagara is associated with the Harrison mantelpiece in the drawing-room of 157 Queen Street, Niagara-on-the-Lake, an extremely charming house (37) whose bland stucco may conceal the scars incurred in the patching and rebuilding of an early house. This was a common occurrence in the homes which rose from the burned-out wreckage of Newark. Legend has it that when the Yankees fired the town on a cold winter night in 1813 leaving four hundred and fifty children and women homeless, a dear old grandmother wrenched this formidable structure from the wall and carried it to safety. Were it not for the legend one would be tempted to believe that the invaders had brought the mantelpiece with them. It is a *rara avis* in Upper Canada but it has a soul-mate in the museum in Cooperstown, New York, a much turned and be-pateraed mantelpiece from Flatbush. No legend attaches to the Davey mantelpiece, a sad lack of invention, one feels, for the Harrison mantelpiece fits the chimney breast to which it is now fixed and the Davey mantelpiece does not.

Another of the legends of Lincoln County has it that the huge mantelpieces, such as the drawing-room mantel from Locust Hall, St. David's (38), found in many of the homes of the 1830's are the work of shipwrights trying to beguile the boredom of the idle winter months. It may well be so. Someone was certainly bored. Unfortunately it may have been the client. There is much evidence of technical competence and a conspicuous lack of architectural conviction in this work and the Woodruffes were accustomed to the superior crafts-manship which had produced their old home at St. David's (39).

As yet there was no sharp break with a style in the first stages of atrophy. Details of proven satisfaction were carried over to the next phase. One such durable item was the spiral stair, another was the decorated cornice. The exterior decorated cornice varied from the simple early Doric, sometimes reduced to mutule and reeding as at Whitehall near Cobourg, to the gay bands of lozenge and triglyph which cavort under the eaves of Poplar Hall (40) and The Manor in Grimsby. Occasionally one sees two spaces just short of either end in the cornice, which at one time held decorative rain-water heads. The rain-water head was a small catch-basin on the down pipe of the eavestrough. The fine examples shown (41) are on the Billings house near Ottawa. This house was built in 1828 by Bradish Billings, one

38. *"Through the long, long wintry nights."*
Locust Hall, St. David's.

of the Ottawa valley's first lumber kings. His descendants still occupy the house, which is one of the few in the province to have a drawing-room above stairs still in use as a reception room and furnished as such.

The Billings house reputedly had verandahs two storeys in height. This does not seem to have been common Loyalist practice. Two-storey porches did occur infrequently. The style was not monumental. The orders of Classical architecture were certainly followed but from afar off — and Roman orders at that. Slim Hellenistic columns have a limited endurance, especially when made of wood, and barrel vaults of the kind so well preserved at The Manor in Grimsby (42) proved difficult to mend. The wood was easy to replace; not so the carpenter. Perhaps the relative simplicity of the hip-roof helped the porch at Whitehall, built near Cobourg by Zaccheus Burnham(43), to endure the freezing and thawing of many years. An early daguerreotype in the possession of the Brouse family of Iroquois is indisputable evidence of the incredible attenuation of the orders used and their relation to the composition of the house and of its surroundings.

Neither verandahs nor porches dignify that last gasp of the Loyalist style, Haughty Mac's house in Perth. It had almost everything else.

Daniel MacMartin built his house in

39. *The valiant beauty of a dying house.*
The old Woodruffe house, St. David's.

1839. It is illustrated here as a drawing (44) because so much of the original woodwork has been removed. Perth at the time was engulfed by British Colonists following the building of the Rideau Canal. It was an insular society given to damping the pretensions of North Americans. The colonial element bestowed the title Haughty Mac on Daniel MacMartin and referred to him as Yankee. He was a Yankee in the same sense that Laura Secord was, that is to say, he was a member of a Loyalist family whose regard for British institutions had brought it again into a wilderness which it had so recently been forced to defend. Haughty Mac's regard was being sorely tried, and being of anything but a pacific nature, he expressed his dissatisfaction in a truly North American manner. He built the biggest house in town.

The house was certainly a gesture of defiance. The Loyalist style favoured arcaded brick. The MacMartin house had also stone quoins. It had window lintels with elaborate keystones and two roof balustrades as well. Other Loyalist houses have a cupola, Haughty Mac's had three.

Daniel MacMartin was a lawyer. His

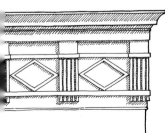

40. *Exterior cornice, Poplar Hall.*

41. *Rain-water heads on the Billings house, Billings Bridge.*

42. *The Manor, Grimsby. A Neo-classic porch*
applied to an earlier Georgian house.

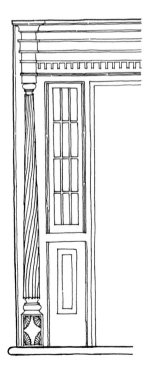

43. *A porch, light in scale, designed for the*
Neo-classic façade of Whitehall, Cobourg.

law office, otherwise adequately furnished, contained but one chair: his own. His clients might stand or they might go away. Neither tradition nor the mute evidence of his house indicates that such churlish behaviour marred his domestic hospitality.

Poor Haughty Mac and his expatriate British neighbours laboured on in a state of mutual misunderstanding. Homesick in their outpost of Empire, and baffled by customs too like their own to be accorded the tolerance graciously bestowed on those of natives in more exotic climes, the Colonists failed to appreciate the magnitude of what the Loyalists had accomplished in so brief a time. Haughty Mac was an exaggeration of the Upper Canadian point of view of 1839. Loyalists who had twice fought for the right to exist as British North Americans — fur traders of the North West Company who had made the paths and the maps which opened up the wilderness, and merchants whose enterprise established the bateau fleets, the stage lines and the banking system in Upper Canada — these were the native Upper Canadians. They had tried so hard to duplicate in the bush the amenities of European life, that any criticism of the result was very hard to bear. The Loyalists had made a great contribution to the founding of Upper Canada, culturally and architecturally. The Colonists had a different role to play, though of equal merit. Time and understanding were to blend the two.

44. The MacMartin house. The limit of Neo-classicism, Perth, 1839.

45. *In the Regency colonial style, design emphasis was no longer centred on the entrance door. It was diffused in villa and cottage by the use of several French windows. Whether the desire was to "cherish the tulip and prune the vine" or whether it was simply to smoke a cigar, the French window was primarily a means of direct communication with the garden. Thomas McKay's Rideau Hall, begun near Bytown in 1838, had five French windows in the garden front, two of which remain.*

66

3
Rule, Britannia

The founding pattern of a colony follows somewhat the recurring movement of the ocean surf. The first human wave flows in, impelled by some relentless force which utterly negates the perils involved, and with luck, consolidates its position before the impetus is spent. The second wave, its path smoothed, goes farther inland with even more impressive effect than the first. It is not the volume of immigration but the quality of the crest which controls the extent of achievement.

In assessing the worth of the United Empire Loyalists' contribution to the architectural heritage of Ontario, it has been necessary to seek out their areas of settlement and to look at the surviving buildings. The course of the second stream of influence is easier to chart. One may hie oneself to the nearest reference library: they spoke for themselves. Whereas the builders of the fine Georgian and Loyalist houses of Upper Canada were literate, the Colonists were literary.

The term Colonist as used here does not apply to all the migrants who streamed across the Atlantic in optimistic thousands from the Old World to the New, but rather to those individuals who came out with the definite intention of "founding the colony" and with a serene belief in their ability so to do. So firm, in fact, was this belief that it sometimes led them to found a town already established. Irritating as this behaviour undoubtedly was to those already on the site, Upper Canada needed in its formative years just such blind belief in a hereditary ability to govern, for with it went hereditary acceptance of the obligations involved. Forceful ancestors had won for the Colonists in the lands whence they came social and economic position which was voluntarily placed in jeopardy when they became settlers in Upper Canada. Those who had the most to contribute to their new country realized that their position could be retained only if they proved worthy of it. Furthermore they understood it to be a life-work.

These were not the governing birds of passage who wrestled with the problems of colonization for a term and then moved on to another outpost, but settlers whose lot was cast for good or ill with Upper Canada. Some of them had, it is true, gained their first knowledge of North America on the staff of either the Governor or the garrison and returned to take up land. The magnitude of the challenge was an incentive to the adventurous. The abundance of game held great attraction for young officers, few of whom paused to consider whether or not their dear life-partners would believe, with Captain Coote of the Eighth Foot, that a swamp full of wild fowl constituted "a veritable paradise." We do not know if many of the ladies were devotees of Diana but even if they were not, they came armed with an insulation of their own. They had all read the Romantic poets and they were prepared to find the wilderness sublime — an opinion with which the descendants of the United Empire Loyalists did not concur. Whoever may have written that most un-Canadian of poems, "A Canadian Boat Song," long attributed to John Galt, it was not a native Upper Canadian. "Fair these broad meads. These hoary woods are grand," was not a North American sentiment. Several generations of struggle with the persistent forest had left the Loyalists with an inclination to assess its grandeur in terms of potash and squared timber delivered at the port of Quebec. Contrary to all the romances, sensibility flourished best in an atmosphere of security and leisure backed by a well-stocked larder. The monumental struggle of the Loyalists to re-establish their way of life had taken its toll. The salt was in danger of losing its savour. However, it was a situation whose challenge the Colonists were well equipped to meet.

The haphazard arrival over the years of cosmopolitan and sophisticated Colonists provided a continual renewing leaven of novel ideas, the latest European fashions, and most important of all, a fresh optimism. Direct British influence in Upper Canada reached its maximum density in the years immediately following Waterloo. With Napoleon safely incarcerated in a pleasant Regency cottage on St. Helena, the younger sons could get on with the job of consolidating the colonies. Years of service abroad had rendered them temperamentally unfit for a sedentary existence at home. Many of them turned to Upper Canada where they had been preceded by veterans of the North American wars. Those who endured and survived and triumphed over the obstacles of toil, loneliness and provincial prejudice were strongly individual and their homes show it. Individuality sometimes appeared in the resolution required to build in the latest architectural style at the extreme limit of settlement or beyond it. Sometimes it lay in the determination with which the current trend was rejected.

High on the list of military and militant Colonists must always rank the names of Colonel Talbot, Dr. Dunlop, John Galt, Susan Sibbald, Hamnet Pinhey and Vice-Admiral Vansittart. It would be stretching the point past bearing to attempt to group their homes into anything like an Ontario colonial style but residence in Canada was in no way responsible for this. Even the most cursory acquaintance with their colourful histories suggests that they would have built to suit themselves in whatever country or century they happened to live. Conformists they were not in any area save that of religious practice and of strict adherence to a code of social conduct.

No individual, however strong, remains wholly uncoloured by his environment. The Colonists were all products of their day and they approached their building problems very much in the Romantic spirit, if not in that style. Those who would have rejected the term Romantic with greatest scorn were those to whom it most applied. They elected to build a style of house which they associated with Home. Unlike the Loyalists who recalled a modest, symmetrical North American Georgian house in stone or brick, the Colonists' thoughts turned to manor-houses in Britain which had grown steadily in size and magnificence over several centuries. At this time exposed timber framing emerged from its long Georgian eclipse to receive the Romantic accolade of being congruent with a sylvan setting. What could be more suitable to a wilderness abode than log construction?

Messrs. Talbot and Dunlop were not indulging in romantic flights when they built with log. Indeed, Talbot seems to have named his Canadian house in a spirit of contempt. Malahide, the heart of the Talbot settlement, whose capital was St. Thomas, was a low, rambling house on an impressive site. At all times it was eclipsed by the personality of its builder, so that few of his guests were moved to record a description of it. There is still a house called Malahide on the site but it is not the house as Colonel Talbot built it. He is known to have taken sad leave of his home in 1850 after it had been altered out of all recognition by the civilizing efforts of his nephew.

While Thomas Talbot was settling his British thousands around St. Thomas, another Empire builder of equal zeal and even greater eccentricity was helping to found the Canada Company. This was the celebrated Dr. William Dunlop, known as Tiger. Legend has it that Dr. Dunlop earned his nickname during the Far Eastern phase of his eventful career when he halted the charge of a man-eating tiger with a well-aimed box of snuff. Nothing as spectacular impeded his colonizing progress on the Maitland River when, in company with the poet-novelist John Galt, he founded Goderich. True, a slight set-back occurred when it was discovered that many wells hopefully excavated yielded salt water only, a source of future revenue which the pioneer did not appreciate.

Dr. Dunlop's famous house, Gairbraid, has suffered from the depredations of time. Two logs, reputedly once a part of his large manor-house, lie in a pile of lumber near the site. Dunlop was not only a raconteur of formidable dimension but he was himself the subject of anecdote. He moves through the history of Upper Canada emanating an aura of pioneering vision, practical jokes and whisky punch. A log house of ordinary size for such a man was unthinkable. Gairbraid, near Saltford, across the Maitland from Goderich, was a log manor-house built according to the old H-plan of Tudor times. Some historians purport to see in this plan and its modifications, the E-plan, a judicious bit of subtle flattery of the great Tudors, Henry and Elizabeth. Subtlety was not a governing characteristic of

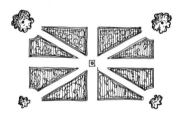

Dr. Dunlop and as he appears to have considered his sovereign to belong to the house of Guelph, he may be acquitted of any but the most practical considerations in adopting the H-plan for Gairbraid. The initials of succeeding monarchs being notably non-architectural, excessive loyalty was later expressed by use of the Union Jack design as a garden plan.

Gairbraid was not the only H-plan log manor-house in Upper Canada. Other British Colonists used the familiar arrangement for their forest homes. One of these, the Beehive (46), survives near Bobcaygeon. It was built in 1839 for the Reverend Hartley Dunsford by his second son Hartley and by George Bick, the family coachman. In the days of the Dunsfords, the great hall served its immemorial function of dining-room. Two doors on the right led to the library and the kitchen respectively and on the left two doors similarly placed opened into the drawing-room and the principal bedroom. Two large octagonal chimney stacks centred in the long axes of the wings served the fireplaces of each storey, which were set in pairs back to back. The total effect of the Beehive with its tall casement windows and gabled roof of steep pitch, broken at intervals by dormers, is of a manor-house of a Renaissance type common to England and northern Europe. But this is not northern Europe. The Renaissance, arriving in Bobcaygeon through the persons of Hartley Dunsford and George Bick, must wisely have sought local assistance. The expert log construction of the Beehive owes its quality to unknown craftsmen bred in the timber tradition of North America. Dunsford and Bick undoubtedly decided that the stair was to rise at one side of the great hall but if, as tradition has it, they actually built the house then they must have assimilated the architectural heritage of eastern Upper Canada with astounding speed as the stair has a striking affinity with the stairs of the Barnum, Blaikie, and Weller houses. However, the name, the Beehive, was imported from England. It derives from the Dunsford coat of arms which displays a hive and seven bees in the field.

A contemporary account of life among the armigerous families of Upper Canada has been set down for us by Anna Jameson in her *Winter Studies and Summer Rambles*. Too many of the houses which she visited have vanished with scarcely a trace — a faint tradition of graciousness, a broken fragment of wall, or a place name to mark their passing. One of these was the legendary and nebulous residence of Vice-Admiral Vansittart near Eastwood. Vice-Admiral Vansittart, according to H. J. Morgan's *Biographies of Celebrated Canadians*, was the youngest son of George Vansittart, Esquire, of Bysham Abbey, Berkshire, and his biographer goes on to say that he was present at the capture of the Cape of Good Hope and later captured twenty sugar vessels off Havana in 1806. The best course of action for a retired youngest son, after the Napoleonic Wars had ceased, was to emigrate. Vice-Admiral Vansittart emigrated to a large tract of land hard by Woodstock, Upper Canada. He seems also to have encouraged others to emigrate, to which end he employed as agent one Captain Drew. Undoubtedly Vansittart considered himself to be a founder of Woodstock. He saw to it that numbers of Englishmen settled in the area and he subscribed at once to the building of an Anglican church. In all probability it weighed with him not at all that the immediate area had been cleared of timber before his arrival by dissenters from New York

46. The Beehive, Bobcaygeon. A Tudor survival in plan.

State under the leadership of a family whose chief source of pride was a collateral ancestor who had served as a personal spy for George Washington. The founding of Woodstock thus provides local historians with controversial monograph material for years to come.

Vice-Admiral Vansittart's merits as a colonizer have been questioned by some. Even the site of his unusual dwelling is uncertain. Mrs. Jameson described it as reminiscent of an African village externally and with so complicated an interior arrangement that he could not have it insured. None of the surviving houses in the Eastwood area, on land known to have been in Vansittart possession, merits the Jamesonian description which seems to indicate that the Vice-Admiral's residence was not planned as a unit but became encrusted with additions as need for more space arose. Lacking any contemporary visual evidence to vindicate his taste, it is unsafe on verbal evidence alone to condemn him as necessarily insensitive to architectural form. Other Colonists built in the cumulative style as well. Two of his most spirited and sophisticated contemporaries, Susan Sibbald and Hamnet Pinhey, left to a grateful posterity houses which accumulated in an interesting and picturesque fashion as remote from each other as both are from Eastwood.

Hamnet Kirks Pinhey, merchant of Plymouth, blockade-runner and King's messenger, had lived both dangerously and profitably through the Napoleonic Wars. He arrived in Upper Canada in 1820. There he took up the land granted to him in March Township on the Ottawa River. The tract was eventually extended to one thousand acres and enjoyed a handsome river frontage. Did Hamnet Pinhey select the fine site for his house with the plans of Horaceville (47) full-blown in his mind's eye or did occupancy of that site, which commands a noble sweep of the river and the Gatineau Hills, dictate a suitable house? The very name Horaceville suggests a community of buildings. At any rate Mr. Pinhey proceeded to build his manor-house, discarding a series of outgrown dwellings as he went.

Close to the site of the existing house is a ruined one-roomed log cabin, which presents an uncompromising windowless chimney wall riverward, the door and window open to the sun. It was a utilitarian dwelling for temporary habitation. The second Pinhey house, also of log and also a ruin, was much larger. Reduced to a sturdy skeleton by the elements to which it lies exposed, remnants of elegance cling about it still. The entrance door, bleached to a silver-grey, retains the delicate mouldings of the 1820's on its six panels. Behind this house and at right angles to it is a rubble-stone kitchen joined at one time to the log

72

47. *The final edition of Horaceville, Pinhey's Point on the Ottawa River in March Township.*

48. The third stage of Horaceville from a drawing in the Public Archives of Canada.

house by a covered passage. A storey-and-a-half log house and attached kitchen may coincide with current ideas of adequate pioneer housing but it did not meet the requirements of many a pioneer. It lacked that absolutely indispensable adjunct of backwoods life — a ballroom. Just as soon as Hamnet Pinhey could locate an experienced mason he remedied the deficiency (48). A two-storey stone structure of greater size than the log house arose beside it. The ground floor housed the ballroom; the second storey, reached by a steep enclosed stair built against the chimney wall of the log house, contained a wide passage and three small bedrooms. A fixed ladder in the passage gave access to the attic, which is finished with plaster and lighted by a single dormer window. Externally, the ballroom wing is a curious blend of inherited and of fashionable taste. The impression is of a Cornish or South Devon farm-house, the disposition of its windows after Nash and the whole executed by a master mason who had served his apprenticeship in the neighbourhood of Brockville, Upper Canada. Since a later Pinhey project was to look even more like Brockville and as architecture is frequently studied to advantage by the comparative method, let us consider the ballroom façade in relation to Horaceville as a whole. Horaceville was completed at a later date presumably in the late thirties or early forties by the addition of an L-shaped house. One can scarcely designate as a wing a building which contains a drawing-room, a dining-room, an entrance hall, a pantry, a kitchen, three bedrooms, several passages and a billiard or sitting-room.

74

By the end of the thirties numerous stone masons, released for domestic building by the completion of the Rideau Canal, were seeking employment in Carleton and adjacent counties. Henceforth Horaceville was to present to the world a façade beautifully laid up in ashlar in a number of muted greys. Standing on a wind-swept promontory high above the Ottawa, the horizontal bulk of Pinhey's house partakes of the Pre-Cambrian massiveness of the Gatineau Hills in a manner to rejoice equally the spirits of the Regency Man of Taste, the builders of ancient Egypt and the shade of Frank Lloyd Wright. The long line of the gable roof, devoid, with a West Country dourness, of any form of decorative cornice, is broken only by the four massive chimney stacks. The disposition of the chimneys and the grouping of the windows symmetrically placed in relation to two false doorways, give the impression of two houses joined, or separated as one chooses to consider it, by a central area devoted to hallways and lighted in either storey by the entrance doorway and the casement window above it. The earlier or ballroom portion of the façade forms a Regency composition of voids and solids whose centre is a false doorway, a narrow opening surmounted by a semi-circular fan transom, reminiscent of an entrance doorway popular in the Brockville area. On either side of the false door and spaced at some distance from it are wide Regency windows, two casements of twelve panes flanked by sidelights a single pane in width. Three small square windows with casement sash light the three bed-

rooms above the ballroom. Window trim is reduced to the bare minimum of stone sills.

The later or drawing-room section of the façade is much closer to the vernacular style of Leeds County, both in the size and in the disposition of the windows about the semicircular-headed false door. There is nothing of the upper St. Lawrence about the entrance doorway of Horaceville, for the builder employed the shallow segmental Regency arch, structurally sound but here visually unhappy. Mr. Pinhey seems to have been as resourceful as he was disappointed. An elm tree planted directly in line with the front door and at no great distance from it effectively obscures the offend-

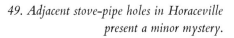

49. Adjacent stove-pipe holes in Horaceville present a minor mystery.

ing exterior Regency arch when one contemplates the façade from the bottom of the lawn.

Internally, Horaceville is remarkable for a processional stairway conceived in the grand manner but carried out by the local carpenter, for an ingenious comfort station of medieval origin, and for the number and diversity of its stove-pipe holes (49). Stoves in the 1830's might be embellished with cupids, garlands, cornucopia, columns and numerous finials but they unquestionably had an aura of heat as well as a certain visual éclat. Furthermore as improvements were continually being made in both the design and manufacture of stoves, alterations in the heating pattern of the house were frequent. The dismantling, cleaning, moving and reassembling of the various stoves and the accompanying labyrinths of pipes was well calculated to replace as a winter pastime, with all but a stubborn minority, the pioneer ploy of moving the stair.

In spite of the fact that as early as 1790, Cartwright of Kingston had been importing cooking stoves from Quebec, the kitchen fireplace was one of the last to be replaced. The kitchen of the later wing of Horaceville had a large one. The earlier rubble-stone kitchen seems to have been demoted to a summer kitchen and laundry. Certainly the small courtyard between it and the kitchen became a bleaching-green.

Horaceville completed, Hamnet Pinhey rounded out his building programme by constructing a very small fort and a slightly larger church. Needless to say local tradition credits the building of the fort to fear of the Indians without specifying which Indians could possibly have been hostile. It would be far more in character for Hamnet Pinhey to have built a root-house on which he ensconced some cannon from his blockade-running days. Be that as it may, it was his church not his fort which came to a violent end. It was blown up.

Neither controversy nor explosion attends the third conglomerate manor-house, Eildon Hall on Lake Simcoe, which owes its present composition largely to Susan Mein Sibbald. Any non-Sibbald flavour is attributable equally to Major Raines, who began the structure, and to the Department of Lands and Forests which finished it. Francis Paget Hett, in his *History of Georgina*, presents a charming picture of the building as it was when Mrs. Sibbald first saw it in 1835: "On a slight elevation nestled an old colonial house, white-walled, green-shuttered and surrounded by a verandah." In 1842 Lieutenant O. Borland, R.N., was inspired to make a sketch of the house with the Sibbald additions and improvements. Among other appurtenances Lieutenant Borland drew the verandahs, both the remnant of the

76

Raines verandah and the Sibbald verandah. The house has been restored without either of them but perhaps this should not cause surprise. A generation which could, in cast aluminum, describe a gentlewoman from Roxboroughshire as a "genteel Englishwoman" is perfectly capable of tearing off the verandah which gave the house its character.

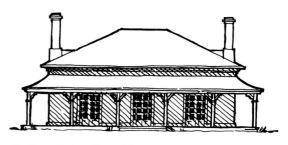

50. Penn Raines, Lake Simcoe, was too small for even a little harem.

Too often the verandah has fallen into undeserved disrepute as a late Victorian intrusion. It is quite true that the verandah had no part in Georgian architecture and but a restricted place in the Neo-classic period. Let us not be misled by Mr. Hett's term colonial, usually taken on this continent to refer to the architecture of the Thirteen Colonies; neither Major Raines nor Mrs. Sibbald was of that order of colonist. Susan Sibbald, described by her friend and fellow countryman, Bishop Strachan, as a "lady of great accomplishments and most agreeable manners," spent her early years at the Mein family seat, Eildon Hall in Roxboroughshire. At that time the literary world was reverberating to the Harp of the North swept by the persuasive hand of that great harbinger of Romanticism, Sir Walter Scott, her father's friend. Eildon Hall on Lake Simcoe was the inevitable result.

Major Raines' Regency cottage, Penn Raines (50), had been picturesquely adequate to the requirements of his household. Mrs. Sibbald added thereto a substantial two-storey house with a tower-like structure between it and the now amputated cottage. The additions made the house even more picturesque in the eyes of Mrs. Sibbald's contemporaries. It must also be borne in mind that Mrs. Sibbald was a widow with a large family to house. Major Raines' household had consisted of two beautiful sisters, who had accompanied him to Canada, and of such servants as seemed necessary to the trio.

Much is known of Susan Sibbald from her diaries and letters; very little beyond his erratic social behaviour is known of Major Raines. This is unfortunate, for Major Raines was, of the two, the more typical Colonist in that he elected to build a fashionable Regency cottage on a picturesque site on Lake Simcoe. No, not a summer cottage, but a Regency cottage, of which the flimsy dwelling in which Ontario keeps holiday is a modified, specialized descendant.

The Regency cottage in Ontario was a house of moderate size designed for year-round occupancy. Until very recently a pleasant example in brick stood in Toronto on the southeast corner of Wellesley and Yonge streets — hardly a resort area even in 1830. Nor was the style limited to the borders of Yonge Street. Regency cottages looked down on the waters of Lake Huron at Goderich. They still stand on wind-swept promontories above the Ottawa and the St. Lawrence, the Grand and the Speed. In Quebec, someone has confused the issue by calling them Anglo-Norman.

Take almost any Regency cottage, backtrack down the list of owners to the 1830's and the original incumbent frequently turns out to be a major if not a colonel. Should research unearth so unlikely a rank as captain a little judicious skirmishing in the files is likely to ferret out the magic letters R.N. It will be recalled that the close association of architecture and the retired half-pay officer has been encountered before in Upper Canada. The Regency officer-colonist was in a better situation than his Loyalist predecessor had been. He was not fleeing for his life. He had won his war. If he chose to encumber his passage with a rosewood sideboard, eight feet long, he might encounter derision but not confiscation. On his arrival in Upper Canada food and shelter, however unpalatable, could be bought. The situation of his civilian counterpart, the gentle or professional immigrant of means, was similar. Increasing stability and urbanity were attracting to the colony clergymen, teachers, lawyers, physicians, architects and engineers.

Although much of the colonization took place and many of the houses were built in the reign of William IV, in this as in every other aspect of life William was overshadowed by his more colourful brother, the Prince Regent. Thus the transitional style between the Georgian and the Victorian is called the Regency, dating roughly from the hopeless madness of George III to the trying sanity of Prince Albert.

The pace of living was increasing. The relocation of population, the shift from an agricultural to an industrial economy, the widening gap between wealth and its source and the increasing numbers of a leisure class with shallow cultural roots rendered professional assistance necessary in the planning not only of individual buildings but of whole areas.

The profession of architecture was not a new one. Whenever religious fervour, personal ambition or civic pride has required monumental expression, a designer has appeared who, by his sensitivity to harmony and balance, could translate an aesthetic ideal into the vernacular of sound building practice for his time and area. In the past such a man might plan a city, a palace, a temple or a garden for his patron, adapting his design to that indi-

78

vidual's requirements or tactfully weaning him away from inappropriate schemes. Now there was a need for multiple guidance, for a large number of trained professional architects, landscape architects and town planners, dedicated to the fearsome task of ensuring that the rights of man and citizen should include that of enjoying surroundings which were architecturally and physically satisfactory both to the individual and to the group. Domestic buildings of the transitional era embody and preserve the logical clarity with which the majority of architects met the challenge. There was need for the reassurance of a clear, unequivocal statement in design. It could be had simultaneously in architecture, in furnishings and in costume, with taste and a leavening degree of whimsy.

Not for several centuries had the world of fashion found leadership near the throne. Britain has not enjoyed entirely felicitous relations with those among her roster of kings who have patronized the arts. Domestic building in the golden years of the great Georgian age, in spite of the name, had flourished under the patronage of a landed aristocracy without either encouragement or hindrance from the monarchs. George IV was the builder of his line. The society which revolved about him as Prince Regent was an urban one. The London season was interesting and residence in town was once more desirable. When the pleasures of town palled, society moved *en masse* to the seaside; when concentrated high living exhausted even its immense vitality, society flocked to the spas.

During the Regency, patronage of design in architecture, furnishings and costume was controlled by the dictates of that self-appointed arbiter, the Man of Taste. Fortunately for all not a few of these gentlemen had good taste. Nominal supremacy belonged of course to the Regent himself but there were enough powers around the throne to maintain a general high level in design. Prinny's own taste was flamboyant and expansive. It sometimes led him to architectural excess. In the onion domes of the Pavilion at Brighton his architect, Nash, gave admirable expression to the Regent's own ponderous gaiety, and as a seaside palace, it was a great success. The challenge to the Regent's vanity had been great. Returning East India Company nabobs were building in the Moorish style. The Regent had to outdo Seizencote. Fortunately no one felt compelled to exceed the Regent. The Regency took its own idiosyncracies with a grain of salt: an ogee arch or a Moorish gazebo sufficed the majority as a gesture to fashion.

The Regency taste desired that all things should be congruent. This they interpreted to mean, with regard to architecture, that town houses should be composed in squares and crescents or set in planned parks to combine urban efficiency with visual harmony, and that country houses should be pastoral and picturesque.

Regency society admired the country more in the abstract and understood it less in the particular than had the Georgians. They sought to rescue its beauty from the rustic inhabitants in much the same spirit as that which inspired Lord Elgin to save the Parthenon marbles from the Greeks. The Regency attitude toward Classical architecture was respectful but reserved. There was greater national concern for the success of the Greeks, then fighting for freedom from the Turks, than there was for the correct use of the Greek orders.

In the interest of the picturesque, professional landscape architects were extensively employed to compose and improve the rural scene. An early manifestation of improvement was the appearance of architectural designs for cottages to house lodge-keepers and labourers. Their primary function may have been to enhance the vista from the drawing-room window but they undoubtedly enhanced the tenants' life as well. Even the Gothic taste made more extensive use of windows than the Middle Ages could achieve.

In the country also, the landscape architect advised the client on the site most advantageous to his residence and on the style most suited to the site. Regency love of the dramatic led to the selection of some vastly imposing but pitilessly exposed building sites. Brick and stone seldom thrive under the lash of sea gales and to ensure survival, stucco or pebble dash became the fashionable protective coating. The resulting uniform surface set off to advantage both the fine proportion of the main massive composition and the linear patterns of current ornament.

This was an era of experiment in composition with simple and complex geometric shapes. Cylindrical and segmental forms were employed in conjunction with a central rectilinear block. Octagonal cottages were built. Roofs were flattened in pitch and allowed to project in a wide Italianate eave borrowed from the Florentine villa, severely plain as to trim. If a Gothic flavour seemed desirable, the roof was raised in height, gabled and ornamented with tracery so plastic in form that it suggests an ancestry deriving from Venetian glass rather than from Caen stone. In either event the chimneys were tall and decorative.

Under the aegis of the landscape architect gardening became a fashionable pursuit.

To ensure maximum visual communion with the garden, villas and cottages were planned to have numerous large windows and, where possible, these took the form of floor-length casements in the French style. Fortunately the Regency architect provided for winter habitation on the picturesque site by inventing the double window. British North America was grateful.

Regency French windows might give direct access to the lawn or to a verandah. The verandah was an amenity foreign by name and nature when it made its brief appearance in Regency England. The Georgian gentleman had been familiar with the Gothic cloister as a design for shelter and he had admired the loggia in Italy when on the Grand Tour, but he felt no urge to build one on his return home. The last thing he needed was shelter from the sun. The Regency gentleman, on the other hand, had had a different background. Grand Tours had ceased with the Napoleonic Wars. If he had sojourned on the continent, it was in the train of the Iron Duke with a prolonged enforced stay in the Peninsula; if he had recently acquired wealth as a civilian, it was more than likely to have been in the Indies, East or West. Either occupation had engendered a healthy respect for the midday sun and a lively interest in the ways of mitigating its lethal effects. At home in England he built stuccoed villas at Cheltenham and Brighton with balconies where cast-iron treillage, mass-produced in the industrial north, replaced the wrought iron used in Spain and Portugal.

Superficial research into the etymology of the word verandah leads one through a morass of Indian and Nepalese terms to the hopeful suggestion that it may be of Portuguese origin. The Regency gentleman, infinitely more concerned with comfort than with semantics, combined Iberian and Eastern designs to produce the verandah of the colonial Regency cottage. Neither wrought nor cast iron was indispensable. Native materials were substituted at will. Whether fashioned of iron, pine or bamboo the Regency treillage and awning roof was to be as much a hall-mark of British colonialism as gin and tonic and for the same reasons: the sun and ague were universal. The Colonists whose destiny directed them to Upper Canada found that they needed both double windows and the verandah and that the mosquito netting of the East was useful too.

There are, scattered about the province, a number of houses of a transitional Regency with vestiges of the Loyalist style. It is reasonable to assume that much the same blend of sophistication and provincialism produced them all. They were built to the require-

51. Inverarden was built at Gray's Creek in 1816 by John McDonald of Garth, wintering partner of the North West Company.

ments of travelled and observant gentlemen who dictated the general allocation of space and overall concept of design but who were impatient with or uninformed about its detail. The local architect then solved the problems so carelessly bequeathed him in the light of personal inspiration, past experience, and such help as could be gained from consulting his copy of Asher Benjamin's latest work. Asher Benjamin was not really of much assistance. To be sure, his instructions for stair building and the like were painfully explicit but the Regency was *terra incognita* to him. It was a British style and seldom met with in the new republic.

Two early examples of the Regency cottage, executed by Loyalist craftsmen, are Thorne Lodge later to be known as Toronto House and Inverarden (51). Both cottages are of stone with half-octagon bays at each end of the façade. Thorne Lodge in Toronto Township was built in the fashion of the smaller British country house on shallow footings directly on the ground. Inverarden, the earlier house, located at Gray's Creek on the St. Lawrence below Cornwall, was built in an area of hard winters and deep frost where pioneer experience had proven the usefulness of a deep excavation. Loyalist builders frequently located a number of the domestic offices in this cellar storey, the kitchen, laundry and storage areas especially. It was such a sensible way in which to meet the extremes of the Canadian climate that it was to become an integral part of the Regency cottage in Upper Canada. The cellar storey of Inverarden contains a kitchen and storage areas and, in addition, servants' bedrooms. Like the Anglo-Norman cottages of Quebec it is a storey-and-a-half house, the storey being above and the half below, with a concealed bedroom storey in the deep roof. It was a house worthy of a gentleman-adventurer.

Although the term gentleman-adventurer is, strictly speaking, a part of the style and title of the Hudson's Bay Company, it is safe now to assert that there were as many adventurers in the rival North West Company and quite as many gentlemen. It would have been unwise to say so in Upper Canada in 1816, the year in which Inverarden was being built at Gray's Creek for John McDonald of Garth.

McDonald of Garth was a partner in the North West Company during the stormiest years of its bitter rivalry with the Hudson's Bay Company. He had just enjoyed the dubious honour of being one of the company of distinguished Canadians imprisoned at the instigation of Lord Selkirk, the eccentric and misguided peer who had made a second unsuccessful attempt to settle displaced Scottish crofters in Canada. His first colony, at Baldoon in Upper Canada, failed because it was not accessible to any source of supply. The second failure was more spectacular. Lord Selkirk brought his settlers to the Red River at the moment when it was the battleground for one of the most violent commercial wars Canada has ever known. The trade war between the Hudson's Bay Company and the North West Company was a military campaign fought with the usual weapons. Innocent people were killed. Lord Selkirk laid charges against prominent Nor'Westers. Neither of the combatant companies was free of blame but Selkirk had friends in the Hudson's

52. The hand of the British joiner can be seen in the decorative panelling executed at Duldregan in 1821 by Edwin Pridham of Montreal, late of Half Moon Street, London.

54. Regency charm in Credit River stone. Thorne Lodge, Erindale.

Bay Company. The North West Company had friends too, and more to the point, they were in York where the trial was held. Furthermore the Nor'Westers had given twelve thousand pounds toward the building of Yonge Street. They were acquitted, but the great days of the North West Company were over, and the partners retired and scattered. Simon Fraser went home to St. Andrews, Upper Canada. His friends, the Welsh geographer and explorer, David Thompson and John McDonald of Garth, settled near him, Thompson in John Bethune's White House in Williamstown and McDonald of Garth at Gray's Creek.

In the exasperating way of so many early writers, McDonald of Garth makes no mention of life in Stormont County in his journals, although he was certainly living at Gray's Creek when he wrote of his life in the Northwest. He does mention his brother, who was a successful merchant in London, and it is logical to suppose that it was he who chose and shipped the Regency furniture sent out for Garth's new home. The collection includes a rosewood harpsicord by John Broadwood of London, "makers of pianos to his Majesty and the Princesses," two sofas, a sofa table, a pair of pedestal card tables, a dining table, sideboard and chairs, a secretary-bookcase, an *oeil-de-boeuf* mirror surmounted, not by the ubiquitous eagle, but by a heraldic

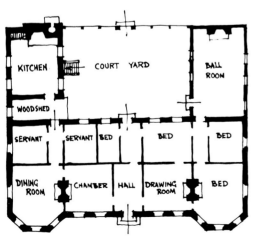

53. Plan of Thorne Lodge, Erindale.

horse. Doubtless this inventory was typical of the furnishings of many a Regency cottage in Upper Canada. In the case of Inverarden there is no need for speculation; the furniture is still in the possession of Garth's descendants.

The interior trim of Inverarden's doors and windows, an elaborate over-attenuated moulding on the panels, is of the school of joinery peculiar to the eastern area of Upper Canada, and which drew its craftsmen from Montreal. Certainly of the houses that boast this trim, Duldregan (52), Inverarden, Maplehurst at Maitland, the MacLean house in Cornwall and the MacDonnell house at Point Fortune had trade connections with that city and two of them with the North West Company.

55. Ridgewood Park sits in Romantic isolation at Saltford near Goderich.

Externally, at Inverarden, Regency taste reigns. The casement windows are set in a stuccoed wall with little or no trim and narrow sills. The cellar windows are square. Placed high in the façade the fan-transomed, sidelighted door is minimized by the sheer bulk of the house. Obliterate the dormer, a later intrusion, and the statement of Regency simplicity is strong — a satisfactory colonial style. Simplicity and a gracious concept of life are expressed in the plan: a wide centre hall, dining-room on the left with a music room beyond it and a bedroom behind; on the right the drawing-room, the library, and a second bedroom, then additional guest bedrooms lighted by rear dormers in the roof, with the kitchen and staff quarters in the cellar.

Thorne Lodge, or Toronto House, is cellarless and hence more involved in plan (53). Of rusty-grey Credit River stone (54), it was built sometime after 1822 by Colonel Peter Adamson, a Colonist on whom the Peninsular War had left its mark. Invalided home after losing the use of a hand, his best friend left for dead on the battlefield, Colonel Adamson settled down in England to a hard-earned peace. Sometime thereafter he married his friend's widow. A daughter was born to them and the future seemed all tranquillity. Then one fine day, some two years later, the friend returned, recovered at last from his near-mortal wounds. Colonel Adamson took passage for Upper Canada, bringing with him his daughter Ellen, his half-brother Doctor Adamson, and enough English hawthorn to plant a hedge. He applied for land in Toronto Township, and presumably planted the hawthorn in 1822. By 1825 he was applying to the Provincial Secretary on behalf of Doctor Adamson for the post of physician to the Indians on the Credit. One assumes that the building of Thorne Lodge had kept both brothers busy in the intervening years.

Thorne Lodge is a one-storey house. Its reception rooms are laid out in a manner markedly similar to Inverarden, although the position of dining-room and music room seems to have been reversed in Thorne Lodge, to facilitate access to the kitchen which was located in a wing. The assembly room, an earlier kitchen wing, and the quarters for farm labourers, all of which completed the walls of the courtyard at one time, were of wood construction. The windows have been resashed and may at one time have had casements. As in Inverarden the chimneys are utilitarian and rather squat for a Regency house. Both houses have narrow eaves. Thorne Lodge has no verandah. Colonel Adamson had quite enough to remind him of Portugal.

The Regency cottage *per se* appeared in Upper Canada in its definitive form in the 1830's. By that date a sufficient number of British craftsmen had permeated the building trades to make possible the execution of a cottage that was Regency within and without. Areas being settled or expanding in the reign of William IV and the early years of Victoria usually have several colonial Regency cottages and vernacular derivatives of the style.

It has been established earlier in the chapter that the typical Regency cottage would be located on a dramatic or romantic site; that it would be a storey and a half in height; that in plan it might be square, octagonal or rectangular with wings or bays; that it would have large windows and a relatively insignificant entrance door; that there would be an awning-roofed verandah with fanciful treillage and tall decorative chimneys.

The most dramatic of Upper Canadian Regency sites is surely that of Ridgewood Park (55). Perched in a dense grove of trees which looks across the Maitland River above Saltford, it retains to this day its villa-in-the-wilderness aspect. Closer inspection resolves the wilderness into an orderly park in which sits a square rough-cast-on-log cottage. The hip-roof is crowned by an ornamental balustrade. The chimneys are paired and decorated with sunken panels and elaborate caps. A highly improbable Renaissance processional stair-

86

way now leads up to the front door. The door is lighted by four large panes of glass on either side and by a transom arched in the flattened Tudor form. This doorway is similar to one designed by John Howard, a Toronto architect, which dates to the 1840's.

One day perhaps, diligent research will discover who built Ridgewood Park. It has been attributed to a Belgian nobleman, Baron de Tuyle. The property was registered by the de Tuyle family in 1841, but Colonel Van Egmond is said to have lived at Ridgewood Park in 1835, and as early as 1827 the de Tuyles were purchasing land in the area. If Colonel Van Egmond once owned Ridgewood, that fact alone would have been enough to obscure the title. Whether he actually led a detachment of Mackenzie's rebel force at Montgomery's Tavern or whether he only arrived in time to share in defeat, he was certainly imprisoned in York where he died of exposure and starvation. Goderich drew a veil of embarrassed silence over the part played in her founding by the disillusioned soldier who left Europe to seek liberty in Upper Canada. Politically the de Tuyles were impeccable, biographically they are elusive. Their title is not to be found in the Almanach de Gotha, at least not now. One fact is beyond debate: the superb site of Ridgewood was selected and purchased for the de Tuyles by Captain Henry Wolsey Bayfield, R.N., who carried out hydrographic surveys on the St. Lawrence and the Great Lakes after the War of 1812. Special mention must be made too of Henry Yarwood Attrill who, after purchasing Ridgewood from Sir Alexander Tilloch Galt in 1873, contrived to build a large house contiguous with it without impairing the character and charm of either building.

A vintage year for the Regency style in Upper Canada was 1833. In that year Admiral Vansittart's land agent, Captain Andrew Drew, was building a cottage in Woodstock; Riverest (56) was rising to the order of John Marston at L'Orignal on the Ottawa River; on Burlington Heights, Dundurn, Sir Allan Napier MacNab's "Fort on the Water," had been under construction for a year; and in York a gay whimsical villa was designed for Bishop Strachan's son-in-law, Thomas Mercer Jones. The Jones villa was the work of an English architect, John G. Howard, recently appointed by Sir John Colborne to the post of drawing-master at Upper Canada College. All that now remains of the Jones villa is the original plan in the Howard papers, but John Howard's own Regency cottage, Colborne Lodge, built three years later (57), stands open to visitors, a familiar landmark in Toronto's High Park.

Colborne Lodge, Riverest and the Drew cottage, admirable expressions of the

56. The gay treillage, lovely garden and tall white pines of Riverest, 1833, at L'Orignal on the Ottawa.

Regency style, are as similar and as different as three individual designers reared in the same tradition could make them. We know the architect of one cottage; the other two share a like quality of taste, of fitness to their site and to their scale of living. It may not be accidental that quite handsome churches were being built close by in both Woodstock and L'Orignal when these cottages were erected. There were architects in the area at the time. All three cottages are, in the Regency phrase, "congruent to their sites." All are low, basically massive buildings, hip-roofed, wide-eaved, united with the gardens by wide verandahs whose posts seem to have grown up to support the roofs, the horizontal composition relieved by dormers and ornamented chimney stacks. Two of them were built on romantic Regency sites. Riverest stands on a bluff above the Ottawa River, a distant prospect of the Laurentian Hills beyond. Colborne Lodge, from a height of land, views Lake Ontario intentionally, the C. N. R. and the Gardiner Expressway inadvertently.

57. Colborne Lodge, 1836, was designed and built by John G. Howard as his Toronto home.

58. Bysham Park, Eastwood, 1851. The texture of the actual building material was seldom allowed to influence the exterior of the Regency cottage. Stucco or pebble dash was the fashionable surface.

The occupation of land agent required that Captain Drew be accessible to his clients. His cottage is set back in a well-planned town lot and is marked by a certain reserve in trim. The tall chimneys are devoid of ornament. Pairs of four by fours set on panelled podia support the verandah roof which sweeps from immediately below the cornice of the house.

Bysham Park (58) near Eastwood was built later than Captain Drew's cottage but shared many of its characteristics. It was built in 1851 by Henry Vansittart, one of the sons of Captain Drew's employer, Vice-Admiral Vansittart. The original verandah of Bysham is missing but the roof lantern is still in place. Two bedrooms receive a modicum of light from this little lantern. A similar lantern, now replaced in function by a dormer, once lighted the upper hall of Captain Drew's cottage, and small dormers at the back light the upper bedrooms as they do at Inverarden.

The apparent indifference of Regency cottage builders to light and air in the bedroom storey is not quite as callous as it seems. While it is true that the majority of Regency cottages had a large bedroom on the ground floor for the master of the vineyard, it is quite likely that he kept his large windows closed at night. Night air was still suspected of being malarial. The Drew cottage has double-hung windows, a concession to town life perhaps. The normal Regency cottage window was a floor-length casement as at Colborne Lodge. Captain Drew's windows are Regency in their scale. Large panes of glass set in spidery muntins, twelve to a sash and double hung, provide windows which extend from the deep baseboard to the ceiling of his cottage. Smaller panes of glass were used at Riverest, and in this charming house Regency taste dictated that not only both entrance doors but all the casement windows as well should have sidelights and semi-circular fan transoms. This is a form of Palladian window (with or without the fan transoms) designated Venetian in nineteenth-century journals. At Riverest the fans are whimsically echoed in the gay scallops of the verandah treillage.

At first glance Colborne Lodge is more sedate than its contemporaries: no awning curves sweep the verandah roof, the

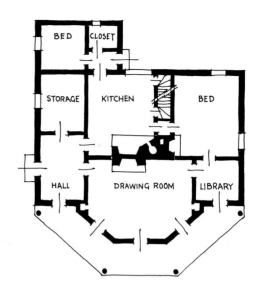

59. This plan of Colborne Lodge is included in the Howard papers in the Toronto Public Library.

91

60. Marble mantelpiece, Colborne Lodge drawing-room. The eye accustomed to the intricacies of Neo-classicism will find the Regency mantelpiece either beautifully simple or just a bit dull.

supports are simply wooden posts, and the bedroom windows, two casement eyes, peer out from under the wide eaves. There is a stodgy two-storey kitchen wing at the back through which, unfortunately, one now enters the house. One could scarcely be further from John Howard's original thought. His plans for Colborne Lodge exist with the later alterations pencilled in. As first designed (59) the Lodge was a basically octagonal one-storey house, its gently pitched, multi-angular roof crowned by the three cylindrical chimneys, which are now located one storey higher up. A curious jog in the dining-room wall beside the existing fireplace recalls the first location of the bake oven, unbearable in summer, and speedily relegated to the cellar. A stairway, inserted in the storeroom now become the pantry, gave access to the new kitchen and increasing prosperity provided the servants whose quarters were located around it. No longer would the visiting Bishop of Quebec find Mrs. Howard doing the laundry on the back porch.

Presumably it was during its second phase that Colborne Lodge acquired its Greek mantelpieces. Regency designers were not troubled by the dearth of mantels in antiquity. John Howard composed a mantelpiece for his drawing-room (60) by applying Greek motifs to a standard Georgian form. A linear pediment surmounts the fire opening, an acroterion at each end, and over all is a bracketed mantel shelf. A pattern for the acroterion exists still, showing rows of pin pricks in a drawing by which the cutter transferred the curves to the marble surface. John Howard knew his Classical orders. He had a folio edition of an eighteenth-century work on the subject. He simply was not interested in copying.

The Colborne Lodge now on public view represents the third phase of John Howard's life there. A designer, architect and engineer, he tried out anything new that appealed to his love of experiment. His house was altered for the last time to install a bathroom, and a kitchen designed to function around a closed cooking stove. The small wing at the back was raised to two storeys in height and a kitchen added. The old ground-floor bedroom was divided to make a stair-hall and a bathroom (61). There is nothing in the plan of Colborne Lodge to indicate the date of the pencilled alterations. The one-storey Colborne Lodge may have existed only on the drawing-board and the stair shown on the plan have gone up to a bedroom over the kitchen rather than down to the cellar. As Howard was going to direct his own builders, he did not need to draw up three sets of plans. There is, however, sufficient structural evidence in the house to warrant belief that it was completed in three

61. *A fixed bathtub in a special room was an amenity sometimes installed at an early date by the Regency architect or engineer in his own villa. Portable hip-baths continued in general use until the end of the century.*

93

stages with the alterations in plan, room use and elevation more or less as indicated.

The compact plan of Colborne Lodge allows for maximum heat circulation throughout the ground floor. Not so Riverest (62) elongated and facing toward the Ottawa and the Arctic. In the partition wall between the hall and the drawing-room of Riverest is an opening, trimmed in accord with the door frames and having a panelled removable screen. This is an early example of the heat hole (63). The screen was removed in the winter to allow warmth from the drawing-room fire to penetrate to the icy hall. The screen is panelled to match the drawing-room doors but with four panels instead of six. The trim is typical of the 1830's interior — a heavy linear moulding, the corner-box plain or turned. Mantelpieces in Riverest and in the Drew cottage (64) are of good proportion and rather austere — cottage Regency at its best. The builders of the Regency cottage in Upper Canada retained the fireplace for aesthetic reasons. At the same time they were likely to introduce small stoves as auxiliary heating in passages and bedrooms, or for summer cooking. The heat hole was to become common by 1841 when the box-stove had largely replaced the fireplace as a heat source and Upper Canada had become Canada West.

From 1854 until 1856 the destinies of the Canadas, West and East, were presided over by Prime Minister Sir Allan Napier MacNab, laird of Dundurn in Hamilton. A Regency gentleman, out of context in the Victorian age, Sir Allan MacNab has suffered for a long time at the hands of posterity. Now that the pendulum of understanding has swung back again, historians are seeking to place MacNab's contribution to the building of Canada in its proper light. To delineate the many-sided character of this patriot and statesman, who was by turns a war hero at sixteen, an actor, a carpenter, first Queen's Counsel in Upper Canada, Prime Minister, a railway magnate and a baronet, is a monumental task, and historians are baffled by the lack of material. His public life is well documented. His personal papers have disappeared.

Born at Niagara in 1798 of Scottish parents, who were in government circles and in debt, Allan MacNab was educated at the Home Grammar School at York. Articled in the Attorney-General's office, he was ultimately called to the Bar in 1826. He moved to Hamilton in the same year. In 1832 he purchased, from John S. Cartwright for twelve thousand, five hundred dollars the land on Burlington Heights, which General Vincent and Colonel Harvey had fortified against the invasion of 1813. What could be more congruent with a great house

94

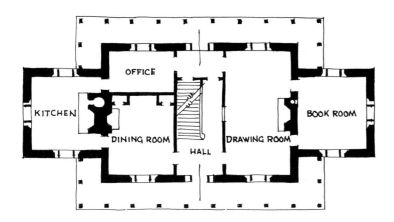

62. The floor plan of Riverest.

63. Heat hole, Riverest. Heat holes were openings in the partition wall opposite the heat source. In summer the hole was closed with a panelled screen. In winter the screen was removed, allowing heat to reach the adjacent room.

64. Dining-room mantelpiece, Drew cottage, Woodstock. Nelson, who built the cottage for Captain Drew, was a cousin of Trafalgar's hero.

95

65. Regency Picturesque Gothic in Toronto. Holland House was built by Henry John Boulton in 1834.

than a site on Burlington Bay, with ruins and earthworks in the garden? To make it even more right and romantic, Dundurn, the title of one of the chieftainships of Clan MacNab means "Fort on the Water."

For three years MacNab worked at his castle. As it appeared when completed in 1835 it was the largest Regency house in Upper Canada and it is the only one of great scale which has survived in an identifiable state. Tradition has it that MacNab was his own architect. It may be true and if so, he was in the best eighteenth-century tradition and in the company of other gentlemen of Upper Canada of similar inclination. Henry John Boulton had just completed Holland House on Wellington Street in York (65). Archdeacon George Okill Stuart built Summerhill (66) in Kingston in 1838. It is quite probable that each of these gentlemen employed a skilled master builder, if not an architect trained in Great Britain, who received such scant recognition for his creativity that it was not deemed worth while to record his name.

Without doubt MacNab discussed his plans for Dundurn with Boulton and Stuart. All three gentlemen were interested in building and all were closely associated in the Government of Upper Canada. Moreover Mary Stuart of Kingston was the second wife of Sir Allan MacNab. Archdeacon Stuart was her uncle and Mrs. Henry John Boulton was her aunt.

Holland House, Dundurn (67) and Summerhill represented for Upper Canada Regency architecture in the grand manner. All three houses were in the style of their spiritual godfather, Henry Holland, architectural adviser to the Prince Regent. Holland's services to the Prince Regent were largely confined to alterations at Carlton House and to designs for the first Royal Pavilion at Brighton. His services to architecture lay in designing elegant

96

country houses. It was left for Nash to transform Buckingham House into a palace, but it should never be forgotten, in assessing the Regency style, that it ran the whole scale of design from the cottage to one of the best known of the world's palaces.

Henry John Boulton may have had access to Holland's drawings; he must certainly have known his buildings, for he spent his impressionable youth in Regency England where he had a connection with the Foxes of Holland House. MacNab and Stuart may have had their introduction to the work of Henry Holland at second hand from enthusiastic descriptions by Boulton and his friend Thomas Ridout, but they were all of the company described

66. One hundred and sixty-eight running feet of domestic ambition, Summerhill was built in Kingston in 1838 by Archdeacon George Okill Stuart, who lived in it for a year. Parliament and power were withdrawn and Summerhill, shorn of its porticoes and parapets, became a part of Queen's University.

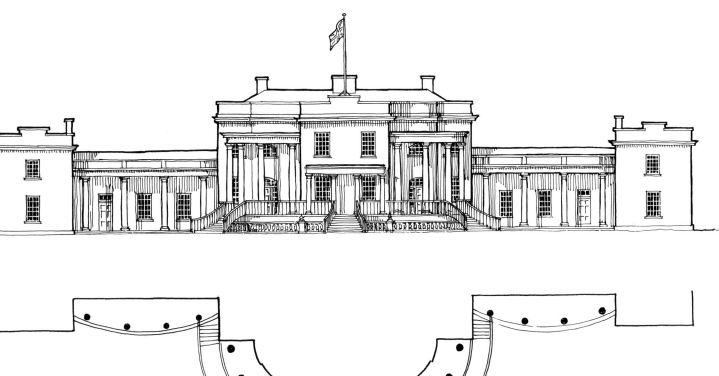

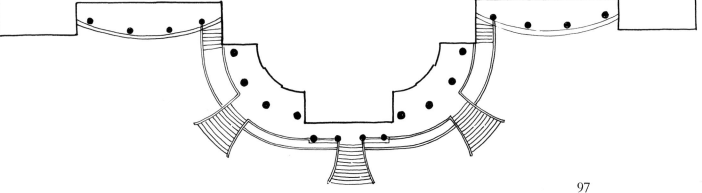

97

by A. E. Richardson and H. D. Eberlein, who wrote of Henry Holland: "He was the unacknowledged leader of a number of architects such as Thomas Leverton, Bonomi and Samuel Pepys Cockerell, together with those surveyors, carpenter architects and masons who had the confidence to work out their own salvation." The Boulton interpretation of Holland's spirit can be seen in photographs in the John Ross Robertson Collection, Toronto Public Library. The denuded remnants of Summerhill now house the medical library and the residences of the Principal and the Vice-Chancellor of Queen's University. Dundurn, more or less intact, is a museum on the eastern approaches to Hamilton.

Both Boulton and MacNab followed Holland's practice of building in brick and covering the surface with stucco. The exterior wall surfaces of both Holland House and Dundurn were bisected horizontally by decorative string courses which became the base line of the verandah parapets. This was a favourite Holland device and one which he used at Southill Park, Bedfordshire. Stuart chose the form of Southill for Summerhill. He used Kingston limestone as his building medium and it is difficult to tell now whether or not he had the surface stuccoed. The relation of the proportions of the central block to the wings was very reminiscent of Southill: the connecting colonnades were almost identical. Then Stuart, or his architect, embarked on a truly remarkable digression from the building practice customary in Upper Canada. Summerhill had a balustraded dry moat as a light-well for the basement kitchen and servants' hall. Three sets of flying steps bridged the moat giving access to the porticoes from the formal garden. The blithe disregard for the winter climate of Kingston demonstrated by this feature of Summerhill does not suggest the hand of Archdeacon Stuart, a North American of the third or fourth generation, but rather the Regency insouciance of one of the English architects, perhaps Edward Horsey or George Browne, who are known to have been in Kingston and Quebec in 1838.

All three major villas possessed in some measure the Regency device of combining half-cylinders or quarter-cylinders with oblongs and cubes in the formal massing of the house. At Wimbledon House, Holland had set a half-cylindrical bow-window on top of the larger half-cylindrical porch at the entrance, and at one side of the façade an arcaded loggia was glazed to form an orangery. Boulton adopted the composition of the half-cylinders for the garden front of Holland House. Stuart used quarter-cylinders in the central portion of Summerhill, while Dundurn acquired the loggia on its garden front. The half-cylinder

67. *Here he lived in state and bounty and in debt. Dundurn, the residence of Sir Allan MacNab, 1835.*

68. *Plan of the principal reception rooms at Dundurn, Hamilton, 1835.*

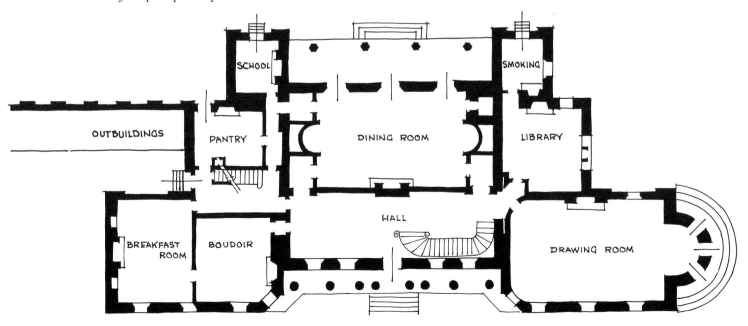

appeared on Dundurn as a bow-shaped bay for the drawing-room. The other end of the drawing-room was curved to match the bay, as can be seen in the accompanying floor plan (68). The scale and complexity of Dundurn has given credence to many legends, all of which may be discounted when one takes into consideration the manner in which the house was built and the taste of its owner. Structurally complete in 1835, Dundurn was actually altered and embellished well on into the fifties as MacNab's credit ebbed and flowed.

Some time after the completion of the building, a major installation of fine joinery was made at Dundurn. The dining-room ceiling was raised, semi-circular alcoves were constructed to accommodate a pair of fine sideboards (69), and handsome two-panelled doors in the Greek taste were framed by wide architrave trim and surmounted by heavy cornices on carved console brackets. In the hall a walnut stair swept boldly, if a trifle awkwardly, up to the principal bedrooms. On this floor later owners of Dundurn have cut into MacNab's plan to the extent that the only MacNab feature of which one can be certain is the view through the windows, from one of which can still be seen the little octagonal building (70) in the garden which housed the cockpit. Cock-fighting, a major Regency pastime, fell into such Victorian disrepute that a later plan of the estate describes this building as the poultry house.

The basement storey of Dundurn contained a large kitchen with a built-in cast-iron stove as well as a fireplace. At the far end of the passage was the laundry. The copper cauldron for heating water is still in place (71), as is the pierced stone drainhead. Between the kitchen and the laundry was the large number of storerooms, workrooms and servants' accommodations necessary to a house of some size. It is unlikely that the vault off the laundry was ever the powder magazine that tradition would have it. Sir Allan was a Regency practical joker, with a family motto of *Timor Omnis Abest* (Afraid of Nothing), but the proximity of the door leading to the garden hard by the cockpit suggests that the little room was more likely to have been a brandy cache.

There was in Upper Canada, in 1838, yet another Regency villa. Lacking the pretentiousness of Dundurn and Summerhill, it was more comparable in spirit to Holland House. It had an interesting silhouette, well-designed interior space, elegant reception rooms, and a well-bred restraint in the choice of ornament. It is quite probable that Messrs. Boulton, MacNab and Stuart had never heard of it. The villa was called Rideau Hall, and it had just

100

69. One of the pair of
monumental sideboards
installed in the larger
dining-room at Dundurn
in 1846.

71. The copper laundry
cauldron in the lower
regions of Dundurn.

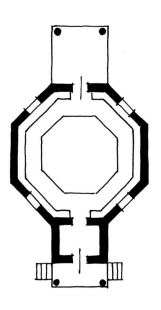

70. An echo of Regency sport: the cockpit,
Dundurn, with accompanying floor plan.

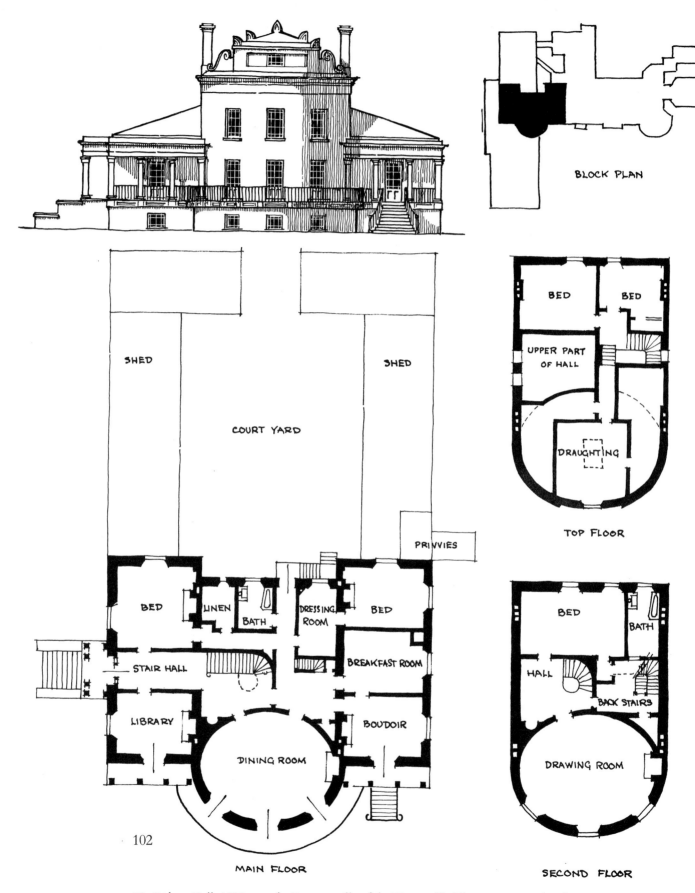

BLOCK PLAN

SHED

SHED

COURT YARD

TOP FLOOR

BED

BED

UPPER PART
OF HALL

DRAUGHTING

PRIVVIES

BED

LINEN

BATH

DRESSING
ROOM

BED

STAIR HALL

BREAKFAST ROOM

LIBRARY

BOUDOIR

DINING ROOM

102

MAIN FLOOR

SECOND FLOOR

BED

BATH

HALL

BACK STAIRS

DRAWING ROOM

72. *Rideau Hall, 1838, was the Regency villa of the Honourable Thomas McKay, legislative councillor, mill-owner, master mason. The later additions to this villa, which made it Government House, are indicated in the block plan.*

been built at Bytown on the Ottawa by Thomas McKay, master mason.

In the infancy of Bytown a citizen named Rankine refused to serve on the village council because it would entail association with McKay who was, he said, "a common mason." In 1856 F. P. Rubidge, engineer of the Department of Public Works, was to describe Rideau Hall in an official letter as "an ordinary house of some eleven rooms." They were both wrong, for McKay, who was to become in succession a contractor, a mill-owner, and a legislative councillor, was an uncommon mason and Rideau Hall was an unusual house by any standards.

As Thomas McKay built it, Rideau Hall was a Regency bow-fronted villa with wings (72). Moreover the bow-front was continued above the cornice to form an attic storey in the style peculiar to the works of Sir John Soane. The attic room, lighted by its little casement window and by a skylight, was most probably McKay's drafting-room. Long after McKay's death when the villa was surrounded by the conglomeration of Government House, that attic room was to serve as the sculpture studio of Princess Louise.

Thomas McKay arrived at the Chaudière Falls on the Ottawa in October 1826 in company with John MacTaggart, Clerk of Works for the Rideau Canal. The Duke of Wellington had personally selected Lieutenant-Colonel John By, R.E., to superintend the building of the Canal. MacTaggart

73. *Two laurel wreaths neatly carved in pale grey marble form the chaste adornment of the mantel in Thomas McKay's elliptical drawing-room, now become the royal bedroom of Government House.*

74. *A graceful Regency stair leads to the attic room once used by Princess Louise as a sculpture studio. It was presumably McKay's drafting-room in the Rideau Hall of 1838.*

was sent out to Canada to be Clerk of Works on the recommendation of John Rennie, the great Scots engineer. Thomas McKay was brought up from Montreal to be master mason, a tribute to his excellent work on the Lachine Canal. All of this is most interesting, but it would be more relevant at this juncture to know which of these fine engineers, designers and craftsmen possessed a copy of *Cottages and Villas* published in 1793 by Sir John Soane. Was it By, or perhaps MacTaggart, whose interest in architecture has already been noted, or was it McKay himself? It is not known, but the Canal was completed, Bytown flourished, and McKay built Rideau Hall, externally a free adaptation of Soane's design for Chilton Lodge, Berkshire.

Elevations and fragmentary plans of McKay's Rideau Hall exist on Rubidge's drawings for the additions of 1868. These, corrected and completed from old photographs and the existing fabric, have provided the authority for the accompanying elevation and floor plans. Soane had taken exception to the Doric portico which his client required him to place in front of the semi-circular bay at the centre of the composition of Chilton Lodge. McKay disposed of the awkward shape by using it twice, as a porch on each wing connected by the gallery which encircled the central bay and which was cantilevered out from the projecting basement wall. Three French windows (45) in the elliptical dining-room opened onto the gallery. The partition wall of the dining-room has been removed with all the partitions of the small rooms behind it to make a large reception room.

The elliptical drawing-room above the dining-room has fared better. Retaining to this day the thistle motif in the centre of its coved ceiling and the chaste elegance of a fine white marble mantelpiece of Regency design (73), the McKay upstairs drawing-room has become the royal bedroom. The long windows have been shortened by a panel at the base to conceal heat radiation.

Unfortunately the main staircase of the 1838 Rideau Hall has had to go to make way for a bathroom and a passage but a graceful Regency stair still winds its way up to the attic (74). Rideau Hall is remarkable for containing one of the few Regency stairs still to be found in the province which could be photographed. Too many of its contemporaries have been overwhelmed by later decoration, the effect of delicate composition of the rail all but obliterated by the pattern of adjacent wallpaper.

Rideau Hall, "an ordinary house of some eleven rooms," quoth F. P. Rubidge in

75. *Blythe Farm, Fenelon Falls, 1837, was built by John Langton, who described it in his book,* Early Days in Upper Canada. *The house is down now but a plaque marks the spot where it fell.*

76. *Regency Classic Revival on Yonge Street at Thornhill, 1845.*

77. *Double scroll newels terminate the stair-rails giving a sense of great scale to a very small space in the Edey house, Thornhill.*

1868; yet two of those eleven rooms were elliptical reception rooms of great elegance and two more, *mirabile dictu*, were bathrooms. The early site plan shows the location of cisterns and drains and a hydraulic ram for supplying water. There was a sunken kitchen courtyard with what appears to have been an elliptical pool at its centre and a vinery leading from the east wing to the tool-shed by the kitchen garden.

In 1855, Thomas McKay died at Rideau Hall and ten years later the house was leased to the Government of the United Canadas. In 1868 it was purchased by the Dominion of Canada to form the nucleus of the official residence of the Governor General.

A more initially romantic Regency house arose while Rideau Hall was being designed when John Langton built Blythe (75) in 1837 on Sturgeon Lake near Fenelon Falls. Born at Blythe Hall in Lancashire, educated in Switzerland, France, Italy and ultimately at Cambridge, John Langton emigrated to Canada in 1833 after the family fortunes, amassed in the mercantile business in Russia, had been lost in speculation in England. Life at Blythe Farm was well recorded by both John Langton's letters to his father and by his sister, Anne Langton, in *A Gentlewoman in Upper Canada*. Miss Langton portrayed Blythe in a series of drawings as well — a most fortunate circumstance, as Blythe itself has been allowed to fall into a lamentable state of disrepair.

Blythe was of planked log construction, the exterior surface rough-cast and grooved in imitation of ashlar; quoins cut from plank bevelled on the inner edges and their painted surfaces spattered with sand to give a stone texture were used to finish the corners. Regency whimsy at Blythe, more in the Gothic taste, was limited to crenellation of the summer kitchen and to a sham tracery on the exterior surface of the windows, a pointed arch behind which lurks a square-headed double-hung window.

Not so the Gothic windows of number 7690 Yonge Street (76), a storey-and-a-half stucco house built in the Regency style in Thornhill by the Edey family in 1845. Here all the windows in the bedroom storey are framed with a pointed arch and fitted with wing-tipped louvered shutters. The Edey house is a personal selection of motifs blended with a lighthearted disregard for correctness of style, which, applied with taste and skill, combined to produce a small house of great charm.

Above the narrow fanlighted entrance door is a small balcony set on brackets. The fine cast-iron treillage of the railing is elegantly Greek. The pilasters supporting the heavy

106

architrave are more or less Greek, that is to say, they have narrow grooves terminating in a fret. In the centre of each capital is a little rosette. We have seen these rosettes before on the frieze of Sir Allan MacNab's garden verandah.

Both the great staircase at Dundurn and the stair of the Edey house, built approximately at the same time, sweep down·to terminate with a flourish in two scroll newel cages. The Edey stair (77) does so with considerable style. On the left of the stair-hall are the drawing-room and the sitting-room with a fine bookcase or china cupboard on one side of the chimney. The glazed doors are arched to match the fanlight above the front door. Immediately beneath the parlour is a large, well-finished cellar kitchen. To the right of the stair-hall are located a pantry, a breakfast room and a dining-room. The Edey dining-room expresses admirably the individual personal quality of the colonial Regency style. Major Edey located his house beside a trout stream. He seems to have heated his drawing-room with a stove but in his dining-room a fire blazed cheerfully in the grate. The mantelpiece is Doric in proportion, lightly trimmed with Gothic tracery and studded with rosettes. Beside it is a deep arched recess in the wall, the private ingle-nook of the Edey parrot.

4

Friends, Romans, Countrymen

Parallel to and coincident with the appearance in North America of a colonial Regency style there had been a flowering in Europe of a serious, academic revival of Classical architecture. This Classical Revival was based on more detailed and scientific research than had previously been possible. The majority of revivals are dedicated, dogmatic, frequently necessary and often humourless. The Classical Revival in architecture was not, unfortunately, to prove an exception.

The Victorians, as they faced the second half of their century, were fortified by two unlikely companion bulwarks, science and sentiment. Sentiment directed them back to the past, removed far enough to seem golden. Science, in the form of archaeology, uncovered for them the architecture of mainland Greece in its great period, the fifth century B.C. The literature of Greece had been part and parcel of the Renaissance. The arts of Greece were also thought to be well known. But the Greece of actual fact, that small, suppressed fragment of the Ottoman Empire that had once been the cultural centre of the world, was unknown. Nineteenth-century archaeology was to uncover it. Nineteenth-century sentiment was to clasp it to its heart. The romance of Greece, fighting for its independence from a decadent Mohammedan empire, fired the imagination of Western civilization, moving in its various ways toward democracy.

The waning of Turkish supremacy which made the Greek revolt possible had also made possible the accurate investigation of ancient monuments in Greece. Measured drawings of the Parthenon were received with consternation by the Man of Taste, totally unprepared by his studies of Greco-Roman Classicism for the strength, virility and sheer bulk of the Hellenic monuments. The blunt force of Greece was still mercifully hidden from his view.

Worse shocks were in store. In 1803, Thomas Bruce, Earl of Elgin, His Britannic Majesty's ambassador to the Porte, received permission from the local Turkish authority to

109

78. The focal point of the Classical Revival house was not so much the entrance door as the porch which sheltered it. The portico of the Bluestone House, Port Hope, is admirably expressed in the Ionic Order.

transport to England a number of tons of Pentelic marble—a literal, official description of fifteen of the ninety-two metopes of the Parthenon and some two hundred and ninety-four running feet of its frieze. Nine years were to pass before Lord Elgin could persuade a by no means grateful nation to accept his treasures. Initial reaction to the sculpture was expressed by Payne Knight thus: "You have lost your labours, my Lord Elgin, your marbles are over-rated; they are not Greek; they are Roman of the time of Hadrian."

By 1820 the Western world had assimilated the scale and breadth of the Hellenic style sufficiently to welcome the Aphrodite resurrected from the waves of oblivion at Melos. The following year marked the beginning of the Greek wars of liberation and archaeology received a severe set-back. The Parthenon was bombarded twice. Scientific investigation came to a standstill, while bloodshed and Romanticism flourished. Delacroix's "Les Massacres de Chio," painted in the new high-flown emotional style and Byron's "The Isles of Greece," written in the same vein, did far more towards spreading the Classical Revival in architecture than did either Aphrodite or Lord Elgin.

The brave struggles of the Greeks inspired the Classical Revival but as usual Rome shared in the victory. The nineteenth century began in a ferment of revolution and democratic manifestoes. The Carthages of hereditary privilege had to be destroyed. They were destroyed, and on their ruins were laid the foundations of political and commercial empires, for the temples of whose success Classical civic architecture was deemed most suitable, whether expressed in the Capitol in Washington, the Madeleine in Paris, the Valhalla at Regensburg, or St. George's Hall in Liverpool. It was an era in which great material prosperity and abysmal human misery marched side by side. The nineteenth-century industrialists did not find their preoccupation with Classical democracy inconsistent with existing mass suffering. Greek democracy had been based on a system of slavery and the equitable laws of Rome did not apply to bondmen or to foreigners. The unquiet, non-Classical conscience of the nine-teenth century was to build hospitals, schools, homes for orphans, libraries, bridges, roads and sewers, not less useful for being in the Classical manner.

Application of the Classical Revival style to civic architecture was logical by nine-teenth-century standards and comparatively simple to achieve. The models which had been selected as arbitrarily right were civic buildings. On the domestic front, the position was more obscure. No serious attempt was made to reproduce an authentic Greek house or even an authentic Roman villa. The climates native to the iron and cotton kings were not Mediterranean in nature. A house with thick, comparatively windowless exterior walls, whose plan centred about a courtyard, was as impractical in Manchester as it was in Pittsburgh. It would have been even more difficult to adapt to the humid reaches of the lower Mississippi. The architects of the Classical Revival wisely did not attempt it. Less wisely they sought instead to domesticate the monumental architecture of Hellenic Greece for their patrons.

The white-columned portico of the Classical Revival house has come to be identified in North America with the cotton plantation of the South, a lingering romantic aura of the last stand of an agricultural society. We tend to forget that the iron-founders of the northern states lived in Classical houses too and that some of the most impressive of the Greek and Roman mansions are to be found in the states of New York, Ohio and Michigan at Troy and Syracuse, Utica, Cincinnati and Milan. The Classical Revival was near at hand but Upper Canada, distrusting republics, Roman or otherwise, looked to her friends for architectural advice.

Early manifestations of the Classical Revival in Upper Canada are almost exclusively of British derivation. Many of the architects and master craftsmen who emigrated to the colony were from the expanding industrial areas of northern England, southern Scotland, and Ireland where a modified Classicism was entrenched. These craftsmen were acquainted with the appearance of Classical architecture. They were also conversant with its terminology. Had one of them been suddenly asked to execute a pseudo-peripteral tetrastyle house, he would at least have known where to look for his model. We, who are content that small bugs, extinct animals, common weeds and the formulae for cough mixtures should have lengthy Latin names, have allowed the comparable terms of the building profession to lapse. Governor Simcoe's Department of Public Works, familiar with the Classical builders' jargon, built at his request just such a house in York, a playful little summer home in the temple form which Rome had adopted from the Etruscans. The extended roof gable formed a pediment which was supported by four stout unpeeled pine logs. Several more exposed upright logs set at intervals along the wall supported the roof. The spaces between the logs were filled up with horizontal logs cut in short lengths. This was Castle Frank, named for the Governor's five-year-old son. Mrs. Simcoe recorded its appearance in 1796. Fortune was not destined to smile for long on either Frank. Sixteen years later, Francis Simcoe lay dead on the field of

Badajoz, and the little log whimsy disappeared in the expansion of the city his father had founded.

In 1818 with the Napoleonic Wars at an end in Europe, and their own conflict safely behind them, we find the Government of Upper Canada seeking plans for a Government House. The principal buildings at York had all been destroyed by enemy action so that it was not a question of tearing down to build greater but one of immediate necessity. It is a measure of the self-confidence of the Government of Upper Canada that they requested their Provincial Agent, Major William Halton, to approach John Soane, the leading architect in the employ of the British Government.

Sir John Soane, now regarded as the greatest of the individual Classical Revivalists was, as a designer, so radical and dynamic, that few of his students were qualified to follow in his steps. Soane's great preoccupations were with the form, the texture and the light in his buildings rather than with an academic use of Classical orders. He designed beautiful houses, monumental in concept, which owed an aesthetic allegiance to the Classical world at no sacrifice of artistic integrity. He designed his buildings as the Greeks themselves might have done given the same conditions. He did not copy the antique, a procedure which made him anathema to the next generation when veneration for antiquity reached the saturation point. The Classical and Romantic revivals were to engulf Western Europe and the United States of America, all but obliterating the principles for which Soane stood, but a small school of domestic building in Canada West derived indirectly from his inspiration.

It is a pity that the negotiations between the Government of Upper Canada and Soane himself were not destined to thrive. Halton laid before Soane the request for a design. This was to be for a "substantial plain house of brick" which was to supply ample accommodation for receptions. It was intended to have a separate building for the Assembly, the Legislative Council and the Courts of Justice, as well as a building for the Provincial Secretary and other heads of administrative departments.

Soane drew up rough sketch plans in pencil and ink, which are dated November 16, 1818 (79) and November 23, 1818. He made short notes and wrote little queries. He seems to have been disturbed by the great width of six-foot fireplaces and by the absence of any request for water-closets. Both plans indicate the position of a musicians' gallery in the ballroom and the presence of a number of Soane's favourite light-wells rising through several

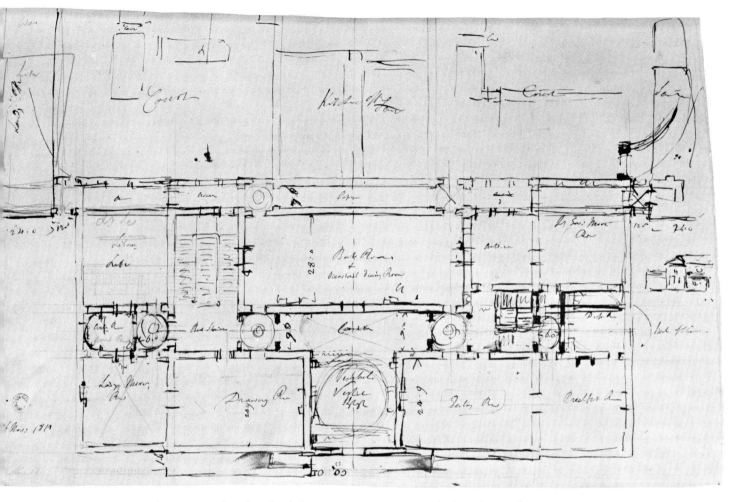

79. In 1818 Sir John Soane made a first sketch for a Government House to be located at York,
Upper Canada. The fine scheme fell through but the sketch remains in the Soane Museum in London.

floors to small domes or lanterns in the roof which were to admit light to the interior.

Although initially intrigued by the commission, Soane was preoccupied with the press of business in England. The Government of Upper Canada, self-centred and impatient, became increasingly irritated by his lack of attention. Halton wrote despairingly that his Government would consider Soane "culpably negligent" if he did not fulfil the obligation he had undertaken. Soane replied that he regretted that he could not complete the drawings in the time allowed, and the fine project was abandoned.

A plain, substantial brick house was built in York, to the design of a local architect,

80. *The clergy of Kingston were well housed in Classicism in 1841. St. Andrews manse is a fine essay in textures. It was designed by George Browne of Belfast, who founded Canada's first school of architecture at Quebec in 1832. The cast-iron balconies of St. Andrews manse are restrained, those of St. George's rectory (below) rather more gay.*

and when the Government next went house-hunting in 1841 and again in 1865, it elected to lease the handsome dwellings of prominent citizens in Kingston and Bytown. By a puckish twist of fate, the house selected in Bytown in 1865 was Rideau Hall, Thomas McKay's Soanean villa. It was absurdly similar to the little elevation drawing on Soane's sketch plan of November 16, 1818. The same capricious fate decreed that the Government of the United Canadas should, in 1841, summon from Quebec as its official architect George Browne, who was to perpetuate Soane's Classicism in Kingston limestone.

George Browne was born in 1811 in Belfast, Ireland, where his father was a practising architect. The younger Browne moved to Quebec City in 1830, practised professionally and set up a school of architecture. It was the first of its kind in Canada, where "instruction and lectures on the Art of Building and Architectural drawing" were to be had for the sum of four dollars a month. Borthwick, in his *History of Montreal*, states that Browne, while in Kingston, was "the architect of the City Hall and Market and a large number of private dwellings and stores."

George Browne's first Kingston commission was to alter Alwington and to add a wing to accommodate the household of Lord Sydenham. In April 1841, Browne wrote to H. H. Killaly of the Department of Public Works that, "the bracketry and cornice of the main house is finished." The bracketry and cornice must have satisfied all concerned as we hear no more of them. All correspondence with the owner, Baron de Longueuil, has to do with the location of the sewers.

George Browne must have derived far greater satisfaction from planning another house commissioned in Kingston in the same year. This was the manse for the Presbyterian congregation of St. Andrews (80). No temple this but a dwelling-place of timeless distinction. Rising from the bed-rock, it is a monument to the individual inspiration of the architect and to the collective discrimination of his employers, who, conscious of having chosen their designer wisely, allowed him to proceed without hindrance. Kingston is a limestone city and there are many fine compositions in ashlar, but in few is the texture of the rock-faced wall such an important factor in the design. Here are no busy mouldings, no elaborate sidelights. The finely proportioned windows and the door are framed by dressed stone trim, monolithic in its simplicity. The strong horizontal of the deep roof projection is repeated in the cornice, string course and base course. A tendency to Spartan austerity is relieved by the subtle break forward of the façade which allows the door and the window above it to be framed in a shallow recess. Skilful use of light and shade has been made in placing the shallow bracketed window balconies, in the serene rhythm of the wrought iron and in the graceful treillage of the side verandah. A like regard for uncluttered detail has provided that the chimneys form the supporting corner members of the roof parapet, that the soffit of the deep eaves be panelled to match it and that there should be certain refinements in the pattern of the glazing bars in the long double-hung windows. Internally the house is spacious and undemanding, designed to accommodate the differing personalities of a series of presumably austere scholarly tenants. A slight irregularity of plan results from the necessity of housing the furnace on the ground floor and of placing all storage and working areas in the kitchen wing, as this house is built directly on the bed-rock of the City of Kingston.

Tradition is strangely silent on the subject of John Solomon Cartwright's town house on King Street. Yet it must have been a startling sight in the Kingston of the 1840's, for here Browne indulged his interest in contrasting wall textures to the full. The house has been greatly altered over the years and appears opposite (81) as a restored drawing. Of much the same size and shape as the St. Andrews manse, the Cartwright house had heavy cut stone quoins at the corners, set against wide bands of smooth ashlar. The remainder of the wall surface was of rock-faced stone and all the openings for doors and windows were faced with a monolithic dressed stone trim.

The Cartwright fortunes were at their zenith in 1842, the year in which John Solomon Cartwright commissioned Browne to design a country villa at Portsmouth. Rockwood (82), now a nurses' residence, is still with us, but not, unfortunately, those famous stables of which Dr. Sampson wrote:

> Oh much I wish that I were able
> To build a house like Cartwright's stable.
> For it doth cause me great remorse
> To be worse housed than Cartwright's horse.

Cartwright himself was housed very well indeed. Rockwood was advertised, at the sale which followed John Solomon's death, as an "Italian Villa." It was an Italian villa according to the Italian interpretation of the term. It was a Palladian villa whose heart was an octagonal rotunda which extended up through two floors, was surrounded by a stout Baroque balus-

116

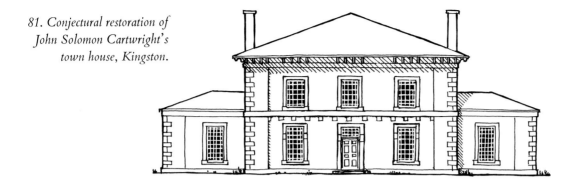

81. Conjectural restoration of John Solomon Cartwright's town house, Kingston.

82. Rockwood, the Cartwright country house at Portsmouth, was likewise designed by Browne but in the unusual medium of stuccoed wood. Shown below is the gazebo.

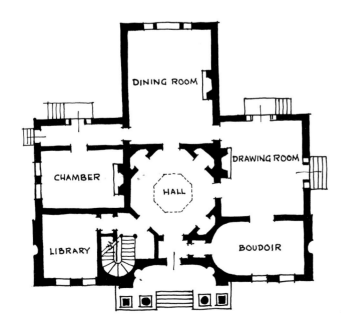

83. Floor plan of Rockwood, showing the octagonal light-well.

117

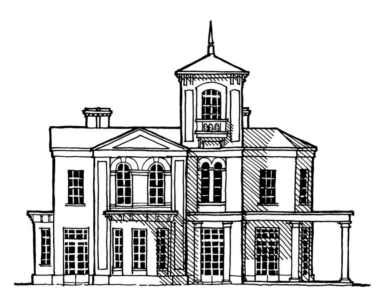

84. Smiley's Castle, Hamilton, was built in 1854 by Robert Smiley, founder of the Hamilton Spectator.

trade at the second level and was crowned by a panelled dome, centred with a skylight of shaded rose glass and lighted by a gay little lantern. The dome still wears the muted Adamesque colours which were designed to harmonize with the coloured skylight.

The medium of this rural elegance is not what one would expect in the heart of the limestone citadel of Canada West. Rockwood was built of wood, stuccoed and lined to imitate an ashlar surface. This was an Italian villa but it was also a Regency Classical villa in the style of Soane (83). There was a fine drawing-room or boudoir with a bowed end wall and a stair of great elegance curving up in a separate stair-hall to the bedroom storey. The large Venetian window in the dining-room looked out across the grounds to Lake Ontario. A frivolous Regency balcony with a tent awning roof adorns the garden front above the Venetian window. Browne was to build a similar balcony on a more truly Romantic Italian villa for a Kingston grocer, and Sir John A. Macdonald was to call the whole confection Teacaddy Castle.

The most thoroughly British Classical of all Upper Canadian houses is not in Kingston but in Hamilton (84). Robert Smiley, the founder of the Hamilton *Spectator*, built a handsome house of brick and stone at the corner of East Avenue and King William Street. He chose a design which has a composition of contrasting vertical panels highly reminiscent of Browne's interpretation of the style of Soane. Robert Smiley and George Browne were both from Ireland, and both men were residents of Kingston in the forties.

118

85. *Echo Villa, Brantford, combines the Doric Order with patterned brick. It was built by the Indian missionary, Peter Jones, and his English bride, Elizabeth Field. Several houses of this type were illustrated in the margins of the map of Brant County in 1858.*

Browne returned to Montreal in 1844 to remodel Moncklands and the Parliament buildings. Smiley went to Montreal in the same year and two years later he moved to Hamilton where he built the house which his fellow townsmen, with a maddening lack of inspiration, called Smiley's Castle. Browne may not have designed Smiley's house but it is certainly of the same school of British Classicism.

An equally handsome house stands on the outskirts of Brantford, at once the best example and the sole survivor of a group of houses built at the same time in a very different school of English Classicism. Echo Villa (85) was one of several houses which claimed the notice of William H. G. Kingston as he journeyed about Canada West. He was to make brief mention of it in his *Western Wanderings or a Pleasure Tour of the Canadas*, published in

1856. "A little before coming to Brantford, we passed a red brick well-built house, with yard and offices belonging, we are told to the Reverend Peter Jones, a full blooded Indian, of the Mississauga tribe. He is a Wesleyan minister, and said to be eloquent, and has married an English woman." But for one slight error, Mr. Kingston's account seems to be entirely accurate. Kahkewoquonaby (Sacred Feathers), or Peter Jones, was the son of Augustus Jones, a land surveyor of Welsh descent, and his Ojibwa wife. Born at Burlington Heights in 1802, Peter Jones married his English bride, Elizabeth Field, in New York in 1831. Apparently a lady of means, Mrs. Jones, immediately on arrival in Brantford, set about having their land cleared and the house built. By the time the *Western Wanderings* was published, Peter Jones' missionary work had ended. He died at Echo Villa on June 29, 1856. His labours on behalf of the Canadian Indians had included an Ojibwa spelling-book published in 1828, an Ojibwa hymn book in 1829 and a translation of the Gospel according to St. Matthew into the Ojibwa tongue published the same year.

Elizabeth Field Jones' Echo Villa is a storey-and-a-half, centre-hall, gabled-roofed house of red brick in Flemish bond with a decorative cornice of buff brick. Engraved illustrations in the margin of a Brant County map of 1858 depict Fairfield Cottage, Burford, and the residence of William Myles, Mount Vernon, as having patterned brick cornices of more elementary character. Both were undoubtedly the work of the same builder-architect. In each house the roof joists form a decorative pattern of widely spaced dentils below the moulded fascia boards. All three had the low-pitched gable usually found centred above the Georgian façade. In the Classical Revival houses of Brant County the cornice has been broken to allow space for a larger window to light the upper hall. At Echo Villa a Palladian window gracefully occupies this space; on the ground floor Venetian sidelighted windows were used. Both here, and at Fairfield Cottage, the stairwell was lighted by an octagonal lantern. All three houses had louvered exterior shutters and square-headed doorways. Interest was lent to the end walls of these houses by allowing the pairs of chimney stacks to project the width of a brick from ground to cap with windows centred between them. Frivolous bits of Regency treillage were allowed to linger on the back verandah. Fashion moves slowly toward the kitchen. Internally these were still Regency houses with a balanced disposition of reception rooms on either side of a centre hall of gracious width, with the stair a light, graceful example of the local Georgian school, and with the trim of mantel, window and doors the wider, simpler moulding characteristic of the British Colonists.

While the gentlefolk of Upper Canada were building in the austere Classicism of Henry Holland and the personal Classicism of Sir John Soane, Soane had been succeeded as architect to the Bank of England by Professor C. R. Cockerell who had spent seven years in Greece studying and drawing. In the years before his Greek expedition Cockerell had shared architectural instruction in his father's office with Benjamin Latrobe, to whom must go the honour of having designed the first Classical Revival building in the United States, the Bank of Pennsylvania. Cockerell and Latrobe were both convinced, gifted Classicists who carried the true beauty of Hellenic Greece to the Philistines of industry and government, Latrobe to the United States, Cockerell to Liverpool, Manchester and Bristol.

While the cotton magnates of Lancashire were expressing civic pride in the Greek temple style, the cotton planters of South Carolina were turning their thoughts toward Athens with the assistance of a young English architect, William Jay. The Classical Revival, in the purity of archaeological accuracy, took firm root in the fertile soil of the United States of America. The breadth and austerity of the Classical Revival style, the very characteristics which failed to recommend it to the Romantics, were the aspects most popular in North America. The visual impact of the best buildings was and still is tremendous.

The Classical Revival temple in North America was handsome in the brilliant sunlight of high summer; it was boldly magnificent against the strong blue sky of March, or rising, black and silver, from the moonlit February snow. Both snow and building, it should be remembered, were clean and white in the first half of the nineteenth century. One can scarcely blame the nineteenth-century North American for being carried away by his archaeological enthusiasm. No effort was spared in securing measured drawings of antique buildings and if the models were often Greek the methodical care with which they were followed was wholly Roman.

The American republic had, with the earnest idealism of the young, identified itself with ancient Rome. The Rome it had in mind was the simple, honest Rome of Cincinnatus at the plow. Unfortunately, its northern neighbour remembered that Caesar was likewise a Roman, and the tendency to equate Classicism with the republicanism led the conservative Upper Canadian to delay his adoption of the Classical Revival style, while his cultural heritage urged him to build in one of the recognized orders of architecture. Every person

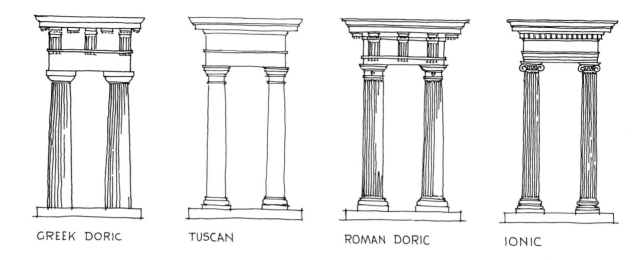

GREEK DORIC TUSCAN ROMAN DORIC IONIC

of any pretension to education in North America knew of, and appreciated, both the virtues and the faults of the Roman and the Greek. As a child he had come to grips with Latin, and to a greater or lesser degree, with Greek. Moreover, from constant contact with buildings and details in the Classical tradition he possessed a well-fostered appreciation for, and sometimes even an addiction to, Classical proportions. In larger centres of population where architects were available, fine houses, Classical in their proportion and in their logical response to function, were built. Builder-architects in outlying areas might eke out flagging personal inspiration by recourse to the pattern-book. Mechanics' institutes and building societies, which were being organized in increasing numbers, set up reference libraries where their members might find the orders and the details of various plans.

The orders of architecture owe their origin to two styles of building in the Greek world of the ninth to the fourth centuries B.C. In mainland Greece, there developed a sturdy style called, after the first Dorian invaders of Greece, the Doric Order. In Ionia, which embraced the coast of Asia Minor plus the islands of the Aegean, a more delicate style developed called Ionic. In the non-Greek Mediterranean world derivatives of the two styles arose. The Etruscans in Italy developed a modification of the Doric style, brought in by the Greek colonists to southern Italy and Sicily. The modification came to be called Tuscan. This Tuscan Order greatly influenced the Romans when they came to build in the late Greek manner, and the Roman Doric was a combination of the Greek and the Tuscan styles. At the time when Roman conformity conquered the Greek world of individualism, a few

122

Greeks were experimenting with a leafy capital on an Ionic column. This became the basis of the Corinthian Order.

By the first century A.D. the methodical Romans had codified the styles for ease of use and for the quick reproduction of obviously Roman buildings in any part of their empire; regional styles had become orders or rules of architecture, Tuscan, Doric, Ionic and Corinthian. By complete chance only one ancient work on Classical architecture was known at the time of the Renaissance. It was the work of a retired Roman army engineer, Marcus Vitruvius Pollio, who lived during the reign of the Emperor Augustus. The influence of this one man was astounding, although he relied on simple rules of thumb and seemed to possess little appreciation of the visual aesthetics of architecture. His bumbling book was to be the basis of the work of men of great brilliance and sophistication for several centuries. Furthermore, it established a precedent for the pattern-book. Just as Vitruvius had provided a spring-board for the creative Renaissance architect, so the pattern-book of the Classical Revival could be an incentive or a stumbling-block, hindering the uninspired but spurring on the gifted architect to greater things.

In the clear air of the Mediterranean almost all daily community activity could be carried on in the open air or under porches; hence the importance in all Classical orders of the column, the horizontal architrave or beam member above it, and the cornice above this for throwing off rain. In the earliest Greek times the Ionic regional way of building was to use numerous small timbers in the roof which projected to support the cornice. These produced a pleasing pattern of light and shade and were retained even after stone had been adopted as the building material. The projections came to be called dentils, or teeth. The early Doric builders appear to have used heavier timbers which rested on simple square beams. To lighten their appearance these large projecting rectangles were given three glyphs, or grooves, and their later derivatives in stone or terracotta were called triglyphs. Terracotta was used in early Classical times as flashing, and, in the details of the Doric Order, there appeared derivatives of what must originally have been terracotta plates pegged to the underside of the flat roof rafters. These plates, in the glossary of the orders, are called mutules and the pegs, guttae. The Neo-classic builders of North America had, under Asher Benjamin's direction, omitted the pegs and allowed

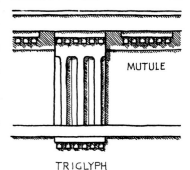

MUTULE

TRIGLYPH

the holes in the mutule to form a decorative pattern. With the rediscovery of Hellenic Greece such departures met with an official frown.

In the Hellenic world the handling of light and shade on surfaces was an important element of design. The Classical orders have a limited range of moulding profiles. Except for one reversing curve called a cyma, specific segmental or elliptical profiles always alternate in their juxtaposition with flat surfaces. The range of enrichments used in the orders was restricted to a very limited number of traditional decorative bands. Their origins are lost in 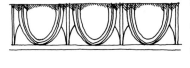 antiquity and many have been given fanciful names such as egg and dart and bead and reel. In Hellenic Greece the comparative rigidity of the order was always associated with religious or civic building and as such it was never disassociated from the irregular landscape for which it had been designed. The disposition of the construction had been worked out over centuries to produce a sense of discipline and repose.

In expanding North America, not yet drowned in industrial smog, the handling of light and shade was an important element of design too. Just as important to the Upper Canadian of Classical background was visual harmony in his surroundings. He did not need instruction in the verities of basic functional building. Either he or his father had built a log house adequate to the physical needs of his family. He was acutely conscious that a house must enclose space for living. He believed also that it might be designed for spiritual enrichment as well.

The important houses of the high Classical Revival were inspired responses to these several needs. They might employ one order, several orders or none; they might have columns of Classical antecedents, blended to taste by a creative planner, for there was no one order which was more correct than another for domestic use. If an academically correct order, or one of personal inspiration, improved his house as a building in any one of its several functions, then it might be granted that the architect was justified in using it.

The streams of influence bringing the Classical Revival into Canada West were still rising from the same well-springs which had produced the Neo-classic style. Eastern Ontario was influenced by England, New England and the valley of the Hudson; Kingston, Toronto and Hamilton continued to attract the British-trained architects, draftsmen and craftsmen as having the greatest concentration of potential clients. The wholehearted Classicism of the expanding United States would enter Canada West, if it came at all, via Rochester, Buffalo and Detroit. This Classicism was likely to be the rich Greek Revival of Minard Lafevre who began his career as a craftsman in the building trade in the Finger Lakes region of New York State and who went on to ultimate success as a professional architect in New York City. While he retained a craftsman's delight in Classical ornament with a marked preference for the anthemion (a stylized palmette), his chief concern was with the design of spatial harmony. The title of one of his later handbooks, *The Beauties of Modern Architecture*, is revealing. One feels certain that Lafevre would applaud the beauty of Greek refinement in the doorway (86) of Roslyn Cottage at Niagara-on-the-Lake.

"Modern" domestic architecture *circa* 1830-1850 was concerned with the problems of planning for a changing society, a changing economy, and a changing technology. There were new methods of lighting and heating, new struggles with plumbing and drainage and ventilation, and there were the unknown quantities of mill-run trim, mass-produced sash and doors, metal roofing and metal casting.

A number of handsome houses of generous size in the Classical Revival style remain, which were, from their beginning, eminently fine places in which to dwell. These were houses designed by the best architects practising in Canada West and built under their supervision for the most affluent members of a cosmopolitan society. A sweeping generalization may be made of characteristics common to many of them: nearly square in plan, set on high cellar walls with high ceilings in the two principal storeys and an attic storey or at least a hip-roof above — the basic geometric shape is that of a cube. One of the finest houses, Ruthven, is fifty-one feet six inches by forty-five feet six inches and is forty-seven feet one inch in height. All the houses have an identifiable derivation from the Classical orders; none is a slavish copy. The houses are formally composed and although all the survivors are

86. A truly Greek entrance door, composed of Classical detail, faithfully reproduced from a pattern-book. Roslyn Cottage, Niagara-on-the-Lake.

set in the middle of large disciplined lawns, any of them might be set down without alteration in a city street. The principal storey generally is bisected in plan by a wide hall, graced by a stairway of importance. On one side of the hall are located the dining-room and the library and on the other side a pair of drawing-rooms divided by a screen. Kitchens, wine cellars, laundries, meat storage areas and all other offices are located in the cellar. A number of the houses have a narrow wing built about ten years after the main building to house a duplicate set of domestic offices above ground. A number of these houses have a stair leading to the roof where a low parapet surrounds the flat central area; in others the roof gallery is replaced by a lantern or monitor for a detached contemplation of the changing world or as a practical means of lighting the attic.

On May 5, 1845, the citizens of Indiana, Canada West, read with interest a notice, to wit:

The subscriber wishes to contract with a competent and responsible person or persons for the following work — viz. For the building of a large brick and stone house, outhouses, etc., at Indiana. For the making of 108,000 first rate stock and 100,000 pressed bricks. The yard and wood to be furnished him. For the clearing and fencing of 100 acres of land. For the purchase of 20 pairs of good working oxen and two spans of good horses. For the quarry and delivery of 300 cords of stone. For the boating of grain, lumber, etc., also for 10,000 pine sawlogs. Any portion of the above work he would agree to to suit applicants.

The notice was signed D. Thompson. Ruthven Park was about to be established. Presumably the one hundred acres which needed immediate clearing was to be the home farm. David Thompson owned two thousand acres all told plus a distillery, some mills and a general store at Cayuga, as Indiana came to be called. Thompson, the son of Scottish colonists, was born at Stamford in the Niagara Peninsula. He had been a contractor for the Welland Canal, and was to be the first Member of Parliament for Haldimand County. Three owners of Ruthven were to represent Haldimand and four generations of Thompsons were to serve in Canada's defence.

Ruthven Park was envisioned as an estate in the British tradition. Quantities of brick were used in building the gatekeeper's lodge, the cow barns, the hen-houses, the dove-cote, the ox-barns and the plant for producing gas to light the house. The kitchen wing, wood-sheds, tool-sheds, carriage barns, and privies were of rubble stone. All stone journeyed to the

126

THE NOBLEST ROMANS OF THEM ALL.

87. Right: Ruthven Park, Cayuga, 1845.

88. Below left: Willowbank, Queenston, 1834.

89. Below right: Glencairn, Queenston, 1832.

site in barges on the Grand River. Ruthven (87) itself was of ashlar in the Doric Order. It was designed by an American architect, Lathrop by name, who was originally from Tonawanda, New York. This may or may not be the Harry B. Lathrop listed as an architect in the Detroit city directory of 1837.

To the architect of Ruthven are attributed two large Classical Revival houses in Queenston, Glencairn built in 1832 and Willowbank (88) in 1834 for the Hamilton family. This is not the Honourable Robert Hamilton's house sketched in Mrs. Simcoe's diary, although the western façades of both houses were much alike. A merchant, shipbuilder, and large landholder of Queenston, Robert Hamilton was born at Bolton in Haddingtonshire. He seems to have made two provident marriages. His first wife was Catherine, widow of John Robinson, in whose honour St. Catharines received its name; his second wife was Mary Herkimer, widow of Neil MacLean. His family prospered. While other members of the family were bestowing their name on the new city on Burlington Bay, his son Alexander Hamilton was building Willowbank.

The Niagara escarpment makes an admirable location for Classical buildings. Willowbank was set on a height so that its eastern front, in the Ionic Order, would be ap-

proached obliquely and uphill. The height of the cellar storey and the narrow processional steps all enhanced the importance of the entrance. One wishes on closer inspection that the architect had given a plainer surface somewhere for the eyes to rest. However, Lathrop's mature style has grace as well as strength. Ruthven shows that by 1845 he had outgrown the exclamatory vocabulary of his Queenston building. Ruthven is a Doric house; Willowbank is Ionic. At Glencairn (89)

90. Left: A tour de force in stair building, Ruthven.

91. Below: Double drawing-rooms, Ruthven.

93. Grille in the frieze.

Grille from within.

both these orders are used on the river front, superimposed to support the double verandahs. If this is the earliest example of Lathrop's work in Upper Canada, it suggests an apprenticeship in youth to an architect devoted to the design of Classical Revival resort hotels on the Hudson.

An element of uniform excellence in the Lathrop houses is the handling of the stair, usually required to reach from the main storey to the roof. Beautiful to behold, pleasant to climb, almost impossible to photograph, rising in a series of gentle elliptical curves for three storeys, the stairwell at Ruthven is lighted by an elliptical skylight (90).

Both Glencairn and Ruthven have double drawing-rooms with screens. The screen at Ruthven (91) is an architrave enriched with many Classical mouldings and supported by two Ionic columns. The rooms were heated by a pair of fireplaces, the dark marble of their

92. The drawing-room door, Ruthven.

smooth plain surfaces a pleasant foil for the delicate enrichment of cornice, pilaster and door frame (92). Ruthven Park, remaining in the hands of the family for whom it was built, has retained much of its original furnishing. Very fine Classical Revival curtain rods, set above the first moulding of the cornice, support long curtains of gold damask which soften the tall window openings without obscuring the fine architectural detail. The windows are twelve-paned, double-hung and set, with a panel beneath, between pairs of pilasters. Early gasoliers hang from plaster ceiling medallions. All the wood trim is light in colour. In town houses of this quality the anthemions and ceiling moulding might be gilded. Wood trim in halls, library and dining-rooms in these houses is plainer in design and darker in colour, frequently of walnut or mahogany. The hall doors of Ruthven are similar to those of the drawing-room but less ornate. The frame of the doorway giving access from the dining-room to the pantry was made very wide to enclose both the door and the dumb waiter in which hot food could be brought up from the kitchen. This was doubly useful in the years before the pantry wing was built.

The pantry wing must have been an addition welcomed by the staff, as it provided additional servants' quarters. However much interest the pierced decorations (93) might lend to the wooden entablature when viewed architecturally, they cannot have given much solace to the domestics whose bedrooms were supposed to receive light by them.

No one has yet suggested that Lathrop of Tonawanda might have designed the small house at Preston (94) so closely related in feeling to Ruthven, or that he had anything whatsoever to do with Mount Fairview in Dundas although they are geographically and chronologically well within his orbit. The Preston cottage (Ruthven in miniature) is of salmon brick and set on a stone basement plinth. It has the narrow processional steps which contrive to convey in all these houses a sense of great scale. The parapet, on its shallow hip-roof, matches the one at Ruthven and is far more readily seen.

Mount Fairview (95) was built by the Moore family on its commanding site when Dundas was a far more important town than Hamilton. The Ionic in this dramatic portico has been executed without fluting in harmony with the Tuscan columns of the wing-like side verandahs. The whole roof at Mount Fairview is a lookout deck, but the designer wisely set a lantern in the midst thereof for those months when it is not summer in Dundas. The house is no longer approached up the face of the hill. The visual impact on the visitor must have been

94. Above: Multum in parvo. The Doric
house in Preston has all the monumental
features of the Classical Revival style but
retains the human scale of the smaller house.

95. Right: Mount Fairview, the laurel on
the brow of Dundas.

in direct ratio to the strain on the horses in the good old days, as the incline was more suited to an escalator than to a carriage drive.

Did the observant Mr. Kingston mention any of the houses at Cayuga, Queenston, or Dundas in his *Western Wanderings* of 1856? He did not, but on his visit to Toronto he had this to say: "At the corner of one of the streets there is a remarkably handsome structure of the finest stone of Corinthian architecture which would attract notice on any street in London." The corner in question was the northeast one of King and Bay streets. The house (96) was designed by Joseph Sheard and was built for William Cawthra in 1851. When Kingston remarked that the Corinthian architecture of the Cawthra house would attract notice on any London street, he was conscious of a fact of the first importance — the place held by this house in the story of architecture in Canada West. Sheard's design for a town house in the Corinthian Order of Classicism, that last and most ornate of the Greek orders, foreshadows the expression of an imminent Renaissance revival which was high fashion in England and Western Europe in 1851. Not only was the design of the building international in its quality but, also, in this house alone of the Classical Revival houses in Canada West, there were no

96. William Cawthra's town house, King and Bay streets, Toronto, was designed by Joseph Sheard, built in 1851, and demolished in 1949 to make way for a commercial building.

97. The drawing-room mantelpiece of the Cawthra town house is now located in the drawing-room at Grove Farm, Port Credit, the home of a descendant of the Cawthra family.

provincial limitations to craftsmanship. The finest Classical detail of Ruthven was executed in wood; the volutes and acanthus leaves of Sheard's Corinthian house were carved in stone.

Architecture which can be described as high fashion is in a precarious position and the taste of 1851 was eclectic. In that year Queen Victoria visited the Crystal Palace, a revolutionary construction of iron and glass, to declare open the Great Exhibition, the first world's fair, "so vast, so glorious, so touching," wrote the Queen. Where the Classicists had been cynical and discriminating the Victorians were enthusiastic and romantic. One of their romantic attachments was to be to the Rococo style of Louis XV. Sheard was simply being ahead of the times in Canada when he installed a Rococo Revival mantelpiece in William Cawthra's drawing-room (97). When this, the finest Classical town house in all Canada West was demolished, the Rococo mantelpiece and the two stone Corinthian columns which flanked the entrance door on Bay Street were salvaged by a Cawthra descendant and transported to a site granted by the Crown in 1804 to Joseph Cawthra when he removed from Guyslely in Yorkshire to York, Upper Canada, to refound the family fortunes.

Well within the limits of all the conditions known to have existed in Canada West which had any bearing on the building of houses is the probability of there having been at least three times as many handbook Classical Revival houses as there were houses designed at the same time by recognized architects. Time has altered the balance in favour of the architect. The houses planned by sensitive and skilful designers of living space were far more likely to continue to please, and pleasing, to escape alteration over a number of generations than those which paid too close a tribute to fashion. Many handbook Classical houses still exist buried beneath a clutter of dormers and sun-porches, the result of initially inept planning which omitted to provide for the admission of adequate light and air. Better examples have fallen direct victims to urban renewal or to misplaced confidence in the bracket chimney. A sufficient number remains, having enjoyed the felicity of competent craftsmen, careful owners

133

and good chimneys, to make a worthwhile study of the handbook Classical house possible.

What might one expect a good handbook Classical house to be? First of all, there would not be a radical change in basic plan or structure from the regional variation of the Georgian house. Porches, verandahs, porticoes, and the "frontispiece," as Asher Benjamin called the entrance doorway with its attendant elaboration, would be taken with little change from plates in the chosen book. Mantelpieces would be likely to bear a close resemblance to those in the same work. If there was a screen between the double drawing-rooms, it would be supported by a Classical Revival order. Interior trim on doors and windows might be eared in the Classical manner; it would certainly have wider moulding, much flatter in profile than any previously encountered. Baseboards would be deep and simply treated. There would be simple plaster cornices and, in early examples, quiet ceiling medallions of ordered acanthus leaves. Doors might be of two, six or eight panels, but the six panels would now be found to be of equal size and often without moulding. All interior trim might be of walnut, mahogany, cherry, or maple or painted to imitate the grain of any of the hardwoods or the veining of light or dark marble. In the large handbook Classical house, the rooms would be of generous size with ceilings of fourteen to sixteen feet in the principal storey. In rooms of this scale the visual weight of heavy wood trim could be accommodated easily.

One of the snares for the unwary in the use of the pattern-books lay in injudicious application of large-scale detail to the smaller house. The criticism hurled at the Classical Revival for building Athens in the wilderness and then painting it brown was largely undeserved. Usually the hand that wielded the brush of brown paint, or yearly coat of varnish stain, was a later Victorian (*circa* 1870) bent on bringing the old house up-to-date. The presiding genius of 1880 was to compound the felony by introducing rapid graining with rubber combs. "Anyone" could do it and usually that is just who did. The painted wood grains and marble veining of the Classical Revival required the hand of a skilled craftsman and the employment of discretion as well as of superior tools.

Perhaps the most widely known and certainly the most imposing of the handbook Classical Revival houses of Canada West is the Bluestone at Port Hope. The name may derive from the limestone walls now hidden by a coat of stucco, or the stucco surface may have been that Pane's-grey known to our ancestors as "stone-blue." The lintels and sills of the doors and windows are of red sandstone. With the Ionic porch, the cornice and all the

98. The Bluestone House, Port Hope. The trim surrounding the sliding doors between the double drawing-rooms is the only heavy-handed element in the design of an extremely handsome house.

glazing bars in white this was a Classical house true to Attic colour. The frontispiece of Bluestone (78) and all its mantelpieces are straight out of *The Practical House Carpenter*, published in 1841 by Asher Benjamin. In the screen between the double drawing-rooms (98) are represented features typical of the Classical Revival style both the commendable and the unfortunate — the deep baseboard, the wide moulding of the door trim (certainly less tortuous than the late Loyalist type but here still rather busy) and the square corner-box with its cast plaster rosette. The plaster corner rosette was a rather pleasing device when used with simple mouldings, but why, oh, unkind Fates, the sudden up-flung clumsiness of the moose-like half-wreath, a little conceit of the master plasterer's own contriving perhaps? Quite likely it was, for there seem to have been practitioners of a school of robust plasterwork busy along the upper St. Lawrence and lower Lake Ontario regions in the late 1830's and early 1840's. The exuberance of their work was subject only to the restraint of their patron's taste. Vestiges may still be found in houses and hostelries from Port Hope to Prescott. The most remarkable for facility and inventiveness are located in a hotel in Grafton and in the town hall of Gananoque, once the private home of Henrietta Maria Mallory MacDonald.

There are throughout the province a number of handbook Classical houses in the temple-with-wings form, three notable examples being Crysler Hall in Upper Canada Village (99), the Chauncey Peck house in Prescott (100) and the Hamilton town house (101) in Peterborough. Crysler Hall, sometime known as Evergreen Hall, was built in 1846 by John P. Crysler. There was nothing to suggest, when its white portico was first reflected by the St. Lawrence, that a turbulent future awaited it. The Crysler family might be pardoned for supposing that they had earned the right to build a temple of Classical repose at some distance from their original site. When John P. Crysler was twelve years of age, a battle was fought in his father's hay field which effectively put to an end American hopes of capturing Montreal in 1813. Colonel John Crysler's imposing Georgian house, which had served as British headquarters during the battle and as a non-partisan hospital afterward, was accidentally destroyed by fire at a later date and its lands were sold to the historian James Croil.

Crysler Hall was reserved for a different fate. It was measured, dismantled brick by brick, and re-erected in Upper Canada Village. It would seem that Crysler had correctly anticipated the official judgment of posterity when he selected the Classical Revival style. In any case Doric was an inevitable choice for one who rejoiced in the middle name of Pliny. Crysler associations, together with its undeniably handsome exterior, ensured that the house should survive. Its successful features and its marked failure dictated its location and its use in a restoration project. Excellence of mass composition and a harmonious balance of areas of fenestration and wall surface, the sweeping horizontal of the wing eaves carried through in the balcony railing, the nicety with which the chimneys were set in relation to the pediment, and the proportion and spacing of the columns — all combined to place the house at the centre of the Village complex. The dull internal space division ruled out restoration as a house. It was reconstructed as a museum with all the partitions in the central block omitted.

Temples have a way of reverting to their original purpose of enclosing space for the ceremonial occasions of groups rather than the private existence of individuals. The Peck house, Prescott, which is now a funeral home, is much more faithful to the handbook than either Crysler Hall or the Hamilton temple house. Crysler Hall had a recessed portico; the Peck house and the Hamilton house have porticoes projecting from the central mass with matching verandahs on their latterly extended wings.

136

100. *The shadow of the cypress is ever near the Classic porch. The Peck house in Prescott is now a funeral home.*

99. *Crysler Hall, Upper Canada Village, was built on the St. Lawrence by John Pliny Crysler in 1846.*

101. *A bold composition of the temple with wings. The Hamilton house, Peterborough.*

102. *The Sills-Moon house, South Fredericksburg.*

103. *Crumbling rural Ionic on the Adolphus Reach. The Sills-Moon house.*

On page 43 of *The American Builder's Companion*, Asher Benjamin gave directions for plaster moulding thus: "Good fine-tempered clay should be provided (pipe clay is best), a template must be made of wood, to fit the moulding. Then run on a board a piece of clay moulding about a foot long. This moulding may be modeled in any pattern and a wax mould taken of it, which will do to cast a great number of feet." Benjamin recommended that for ceiling plaques, "water leaf, parsley leaf or acanthus leaves" were best, but that the builder could use his own discretion. The builder of the Peck house was moved to embellish the ceilings of the double parlours with large medallions of windblown acanthus leaves. He expressed both the character of the land and the ancestry of the people by adding a small wreath at the centre composed of pond lilies and tulips.

Each of the three temple houses presented a different wall surface to the world. The Crysler house is of local salmon-red brick, the Peck has a white stuccoed surface with heavy quoins at the corners, and the Peterborough house is of stone. It is handled with a breadth and exuberance of composition which suggests a much later date than the eastern examples. The sweeping boldness of the wing architraves could only be supported visually

138

by pillars of such weight that they may be considered piers. Perhaps this builder owned a pattern-book. If he did, he shut it firmly before he began to draw. This is a Classical temple in the vernacular, the countryman's Classic.

One might travel far before encountering a small Classical Revival house which would surpass in monumental quality, in harmony of proportions, in wood craftsmanship, in the beauty of its setting or in the imminence of its disintegration the Sills-Moon house (102) on Lot 3, South Fredericksburg. The rural Classical Revivalist apparently considered that the proper study of mankind was man. Many houses in Canada West were faced toward the Queen's Highway with no regard to the aesthetic value of the site. The Sills-Moon house has its back firmly set to the south and the sparkling waters of the Adolphus Reach. Dramatic patterns of swaying shadow are cast over the summer kitchen and the gable walls for much of the year, but only the late afternoon sun of midsummer ever touches the fine wood carving in the deep volutes of the Ionic capitals of its porch (103). The Sills-Moon house is in an old farming community, in one of those fortunate areas of Ontario whose primeval irregularity of shoreline ensures that the super-highways will pass by forever on the other side.

While the temples of Upper Canada were being built, a regional Classical Revival style, which was to make its presence felt in Canada West, had been evolving along the south shore of Lake Ontario. The style was to retain those features of the Classical orders which were most closely allied to wood construction, the basic post and lintel form, (or columnar and trabeated if you prefer) and was to interpret them as a new canon of proportion.

The point of departure was the Doric Order. There was a sparing use of columns: usually one was placed on either side of the entrance doorway, or a pair supported the shallow porch. More frequently the design of the Doric anta was employed either as a pilaster or as a pier. In both instances the entablature supported was Greek Doric in proportion, but it lacked the rhythmic pattern of triglyphs and metopes which distinguishes the Classical building. The breadth of the resulting composition could and did accommodate a handsome number of windows on the ground floor. It was especially successful when the windows attained the scale of French doors and were partly shadowed by a deep continuous colonnade. There remained, however, the vexing question of lighting the bedroom storey. The most frequently recurring solution was to use the roof lantern. The lantern would seem to be the

139

104. Hamilton Place, Paris, is a highly photogenic member of an interesting group of Paris houses built in the regional cobblestone style of Upper New York State. A detail of the surface textures is shown, left.

logical extension, in a climate of extremes, of the skylight. It looked very well on the drafting board; it looked equally well from the ground. However, it is not uniformly satisfactory from within. An alternative solution was to insert decorative grilles in the frieze. The choice, as far as the prospective occupant of the bedroom was concerned, lay in whether he preferred to have light and air admitted at floor or at ceiling level.

The development of a vernacular Doric in Upper New York State coincided with the migration across Lake Ontario of a number of craftsmen and industrialists intent on developing the natural resources of Canada West to the mutual advantage of themselves and the province. The iron-founders, plaster barons, stone masons — the Caprons, the Boughtons, the Maus, the McQuestens, the Van Normans — were to play important roles in the commerce of the province, and when they built homes in their adopted country they

employed their native idiom. A number of most interesting houses are located in and around Paris, which received its name from its most lucrative export, plaster, and not from a Classical allusion to a Trojan prince. Hiram Capron, the plaster king, built an imposing Classical house. It was illustrated on Tremaine's map of Brant

105. A ceiling medallion, almost as wide as the hall, caught the glow of the hanging lamp. Hamilton Place.

County, published in 1859. It has been altered out of all recognition. The Capron house was of ashlar but the distinctive stonework of Paris is cobblestone.

Cobblestone is the natural building medium of a glacial ridge running along the southern shore of Lake Ontario. It would seem to have derived from the incidence of the glacial deposits in that area and not necessarily from the flint tradition of Europe. The immigrant New Yorkers brought the use of the medium to Canada West. The mason of the cobblestone in Paris was Levi Boughton from Albany County, New York. It seems likely that he was employed for the masonry of Hamilton Place (104).

Hamilton Place is the apex of the vernacular Doric style in Canada West. It was designed by an architect, one Andrew Minny, and built in 1844 for Norman Hamilton, miller and brewer. Hamilton Place is a three-storey house with a basement kitchen which contrives to appear to be a storey and a half in height. The windows of the second floor, set in light-wells in the verandah roof, are concealed from casual view by the deep architrave of the verandah. The roof lantern, a room of some size, presumably served as a sunroom when the subaqueous light of the bedrooms became depressing. All rooms on the first floor are lighted by fine triple-hung windows with panelled interior shutters. Four reception rooms occupy the ground floor, double parlours, a dining-room and a library on either side of the central hall. Interior trim throughout the house is of a monumental Doric vernacular (106). In the hall it retains its original painted graining. Restrained Classicism is evident in the plain, bold moulding of the plaster cornices and in the severely disciplined acanthus leaves of the ceiling medallions (105).

There had been a natural revulsion away from the tortuous fine-drawn linear quality of the Neo-classic in its

106. Classical Revival architects managed to use a remarkable quantity of wood. The drawing-room door, Hamilton Place, retains its original painted graining.

107. *A Classical Revival parlour. The doctor's house, Upper Canada Village.*

108. *Pipes from a Greek stove create a labyrinth in the doctor's dining-room in Upper Canada Village.*

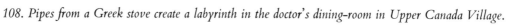

decline, and for this the strength and dignified simplicity of the Classical orders had seemed to be the solution. This was true even of the small house constructed by a minor builder who limited his Classicism to harmony of proportion or to interesting, individual application of Greek decorative detail. When the house was furnished with the quiet elegance within the means of a citizen of moderate income of 1845, as shown here in the drawing-room of the doctor's house in Upper Canada Village (107), a small dwelling of great charm and distinction ensued. Many smaller houses were designed to permit better circulation of heat from the new multiplicity of stoves. The stoves themselves were frequently designed to increase the Classical character of the room. Greek columns served as heat radiators of the stove in the doctor's dining-room (108), complementing the Greek chairs around his well-laid board. Additional heat was felt to be ample compensation for the unsightly tangle of overhead stove-pipes, but an Ionic stove is closer in spirit to Romanticism than it is to Classicism.

Rural Canada West enjoyed the Classical Revival in minuscule. At its best, the style was pleasant, dignified and comfortable. As it declined, lesser carpenter-builders were to use deeper cornices and coarse, thick trim and to insert large, heavy two-panelled doors in small, low-ceilinged rooms whose baseboards attained the height of a dado. The impetus was spent and the end was near. An antique style had been revived, and for a time it flourished. Then it died, a Spartan obedient to the laws.

109. *It has been remarked with some truth that, whereas anyone may adopt a style, only an architect can compose in it. Fortunately for Upper Canada, the Romantic styles were brought in by architects who composed with Picturesque freedom. It may have been sentiment which led William Thomas to bedeck the entrance of Oakham House, Church Street, Toronto, with battlements and sculptured heads, but it was informed not pedantic sentiment.*

144

5

Ye distant spires, ye antique towers

As the last stroke of midnight ushered in the cold first day of January 1837, did an expectant thrill quicken the imaginations of Upper Canadians? It ought to have done, for they were beginning a momentous year. On the contrary, the wakeful were doubtless discussing with heat the political controversy, unaware that before the year was out they would all have become Victorians if not victorious and shortly, although still Canadian, no longer Upper.

By common consent, writers of Canadian history pass quickly from the causes of the Mackenzie rebellion to its ultimate constitutional effect. The tragi-comic incidents of the actual conflict are treated, as they probably were by the active participants, as a political campaign waged with slightly more than ordinary vigour. So wholehearted has been public acceptance of the dictum that the rebellion was ill-bred and unnecessary that many residents of the province are not aware that there were causes more immediate than the fiery temper of the first mayor of Toronto and results more edifying than the execution of Lount and Mathews. The fact which eludes the greatest number appears to be that, following investigation by a Royal Commissioner, one of the recommendations put into effect was the union, in 1841, of the Canadas, Upper and Lower, and that they were henceforth to be known as Canada West and Canada East.

Unity has yet to be achieved by legislation alone. The union was a temporary expedient destined to be absorbed after the passage of twenty-six years by Confederation, but the social history of the quarter-century should not be ignored. In the field of architecture, it was marked by the North American hey-day of Romanticism.

The Classical Revival was, at birth, a romantic style, the sole repository of the True, the Beautiful and the Ancient. It blossomed as the darling of the poets and the painters, flourished in the light of archaeological recoveries, and faded at last from an excess of correctness. The Classical was not, however, the only style revitalized by the poets and painters of

145

the early nineteenth century. Their repertory was enlarged by other styles which drew inspiration from another fertile source, that of the Romantic novel.

Early in the field of English letters with a blood-chilling tale, Horace Walpole was probably first in the running with a Gothic house. He built Strawberry Hill in 1750, an aristocratic eclectic whimsy of a house, and as no one had yet given serious consideration to the Gothic as an architectural expression, everyone was pleased to be amused. As early as 1747 Battey Langley had written of the charms of something he called "rustic architecture," which was in fact Gothic surface decoration for domestic buildings. His intention was to present a novel style as an alternative choice to patrons who might be bored with *chinoiserie*. Mid-eighteenth-century England was set too firmly in the Georgian mould to do more than apply some Gothic detail to decorative use. National temperament, which had in England curtailed the gaiety of the Rococo and by a sobering admixture of Palladianism had produced the Georgian style, had also rejected the Gothic fantasy as architecture. The time was not ripe, for as Heinrich Wölfflin, the art historian, declares: "The picturesque style . . . has always come only when its hour has struck, that is when it was understood." Almost a century of idealistic philosophy, imaginative painting, colourful verse, stirring prose and earthshaking events lay between the publication of Battey Langley's *Gothic Architecture Improved* and the year which brought Victoria to her throne. The balance was heavily weighted on the side of the Picturesque in 1837.

The major patrons of architecture in the nineteenth century were drawn from a wealthy mercantile society. This was also true of the Renaissance. Both eras were remarkable for an exuberant vitality and a fearless arrogance of belief in human accomplishment which could be considered naïve but which would prove to be, like the little Queen of Britain, vigorous, enthusiastic and durable.

The early Victorian palpitated with eagerness to experiment with all manner of things, architecture among them. Lured by shadowed towers in the landscapes of Poussin and Claude Lorrain, entranced by the marvellous, if inexplicit, descriptions of Victor Hugo and Walter Scott, he set out to discover the high Gothic and the Renaissance. He was to view fair Melrose and Notre-Dame, to be led over the stones of Venice by the authoritative hand of John Ruskin, to go up to the villa and down to the City of Florence with Browning and to see the ancient world silhouetted against acres of Turner sunsets.

146

Early Victorian Gothic had very little to do with the medieval world. It was not an archaeological study but a colourful excursion into "realms of gold," the decorative, imaginative Gothic of the black-letter manuscript. There were no frightening orders, no rules to break, no jealous Olympians to make nasty comments. There was not even a textbook. Augustus Welby Northmore Pugin was, it is true, off in a corner somewhere writing *The True Principles of Pointed or Christian Architecture* which was to paralyze invention by calling it heresy, but in 1837 the Romanticists held the field.

In the early nineteenth century there were in Great Britain and western Europe numerous castles, *châteaux* and *Schlösser*, both romantic and habitable. Old landowning families, desirous of a medieval atmosphere, could at will return to the ancient family seat or the earliest portion of the house in which they were presently residing. The new patrons, the Captains of Industry, bought mellow estates steeped in history from an improvident aristocracy or when the required style, site or size was not forthcoming, they had castles built to order. The lesser industrialist, whose aspirations did not rise to keep, moat and barbican, desired a manor or a villa. It was the architectural response to the requirements of the latter group which was to form the nucleus of export Romanticism for Canada West.

Numerous villas were designed in the Classical Revival style in Great Britain, and some were even perpetrated in the Egyptian taste. However many English architects, who considered the Classical style to be either too monumental or too sacrosanct to be domesticated, were assaying the vocabulary of the Perpendicular, the Tudor and the Jacobean. When Wordsworth and the other Romantic poets espoused the cause of Switzerland, the Gothic plan was ousted from the drawing-board by the chalet. Then the designers crossed the Alps and descended on Tuscany.

It is of some significance that Queen Victoria, who had on her accession moved into a Regency palace and a refurbished Windsor castle, built, with her beloved Albert, two houses in the forties. The houses in question were Osborne, an Italian villa on the Isle of Wight, and Balmoral, a baronial castle of Rhenish inspiration on the Dee. It is equally important to recall that the royal pair was following fashion, not shaping it, and that both houses were built with careful savings. Alexandrina Victoria was the epitome of the nineteenth-century patron, a Romanticist whose diary was awash with superlatives, and an alert business woman who sat at the centre of, and in complete rapport with, the most powerful mercantile empire of the century — an unlikely combination, one might think, but typical of the era.

Loyal Canada West did not break out in a rash of Italianate villas and Gothic manors in emulation of their sovereign's choice in domestic architecture. Queen Victoria noted in a letter to her Uncle Leopold, King of the Belgians, "We moved into our new house today." The letter was written at Osborne and the date was September 14, 1846. In 1836, a full ten years earlier, Allan MacNab had moved into his new house, Dundurn, with its two squat Tuscan watch-towers and Italianate dove-cote. Sir Allan was pleased that Her Majesty now enjoyed similar felicity. As for the Gothic Revival, Balmoral, "dear Albert's own creation," was finally completed in 1855 with the professional assistance of William Smith, city architect of Aberdeen. This was the year in which Auchmar was rising on Hamilton Mountain to grace Claremont, the domain of the Honourable Isaac Buchanan. Claremont was named in honour of that other Claremont where, for so short a time, the Regent's ill-fated daughter Charlotte lived with her husband Leopold of Saxe-Coburg, who later became King of the Belgians.

Dear Claremont, dear Coburg, dear Uncle Leopold one tends to forget, while contemplating the tremendous social contributions of the Victorian era, that Romanticism enjoyed its trial run in Regency England and that the road companies had reached the provinces. The advance guard of architects who brought the Romantic revivals to Upper Canada, even before it became Canada West, were most frequently young men who had received their training in Great Britain and Ireland in the happy tradition of the Picturesque. The doctrine of the Picturesque, which may be equated in part with the "painterly" of Heinrich Wölfflin, was advanced in 1794 by Sir Euvadale Price as a counter-theory to the whole philosophy of aesthetics but more particularly to the philosophy of the Sublime and the Beautiful as advanced by Burke. The Picturesque was concerned, not with archaeology and engineering, but with composition and visual effect.

The architect was in a position far more tenable in reviving the Picturesque than he had been in designing the Classical house. The definitive expression of the Classical style was the Greek temple. The little houses, even the large palaces, of Athens and Rome were forgotten. The Picturesque revivals, on the other hand, were all derived from domestic building. The Gothic, Tudor or Jacobean, whether it be manor-house or cottage, was still in use. Although Italian villas and Swiss chalets might be old, they were certainly occupied. The

148

purpose of the building had remained constant. Virtuosity and the evocative were qualities most admired in every field of creative activity during the Victorian era. What element was common to the widely diversified styles of the Picturesque which made them interchangeably acceptable to Romanticists? What quality was conspicuously lacking in the temples of Greece and Rome?

Classical temples were distinguished by a great and monumental repose and a rigidity of plan utterly unsuited to the patriarchal character of the Victorian household. The domestic Picturesque models were all, to a greater or lesser degree, tolerant of asymmetrical composition, both in elevation and in plan, and were capable of addition and subtraction in any direction at will. Irregularity of outline, contrast of light with shade, variety of texture — all were requirements of the Picturesque which could be satisfied by domestic building in either of the two preferred styles, "old English" or the "modern Italian." The City of Kingston has an excellent example of each in Elizabeth Cottage and in Teacaddy Castle.

General statistics of the survival of the Picturesque houses of Ontario are rather surprising. Toronto, which enjoyed a great measure of prosperity in the days before Confederation and had at its disposal the talents of the best architects of Romanticism practising in Canada West, has been at such pains to eradicate the Picturesque that very little of it remains. Victorian Hamilton built its castles upon the rock and time has proven the efficacy of the biblical injunction. Kingston, never a convinced Romanticist, put up little that was self-consciously Picturesque, but has retained its whimsies.

Teacaddy Castle, or Muscovado Manor (110), received its derisively apt name from an illustrious tenant, John A. Macdonald. What its owner, Charles Hale, a prosperous grocer, thought of this is not known. The design, it is believed, came from the drawing-board of the versatile George Browne, architect of Kingston City Hall, St. Andrews manse and many other fine buildings. In the St. Andrews manse and at Rockwood, Browne may be seen working in the Soane tradition. Teacaddy Castle is in his Picturesque vein and it follows the Italianate manner employed by John Nash just ten years earlier in Park Village East in London.

Browne seems to have chosen as his exemplars the two most brilliant architects in England at the turn of the century, John Soane and John Nash. The fine simplicity of Soane was misunderstood in his own day and by his fellow countrymen. Nash was a slap-dash opportunist whose building practice did not always keep pace with his hurtling ideas. Canada

110. *Bellevue, Kingston. When he lived there, Sir John A. Macdonald called it Teacaddy Castle or Muscovado Manor as the fancy struck him. Charles Hale, who had it built, bestowed upon it the more pedestrian but typical name of Bellevue.*

150

West was saved from a vast weight of monumental Greekery by the quality of Soane and the happy *bravura* of Nash which had fired the imaginations of young architects on the brink of departure for the New World.

Teacaddy Castle is Italianate, that is to say, it was derived from the villa architecture of Italy. The Picturesque school did not indulge in archaeological surveys of Hadrian's villa or delve in Herculaneum. For their purposes, the Italian villa was taken to be a composite of the small country houses of Tuscany. The arch-type would be of irregular shape, perhaps an L-plan. The walls would be thick, and the door and window openings crowned with semi-circular arches. The roof would be a gable or a hip of wide projection with exposed rafter ends, or it might be supported by ornamental brackets. There would be a number of small balconies and a short square tower. The walls would be made of brick and covered by stucco. Brick, stucco, concrete and tile have been the builder's media in Italy from the time of the Etruscans to the present. The short watch-tower may be considered the legacy of the Middle Ages, post *Pax Romana*, when each householder had to look out for himself. The round-headed windows and the gay little balcony can be considered contributions to or from both the Romanesque and the Renaissance, as both are structural in origin. The Tuscan villas were usually simple in the matter of interior decoration. Consequently the Italianate house will be found to be austere within. Whether the effect was one of gracious space or of un-remitting dullness depended entirely upon the degree of taste employed in furnishing it.

Stuccoed brick, the medium of the Italian villa, had been put to traditional use by Sir Allan MacNab at Dundurn where two Tuscan towers add an Italianate fillip to his symmetrical Regency house. Brick was not the logical choice in Kingston, so Browne designed Teacaddy in limestone and cloaked it decently in stucco. Not only was this in keeping with the style, but it provided the necessary unbroken background for the dramatic shadows cast by the scalloped verge boards of the awning roof. Teacaddy Castle looks its Picturesque best in the long, low rays of the setting sun when deep shadows engulf the alterations of later years.

Light and shade are equally important to a row of charming attached houses on King Street in Kingston (111). Hale's Cottages were built by Teacaddy's owner, Charles Hale, during the boom of 1841. They were designed to accommodate the Governor's staff and to that end were erected across the street from Alwington. Unfortunately it was in front

111. Hale's Cottages, Kingston, are row houses in the Picturesque style built in 1841 when Kingston was the capital of the United Canadas.

of these little houses that Lord Sydenham's horse took fright at some horrible object, possibly a pile of lumber or stone, and threw its exalted rider, dragging him along the highway. Hale's workmen caught the runaway and carried the Governor to Alwington. The Governor died. The seat of Government was moved to Bytown on the Ottawa and the tenant of Teacaddy Castle, the lawyer from Kingston, became the first Prime Minister of Canada. Truly the stuff of high romance, but where is the novel that tells the tale of Teacaddy and John A., of the Cottages and of the household, of the chaplain and the commissioner, of Lord Sydenham and Alwington? And what became of Amy Washer? Steadily through the unrecorded annals would run the quiet story of Charles Hale, grocer, and George Browne, architect, who could and did produce row housing of timeless charm.

Hale's Cottages are Regency houses of stuccoed Kingston limestone. Each unit is thirty-eight feet by thirty-two feet and a storey and a half in height. Kitchens were located in the cellars. All interior trim was plain and slightly Greek. Romanticism gave a scalloped awning edge to the verandah and sympathetic planting of the little gardens has carried out the Picturesque intention.

Regency Tuscan has awning roofs; it may or may not have towers. Bow Park (112), from Tremaine's map of Brant County, illustrates the transitional early Victorian Italianate. The awning roof, although gaily striped, has a pierced rather than a scalloped edge. The gable roof of gentle pitch was supported visually by ornamental brackets and the central gable, crowned by a masonry outcrop, was pierced by an arched aperture. In Italy the opening would contain a bell, but in villas on the Grand one suspects that the supporting members were chimneys, as they are on Dundurn.

Brant was, among the counties, fortunate in its cartographers. Bow Park was

112. Bow Park, Brantford, was purchased by the Honourable George Brown and as the scene of his agricultural experiments it became his pride and his despair. Ontario was not yet ready for an experimental farm.

delineated with precision, the shadows mathematically calculated, the house presented with as much pride as the marshalled ranks of sheep and shorthorns. It should not be inferred from this illustration that Canada West followed the Italian farm practice of housing its livestock under a roof contiguous to human habitation. Civic pride, not custom, placed the purebred flocks and herds before the door to edify posterity. At other times, a stout fence would curb encroaching animals if they did not, as good Victorians, know their place.

Deep shade obscures the brackets of Bow Park which appear to be cut from plank with a cyma-reversa profile, that is, a double curve, concave at the base and convex as it rises to support the eave. As the century advanced, the complexity of the bracket increased until it attained such surface importance that one reads of the Italianate or Bracketed style, a term only superficially correct. More than a bracket is needed to make an Italianate house. Many brackets in this province and elsewhere on buildings of the sixties, seventies, and even the eighties and nineties have little to do with Italy and even less with romance.

There were pitfalls in the Picturesque which had been pointed out as early as 1830 by John Claudius Loudon, who had this to say of the Tuscan:

> The modern Italian style of architecture, the characteristics of which may be given in two words —"painter-like effect," has in this country a recommendation of novelty; a quality which always makes a strong impression on the general observer. It is not, however, a style which can be trusted to the hands of any architect not a master in the art of composition. The great object in designing every building as far as exterior effect is concerned is the production of a whole: now, in regular symmetrical architecture, this is comparatively easy; for a centre being fixed upon, the two sides can easily be made to correspond with it. A beautiful design may not be the result, but, whatever it may be, it will have pretensions to being a whole. Italian architecture, on the other hand, is characterized by irregularity, by strong contrast and by other painter-like effects.

The painter-like effects of 495 Sherbourne Street, Toronto (113), were designed by Frederick William Cumberland, who elected to dispense with the watch-tower but retained the round-headed windows singly, paired and in Palladian combination. The Italianate flavour extends to the chimney in a blind arcade and patterned cornice. Internally, the house has suffered a twentieth-century Georgian revival, from which only the entrance hall has escaped comparatively unscathed. Cumberland was a gifted designer and he employed his

154

113. Sherbourne House, Toronto. A Tuscan villa designed by F. W. Cumberland for his brother-in-law.

114. *Idalia, Port Hope. A villa in the Italianate taste, somewhat altered by time.*

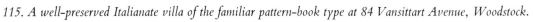

115. *A well-preserved Italianate villa of the familiar pattern-book type at 84 Vansittart Avenue, Woodstock.*

considerable talents in making Toronto picturesque in partnership with William Storm. He designed University College in the Romanesque style, St. James' Cathedral in the early English, 10 Toronto Street in the Ionic and with Storm completed Osgoode Hall in the manner of Andrea Palladio. Cumberland found time in his spare moments to organize the Royal Grenadiers, of which regiment he was first Lieutenant-Colonel. It is typical of the city in which he designed so much that he is remembered in Robertson's *Landmarks of Toronto*, not as an architect but as Colonel of the Royals, and that when, in 1962, the colours of that regiment were, in the presence of the Colonel-in-Chief, Her Royal Highness the Princess Royal, laid up in the cathedral which he had designed, Cumberland was not mentioned at all.

Italianate villas graced a number of cities of Ontario but the pruning hook of time has cut them down. Some were destroyed by fire, as was Barton Lodge in Hamilton; others have been mutilated beyond recognition. Idalia (114) in Port Hope and 84 Vansittart Avenue, Woodstock (115), survive with only minor abrasions. Both villas have balconied watch-towers, paired round-headed windows and gay brackets under their wide eaves. The brackets of Idalia are joined by a narrow moulding to form a decorative cornice. The Woodstock villa has pairs of brackets set on a string course of projecting brick. The entrance door of Idalia is Italianate with a semi-circular transom. The other villa has the later door head which continued in fashion into the seventies. It is disproportionately high and this is the only feature, other than a singularly dull later porch, which gives cause for regret in a fine composition. Idalia suffers from a turret, an outsize chocolate drop, perched by insensitive alteration on its picturesque roofline. Idalia is asymmetrical in plan. An obstacle encountered by architects of the Picturesque was the unwillingness of many clients to depart from the traditional, comfortable centre-hall plan. Our friend John Claudius Loudon had warned that this would be so.

It seems likely at the present stage of investigation into the architectural source material in Canada West that the greatest single advocate for the Picturesque was a corpulent volume entitled *An Encyclopaedia of Cottage, Farm and Villa Architecture and Furniture: containing numerous designs for dwellings, from the villa to the cottage and farm, including farm houses, farmeries, and other agricultural buildings; country inns, public houses and parochial schools; with the requisite fittings up, fixtures and furniture: and appropriate offices, gardens and garden scenery; each design accompanied by analytical and critical remarks* by John Claudius Loudon, F.L.S., H.S.,

C.S., Z.S., etc., first published in London in 1830. Loudon's *Encyclopaedia* is exhaustive; it is also concise, explicit, persuasive and fascinating.

In a single useful reference work were to be found discourses on aesthetics and architecture, on horticulture and furniture, on the installation of furnaces and awnings, and theories on ventilation and the circulation of heat. There were directions for fashioning refrigerators, water-closets and shower baths, and there was the recommendation of a new device whereby a small frame inserted in a dress or coat permitted the garment to be suspended from a rod rather than hung from a peg in the wardrobe. The potential client was being conditioned to change but not always to change in house plans.

Neither Loudon nor his American counterpart, Andrew Jackson Downing, lived to enjoy the Romantic harvest of their sowing, but Ontario is greatly indebted to them. In rural areas, the practical instructions for farm improvement were of value, as were the directions for construction of the simpler forms of Italianate and Gothic houses. The importance of Loudon's work to urban areas lay in his analysis of style, as he understood it, and his insistence on the need to plan the surroundings as well as the villa.

Some time after 1843, a large stone house was built for Richard Duggan at the southwest corner of Jackson and Macnab streets in Hamilton, Canada West. Duggan and his architect appear to have decided, not without justification, that the proper place for a villa was in the country and that residence in a city with a future necessitated the building of a town house. The town house acquired neat little brackets under its eaves; and matching pairs of brackets supported the flat roof of the Ionic porch, which was crowned by a Renaissance balustrade. A pair of French doors, which opened from the upper hall onto the balustraded porch roof, are set in a frame of monolithic stonework headed by a semi-circular keystoned arch. The tympanum of the arch is fan-reeded, as is the elliptical false fanlight in the pediment above the roofline. The edifice was called Willow Bank, which seems to have replaced Locust Grove as the popular name for a house in the 1840's.

In 1852 Willow Bank was sold for eight hundred pounds to Calvin McQuesten, M.D., iron-founder, late of Bedford Town, New Hampshire. Dr. McQuesten, who had had Hawthorne, Longfellow and Daniel Webster as fellow students at Bowdoin College, Maine, was a man very much to Loudon's taste, a humanitarian who enjoyed gardening and a businessman who valued invention. Doubtless the guests gathered about his hospitable board

158

were often grateful that the McQuesten dining-room (116) had, besides a handsome mantelpiece, a neat circular register in the baseboard (118), mute but comforting evidence that one of Hamilton's first furnaces was at work in the cellar. This was the home of a scholar and a ruling Elder of the Presbyterian Church, so it is likely that the gentlemen soon joined the ladies in the drawing-room (117), furnished then very much as it is now. Willow Bank, renamed Whitehern by Dr. McQuesten's daughter-in-law, remains in the McQuesten family, and it is undoubtedly for that reason that Whitehern is one of the few of the many comfortable, worthy bracketed houses of its day which is sufficiently unchanged to warrant study. The loving care which preserved gracious living within was extended to the garden. Laburnums still drip golden rain behind a high stone wall close to Hamilton's City Hall. Sunflowers smile perpetually from that garden wall, undisturbed by the occasional breeze from the steel mills on the Bay. The laburnums wax and wane with the seasons; the sun-flowers remain, for they, like the products of Calvin McQuesten's foundries, were cast in iron.

The operative basis of the Picturesque was the lively imagination of its patrons, and it is not always possible at this distance in time to gauge their reactions to new ideas. Few activities could evoke as little romantic fervour now as the installation of a furnace, but was it always so? A whole series of octagonal and cubical houses was designed to prove a theory of the circulation of heat. As the circulation of heat in domestic buildings has never held the attention of English architects for very long (with the possible exception of eccentrics like Loudon), it is not unnatural that octagonal and cubical houses are largely products of North America. The core of halls, which forms such an admirable heat and ventilation well, is somewhat deficient in light. To remedy the situation, houses of this type raised a monitor or belvedere on their shallow hip-roofs. As the vast majority of these houses were built in the central United States before the Civil War and in Canada West before Confederation, they were either Greek or Italianate, or both, as the client chose.

The Tuscan quality of houses such as 76 Arkeldun Avenue, Hamilton (119), some of whose most prominent decorative members are frankly Greek, might puzzle a Florentine, but a diligent peruser of pattern-books would locate it at once. The square hip-roofed tower of the Italian farm-house has been set in the centre of the roof and all the eaves are bracketed. Simpler examples of this derivative style can be seen in many towns and villages of Ontario, but rural examples are unlikely to boast console brackets carved in stone to support the lintels

116. *Opposite: The furnishing and decoration of the dining-room was as solid and dependable as the food consumed in it. Whitehern, Hamilton.*

117. *Above: Untouched Victorian opulence in the drawing-room of Whitehern.*

118. *Right: Heat register of the early furnace.*

which surmount the window and door openings, as this subtly Italianate house does.

Only in Guelph will stone brackets (120) of similar quality be found on small houses, and these houses are not examples of the Italianate style. The small stone houses of Guelph are part of the North American success story, picturesque romance of a different genre. Master masons and stone carvers who had spent many years chipping Palladianism from the rocks of Great Britain and Ireland had gathered up their families, their gear and their courage, and emigrated to Canada West. The little stone houses along the Speed acquired console brackets, pedimented windows and even the odd Roman frieze. Perhaps the working drawings were prepared by David Allan, the Edinburgh-born architect of a good deal of Guelph, including the jail and courthouse, his father's mill and St. Andrew's Presbyterian Church, but spiritual satisfaction for the stone mason lay in the fact that in Guelph, Canada West, at long last, he was free to carve his best ornament on a house in which he himself might live.

Romanticists of the early nineteenth century wished to gaze upon narrative painting, to listen to sweet music, to read lyric poetry and to be told affecting histories. The story of Chiefswood (121) on the Grand River near Brantford was very much to their taste, for in this bracketed Regency house was born Emily Pauline Johnson, poetic voice of the Mohawks. Here died her father, Chief Johnson, martyred by ruffians who wished to exploit his people.

Chiefswood was built in 1856 by Johnson as a gift for his English wife, Emily Howells. It is basically a hip-roofed Regency villa of the simple centre-hall plan, in other words the well-proportioned Georgian form stripped of Renaissance detail, the identical façades relieved by central gabled projections. The stark simplicity of exterior trim and of the door and window openings gives an air of great importance to the bracketed cornice, which would have been immeasurably increased had the composition been allowed to accelerate in drama until it achieved the belvedere for which framing exists in the roof. The belvedere was never built, and interest was transferred to the doors, which were given ogival arches of Picturesque Gothic, here to be seen in peaceful rural form in the country villa of a Six Nations chief.

One might well expect playful Gothic to be given more vivid expression by an English architect in the design of his own home; one might be forgiven for not seeking such an expression amidst the rugged limestone of Kingston. Nevertheless, quite the gayest

162

119. The North American Tuscan or Bracketed style at 76 Arkeldun Avenue, Hamilton.

120. Right: Stone consoles. McTague's cottages, Guelph, 1854.

Regency cottage of Canada West stands with later Victorian accretions at 251 Brock Street in that city. It was built some time before 1850 by Edward Horsey, late of Sherborne, Dorsetshire. It was called Elizabeth Cottage and such relationship as it bears to the medieval is in the order of Peacock's Mr. Chainmail, "that blissful middle period after the Jacquerie were down and before the march of mind was up" — more or less Tudor — but Elizabethan in this instance only in the sense that it housed Elizabeth Horsey.

Architects of the Regency *cottage orné* tradition were very much concerned with an interesting silhouette, with the charm and character inherent in the composition of form enhanced by supplementary ornament. The accompanying drawing of Elizabeth Cottage (122) identifies Horsey's successful essay in the playful Tudor — a central block of two storeys, defined by three pinnacles, reminiscent of the Abbey in Sherborne. The verge boards are edged by a highly plastic moulding which retains the same profile as the charming tracery of the little oriel window (123). The tracery is repeated in the narrow double-hung windows, set under Tudor labels, or dripstones, which flank the oriel. The quatrefoil repeat pattern which Horsey used with telling effect on the parapets of the wing derives from Sherborne Abbey too.

163

The Gothic was a supreme expression of stone construction, and undoubtedly Edward Horsey appreciated it fully. But he can be readily forgiven for hiding the heavy masonry of his little cottage behind a coat of stucco. He had had, at one time, a hand in directing construction of the grimmest expression Kingston limestone was ever to find in the building of Portsmouth penitentiary. Planning the skeletal sham buttress (124) of his little verandah must have made a happy contrast for him.

121. Chiefswood, Brantford, was built in 1856 by Chief Johnson of the Six Nations Indians for his English bride. The little balcony is a restoration.

The verge boards and the tracery of Elizabeth Cottage, the latter less frequent in the early Gothic Revival in Canada West, were distinguished by imaginative linear use of a strongly articulated moulding of bold profile. On the verge board, the moulded pattern is applied to the edge of the board, which actually protects and conceals the end framing of the steeply gabled roof. An excellent example of the linear style decorates the cottage (125) in Picton, Prince Edward County. The Picton cottage has an oriel window and a buttressed porch, but its oriel is simpler than that of Elizabeth Cottage and the buttresses are of authentic structure even if not strictly necessary.

Success in the Picturesque style depended entirely on the ability of the architect as a designer. He had to exercise a nice discretion in his composition, to balance his daring with restraint. Let us consider the drawing-room chimney-pieces which were, respectively, designed for Elizabeth Cottage (126) by Edward Horsey, and carved for Sunnyside, Guelph (127), by John Kennedy. The two mantelpieces are Picturesque Gothic and for many years both have been a source of endless enjoyment to their owners for very different reasons. The white marble mantelpiece of Elizabeth Cottage recalls the laudatory comments of a day long gone, when "chaste," "elegance" and "propriety" were household words. The scale is admirable for the house, the city and the era. The Gothic detail of cusps and quatrefoils, escutcheon and oak leaves is Romanticism of the ancient harp and the minor key. The mantelpiece in the drawing-room of Sunnyside must have been second to none in Canada West as a conversation piece, and if the man who carved it did so as a hobby to while away long winter evenings, his efforts exceed even those of the shipwrights

164

122. *Elizabeth Cottage, Kingston. Edward Horsey's little Regency Gothic fantasy.*

123. *The mullioned oriel window of Elizabeth Cottage.*

of Niagara who beguiled their boredom in the same way.

Sunnyside, where this remarkable artifact stands, was built by Charles Davidson on the bank of the Speed in 1854. The building date was helpfully carved on the imaginative Ionic porch by Davidson's father-in-law, John Kennedy, who came to Guelph from Philadelphia. A low-relief carving of Abbotsford adorns the porch and indicates that whether Kennedy sprang from the Kennedys of Ulster, or of Strathclyde, he was a Romanticist at heart. Another house is depicted on the centre panel of the Sunnyside mantelpiece which has greater claims on the attention than Abbotsford, far greater even than the stone facsimiles of early English bench-ends which flank the grate. Here, faithfully depicted, is the only contemporary evidence of Ker Cavan, unaltered and unrestored.

Ker Cavan, once known as Ter Kathleen, was built as a rectory for Archdeacon Palmer in Guelph in 1855 and has the distinction of being the only house to have been built in Canada West from plans reputedly

124. *Openwork sham buttresses replace the usual posts in supporting the verandah at Elizabeth Cottage.*

125. Left: Picton's Gothic cottage has real, if unnecessary, buttresses.

126. Below: Regency Gothic was light and gay inside and out. The drawing-room mantelpiece, Elizabeth Cottage, Kingston.

127. Bottom: Sunnyside, Guelph, has a mantelpiece carved by John Kennedy showing Ker Cavan in low relief.

128. The dining-room at Ker Cavan, 1855, has corn-ear moulding, introduced to fashion by John Latrobe in the Capitol in Washington.

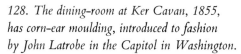

by Sir Charles Barry. Did Barry's pupil, Frederick Rastrick, by any chance watch over the building of Ker Cavan? He was very near, having set up practice in Hamilton in 1853, but as usual information is not forthcoming. The interior of Ker Cavan is surprisingly Greek in character for a Church of England rectory of the nineteenth century, and the plaster trim of the dining-room ceiling (128) leads to other conjectures. Did Barry feel that a moulding of maize would please Archdeacon Palmer's North American parishioners, or was the corn-cob moulding run by a master plasterer fresh from the Latrobe tradition of John Kennedy's native Philadelphia? The Tudor roses and Classical rosettes above it were elements of the British heritage of decorative motifs common to Upper Canadians whether they had come directly across the Atlantic or had made stop-overs in New York and Pennsylvania.

Hamilton seems to have numbered among its dwellings the highest percentage of titular castles in Canada West. There was Dundurn Castle, and Rock Castle, and Smiley's Castle, and the Colin Reid house on James Street South called, with unwarranted complacency, simply The Castle. There were also several large houses of picturesque medievalism for which the designation "castle" was not claimed. A parallel list of excellent architects of the fifties can be assembled which would include William Thomas, F. W. Cumberland, F. J. Rastrick, Lucian Hills, John Buchanan, William Boultbee, and many others who are known to have practised in Hamilton. It is not so easy to assign surviving buildings to their respective designers. There is a dearth of documentary evidence. Even less is known of the architects who designed houses for Hamilton in the thirties and forties.

The first of the castles in Hamilton was, of course, Dundurn, in 1836. The second appears to have been Rock Castle (129), built some twelve years later for one of the expatriate American iron-founders. Probably on a clear day, Mr. Carpenter could see Carpenter and Gurney's factory from his castle, which still stands beside the shelving grade of Arkeldun Avenue. The site is both magnificent and precipitous. Rock Castle, which is basically a rectangular centre-hall house, satisfied the Picturesque requirement of irregularity by the number of levels which adjustment to that site dictated. The house is three storeys in height on the Bay side, two on the Mountain side and one at the Arkeldun Avenue level, where the carriage room at the top of the kitchen wing has direct access to the street. Rock Castle is set at a right angle with the street, the entrance façade toward the garden. This disposition ensured for

Mr. Carpenter the maximum fenestration on the Bay side and allowed the principal reception rooms to command the finest prospect. The garden front has the central gabled bay so frequently found in houses of the late forties. The gable enriched by the cusped barge board, recommended by Loudon for small villas, is here further decorated by a tiny trefoil window in the apex and by a pointed Gothic double-hung window below. The doorway has fine restrained Picturesque Gothic detail: a Tudor label terminated by two plain escutcheons surrounds the pointed arch. Both label and arch are the work of a master stone-mason. The sidelights and pointed transom have metal glazing bars which form a pattern of clipped ellipses made Gothic by angularity. The motif of the pointed arch within a square head is repeated in the door panels and in the sham frames of the double-hung windows of the second storey. Mr. Carpenter reserved his most Gothic whimsy for the Bay and Mountain gables of Rock Castle (130), placed under the eaves not to impress the passer-by but to delight the inhabitant. The ogival false gable with its hexagonal pinnacles and corona of heraldic feathers also boasts a blind lancet arch and a coat of arms.

Rock Castle was a bracketed house but it had no Tuscan associations. Its brackets were Gothic and the free-standing tower (131) behind the kitchen wing was not a campanile. It was a two-storey privy, originally reached on the upper level by an open bridge, the view from which must have been magnificent. Today it encompasses most of the City of Hamilton, the Bay and that bridge of far greater expanse, the Burlington Skyway, made possible by steel mills of the kind which grew from small foundries such as that operated by Carpenter and Gurney.

Toronto was to languish castle-less until 1910, but in 1848 there was erected its best example of domestic Gothic. Oakham House (132), whose impressive shell still stands at the southeast corner of Church and Gould streets, was designed and built by William Thomas as his house and office. Thomas, who shared with Cumberland the honour of having designed the finest pre-Confederation buildings in the City of Toronto, was born in 1800 and died in 1860. His special field was ecclesiastical architecture. St. Michael's Cathedral was one of his churches and the only one, much altered, to survive in Toronto. His last work was the central portion of the Don Jail; his best surviving building is St. Lawrence Hall. The most recently demolished of similar major works was the Normal School on Gould Street opposite Oakham House. The educational institute, which saw fit to level the Normal School, also

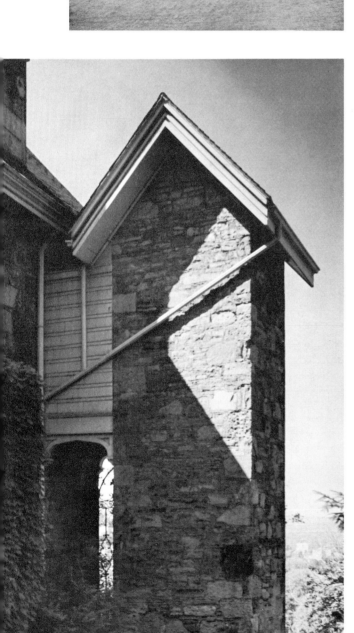

129. Upper left: Rock Castle, Hamilton,
was built by the senior partner of Carpenter
and Gurney on the side of Hamilton Mountain.
It commands a magnificent view of the City
and the Bay.

130. Above: Gable wall, Rock Castle.

131. Left: The unique feature of Rock Castle
was its free-standing two-storey privy. An
open bridge once connected it to the house
at the second-storey level.

169

efficiently gutted his house. One must be grateful in proportion to the degree of conservation and be thankful that the "external Picturesque" of Oakham House has been graciously allowed to remain to us.

In order to acquire a clear idea of the domestic Picturesque Gothic as designed by an architect of considerable stature, it would be well to consider the merits of Oakham House in Toronto with those of Inglewood in Hamilton, which also appears to bear the hall-marks of a Thomas design. A third house of similar character and quality, Highfield, in Hamilton, which could with equal justice be attributed to Thomas, was demolished in 1932. By a happy chance, the architect's coloured perspective drawing of Highfield, regrettably unsigned, has found its way to an honoured place on the walls of Inglewood.

In Oakham House a Thomas design has survived externally; in Inglewood, skilful partitioning by a sympathetic architect has preserved the interior, although the exterior has, of necessity, suffered somewhat in being converted to multiple occupancy. Both houses express architectural truth in their media. Oakham House was built of the natural material of Toronto, brick, and Inglewood in that of Hamilton, stone. In both houses, Gothic mullions divide windows, which are set in rectangular openings. The windows of Inglewood have a central mullion of simple form giving the window two lancet lights. Oakham has very similar mullions on the second storey but has three lights, and the ground-floor windows have an enriched tracery related in character to that found on the almost identical entrance doors of both houses. Consistency of design is maintained in the modified tracery of the panelling of all ground-floor internal shutters, one of which can be seen on the oriel window off the dining-room of Inglewood (133).

The dining-room in the ideal Picturesque Gothic villa as set forth by Loudon from the designs of various English architects was always the largest reception room in the house, and was usually distinguished for the fine plasterwork of its ceiling and by the added Romanticism of an oriel window. It was the lineal descendant of the great dining-hall of the medieval house. The design was usually conceived on a broad scale and carried out boldly. Less energy and greater refinement, as well as diminishing scale, marked the drawing-room and boudoir. Groined ceilings were reserved mostly for the hall and the entrance hall, or porch, if there was one.

Inglewood fulfils all of the above requirements and is an ideal villa. The dining-

170

132. Oakham House, Toronto, was built as a combined home and office by William Thomas in 1848.

room (134) has an oriel window with quatrefoils and border of golden stained glass and large lights of clear glass which permit a handsome view over the city. Heavy Gothic moulding outlines the oriel and corresponds in depth to the baseboard. The white marble mantelpiece, carved in authentic Perpendicular Gothic motifs, has the depressed four-centred Tudor arch. The ceiling (135) is a truly magnificent excursion into the curvilinear tracery of the Decorated style and is enhanced by its present colour scheme of pale greyed-turquoise picked out with gold against a Pompeian red ground.

The stair, set in a stair-hall at right angles to the principal corridor, consists of a straight central flight to a landing and a pair of return flights from the landing to the upper corridor. The stair-rail (136) is a continuous pierced screen, well related to the tracery of doors, mantels and shutters throughout the house. The newel pendant is similar in form to,

134. The dining-room of Inglewood showing the oriel window.

*133. Gothic panelling on an inside
shutter at Inglewood, Hamilton.*

135. The glory of Inglewood's dining-room is the ornate plasterwork of the ceiling in the Decorated phase of the Gothic style.

136. The stair at Inglewood shows that stair-rails in the Picturesque vein were much heavier than their Upper Canadian predecessors.

but much simpler in treatment than, the pendants centred in the ceiling of the dining-room, drawing-room, library and ante-hall, or interior porch. This latter small apartment set between the entrance doors and a second walnut door of similar framing and glazing is, in Inglewood, distinguished by fan vaulting (137). The picturesque Gothic of Thomas, if this indeed was Thomas, was markedly reminiscent of the gay Gothic of Nash and in particular this little fan-vaulted room of Hamilton, Canada West, was closely related to the vaulting of Shanbally Castle in Ireland, illustrated by Terence Davis in his *Architecture of John Nash*.

It is not fan vaulting in stone but fan vaulting in lath and plaster and in consequence, shudders run through the purists from Pugin to the present. The Romanticists were of a less jelly-like consistency and believed that the inner porch should be "much enriched with sculptured ornaments, heraldic devices etc. . . . because the stranger is supposed to observe it carefully while he is waiting to be admitted to the house . . . the door and doorway highly ornamented, because exposed to minute examination." The visitor stranded on the steps of Oakham could while away his time by contemplating the heads carved on the corbels which support the pinnacles or those which serve as terminals to the door and window labels (109). The corbel head, so much a part of Gothic tradition, not only adorns Oakham and Inglewood,

137. Few architects of the Picturesque attempted even sham vaulting in domestic buildings. The plaster vaulting of this little room at Inglewood follows the style of Nash at Shanbally.

it has found its way as well (as had the console bracket) to the small house of the artisan.

The House of the Heads (138) on Water Street in Guelph possesses an impressive collection of corbels. It has also, partially obscured by the shadow of its barge boards, the best example surviving in the province of Gothic crockets carved in stone. Similar crockets, the foliations used to decorate a raking edge in Gothic building practice, once formed a part of the entrance complex of Highfield.

The castles, Tudoresque manor-houses and medieval halls of Canada West may never have attained to the grandeur of their British prototypes, but they were destined to a similar fate. Too large for single family occupancy, they have been partitioned into apartments, successfully as are Rock Castle and Inglewood, and ruinously as was "Rastrick's masterpiece," the castle which he had designed for Reid. Many have become institutions. Trafalgar Castle, Rodman Hall, and Auchmar are all institutions, religious, educational or public, and each of them can be described as a picturesque Tudor Revival manor-house.

The Tudor great houses were usually built by a group of *nouveaux riches*, as were our Canadian manors. The Tudor house might be designed as a unit or it might accumulate about a former religious institution on whose decline its prosperity was founded. Auchmar represents a reversal of this process in that it became a religious institution in its latter years. If the Tudor house was designed from scratch, it was likely to exhibit a few suggestions of the Renaissance grafted on the basic Perpendicular style. An architect designing in the manner of the Tudor was free to transpose and his plan might retain Renaissance symmetry while the elevations gave evidence of Gothic variety. Rodman Hall was designed in this manner.

Rodman Hall (139) was built in St. Catharines in 1853 by Thomas Rodman Merritt, son of William Hamilton Merritt, guiding spirit of the Welland Canal. As one might anticipate, it is an ashlar building, commodious and sensible. The Picturesque is relegated to the attic storey, where it emerges in late Elizabethan gable ends and dormers. Easel-painting and the Renaissance emerged together, so it is quite fitting that Rodman Hall should, after one hundred and seven years in the Merritt family, have become the property of the St. Catharines and District Arts Council.

Few records or traditions are preserved of Joseph Sheard, the Yorkshire wheelwright and journeyman joiner turned architect, who designed Trafalgar Castle (140) in 1859. It was built in Whitby for Nelson Gilbert Reynolds, first sheriff of Ontario County. Very little

174

138. Romanticism on the Speed.
The House of the Heads, Guelph.

139. Rodman Hall, St. Catharines, was built in 1853 for Thomas Rodman Merritt. The Romanticism of Rodman is transitional from late Gothic to early Tudor to Jacobean.

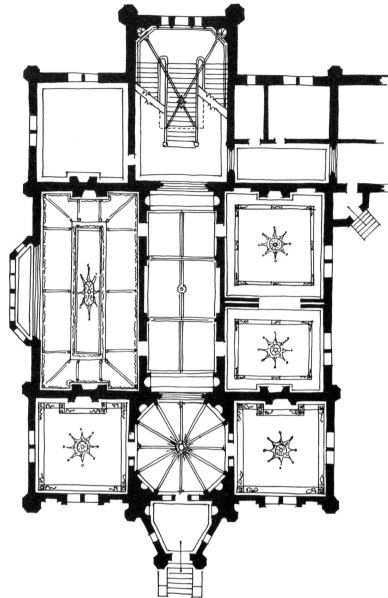

140. *Upper left: Trafalgar Castle, Whitby, was built in 1859 for Nelson Reynolds from a design by Joseph Sheard.*

141.   *Above: The floor plan of Trafalgar Castle by Joseph Sheard. The fine lines indicate the divisions of the plaster ceiling design.*

142. *Left: Double drawing-rooms, Trafalgar Castle.*

143. *Right: The hall of Trafalgar Castle, a most exotic apartment in the Whitby of 1859, retains most of its original furniture.*

more is known of Sheriff Reynolds. These are most unfortunate lacunae, for surely they must both have been memorable men, the one to envision for his client the only crenellated "castle" in Canada West and with sufficient prescience to employ the collegiate Gothic; the other to build the only Methodist castle in existence, and when he could no longer maintain his estate, to have become a charter member of the Board of the Ontario Ladies' College which assumed ownership. As a romantic Picturesque house, Trafalgar Castle was and is a huge success. It has octagonal turrets, battlements, buttresses, stone labels and string courses in the manner of Perpendicular secular building. It is a telescoped St. John's College, a miniature Hampton Court. The great Tudor predecessors were red brick with dark mortar and supported great plastrons of heraldic import. Trafalgar Castle is buff brick. The stone drip moulding is above reproach and whatever may be said for or against Reynolds' right to the name of his house, his right to the coat of arms carved above the door was probably as well founded as was the claim of the Tudors to theirs.

144. *The turreted doors at Trafalgar Castle were a part of the comprehensive installation of elaborate joinery by William Robinson.*

The floor plan of the principal reception rooms of Trafalgar Castle is shown (141). The fine lines indicate the moulding divisions of the plaster ceilings with the medallions and pendants. The room use most probable in 1859 has been inferred from similarity to Gothic villas in Loudon. Pendant fluorescent fixtures, inserted with a skill which leaves the fine plasterwork of the ceiling unimpaired, preclude illustration of the handsome dining-room which has now become the student library. The Romanticists would have balanced the dining-room composition by placing a monumental Gothic sideboard opposite the oriel window and would have crowned their achievement by installing a huge mirror above the sideboard which would not only reflect the mullions of the oriel in its surface but would echo in its frame the pendant tracery of the oriel arch. One of the original pair of white marble mantelpieces survives. Its carved ornament is authentically Perpendicular. The consistent, unifying motifs throughout Trafalgar Castle are the tablet flowers of cornice moulds and mantelpieces and the little battlements which surmount the door frames, large and small.

The battlements appear above the large frames of the folding doors, both those which separate the drawing-rooms (142) and the identical pair which stands on either side of the upper hall, and when opened, convert two vast bedrooms into a ballroom. The bedroom mantelpieces are white marble, those in the drawing-rooms, *rosso antico*.

Consider the hall in the light of what Loudon has to say of that part of the beau idéal of the English villa: "Opposite the door by which you enter is a broad arch through which appears the staircase and the lower division of its painted windows." How right he is, and if one turns about, the painted glazing of the doors of the ante-hall is visible. "There should be handsome chairs and benches of carved wood ornamented with the family arms." There they are, the chairs on either side of the entrance door and the benches with the stag and the scallop shell crest farther down the hall in wide niches built to receive them. There are narrow niches (143) for statues or lamps, four in the hall, four in the ante-hall and two in the stair landing. "The design of the doors is somewhat unusual and more ambitiously decorative than the strict adherence to actual precedence in the domestic style would warrant." He could have been actually describing those in Trafalgar Castle (144). Loudon would have expressed wholehearted approval of the manner in which the architect provided for the hot air registers in the baseboards of Trafalgar's principal rooms, even if he could not quite like its little battlemented door turrets.

Canada West seems to have worn its coronet uneasily. The castellated style was too ambitious. The enriched steep gable and decorative chimney cluster were to be perpetuated as far more suitable to a placid democracy than the pseudo-defensive superstructure of fanciful medievalism. A shining example of the solvent Picturesque was Auchmar (145) built in 1855 by Isaac Buchanan, one of the first international financiers of Canada West. H. J. Morgan, in his *Biographies of Celebrated Canadians*, devoted twenty-eight pages to extolling Buchanan's business and political acumen. Buchanan's activities were so comprehensive, as cited by Morgan, that one wonders what he left for other civic-minded gentlemen to accomplish.

Auchmar received its name from the fourteen-hundred-acre Buchanan family seat

145. *Auchmar, 1855, the modest Gothic home of Isaac Buchanan, was situated in the middle of Claremont, his estate above Hamilton.*

146. *The gatehouse of Claremont follows the style of the main dwelling.*

on Loch Lomond, which was sold in 1830 to the Duke of Montrose by Isaac and Peter Buchanan, who promptly invested the money in Canada. The Canadian Auchmar began as a summer home of stuccoed brick on top of Hamilton Mountain. As it grew, it was decided that it should be made two storeys high and become the permanent manor-house. This was done in the Picturesque style much in the vein of Elizabeth Cottage, a style so unpretentious that the little lodge gate of Buchanan's estate (146) could be Auchmar in miniature. As early as 1862 Buchanan was subdividing his estate, Claremont, into villa lots, and twenty years later the house itself was sold by the Buchanan family. It is now the retreat house of a religious order.

The gatehouse of Claremont was designed as part of the estate complex of a wealthy man of discriminating taste. It happens to represent the small Picturesque Gothic house in stuccoed brick. Other principal building media of Canada West are well represented in Picturesque Gothic also. These were the work of gifted designers obviously, but whether the plans came directly to the site from the hands of the architect or through the medium of Loudon, Downing *et al.*, tradition does not relate. The ships that brought out the architects brought out the handbooks as well. The weather-boarded Picturesque Gothic finds admirable expression in a house near Sharon in the County of York (147). The clustered colonnettes that support the verandah with delicate strength and the rhythm of expanded and contracted arches between are of the order employed in the Perpendicular style for the screens of chantry chapels. It is employed here to accommodate the wide opening necessary for the Gothic door.

Romanticism in Flemish bonded brick (148) still stands by the Queen Elizabeth Way in Burlington but now, alas, a shadow of its former winsomeness. When the accompanying photograph was taken, one pair of chimneys had already gone. The next day the fine Gothic porch was demolished and the central window mutilated.

The more stolid, serviceable Picturesque of Earnscliffe (149) seems destined to survive, not because it is a finer building architecturally (it comes perilously close to being vernacular) nor because it is constructed of hewn stone, but because it was the last home of Sir John Alexander Macdonald, first Prime Minister of the Dominion of Canada. Sir John did not build the house, nor was he living in Earnscliffe in 1867. He seems to have been content, while building a nation, to dwell in Picturesque houses built by his fellow country-men in the successive capitals of Canada West.

*147. A rural Gothic house of
a high order near Sharon.*

*148. Watching the world go by on the
Queen Elizabeth Way near Burlington.*

*149. Earnscliffe, Ottawa, built in
1856, was the last home of Sir John
A. Macdonald. It is now the residence
of the British High Commissioner.*

The sturdy workman-like Gothic house was built of cut stone in 1856, probably by the stone masons Donald Dow and Peter Fraser. It was commissioned for John MacKinnon, the son-in-law of Thomas McKay. McKay had a contract with John Redpath for the stonework of the Rideau Canal. Redpath went back to Montreal to the sugar business and McKay set about establishing his dynasty in Rockcliffe Park, then called McKay's Bush. By 1866 MacKinnon was dead and the MacKinnon house redeemed from pressing creditors by another McKay son-in-law, one Thomas Coltrin Keefer. Keefer had helped to build the Erie and Welland canals and was the only foreigner ever to become President of the American Society of Civil Engineers. In 1868 the house was sold to Thomas Reynolds, the manager of the St. Lawrence and Ottawa Railway. Reynolds leased it to the Royal Engineers and a plan of the house exists from this date showing the proposed alterations. However, Reynolds occupied the house a year later and it was during his personal tenure that his friend, John A. Macdonald, gave it the name of Earnscliffe. In 1883, Macdonald purchased the property. He appears to have leased the house on and off before this and to have been sufficiently pleased with it to purchase it, although additional space was required almost immediately, and William Hudson was asked to plan the alterations. Earnscliffe still enjoyed a magnificent view up the river in the last days of the Old Chieftain, who could see from his summer house the cities growing on both its banks. It was a long way from Teacaddy Castle to Earnscliffe, and whether it was patriotism or feudalism or the marked dissimilarity between Bytown and the Mediterranean, the die was cast for vernacular Gothic as the official monumental style of the true North, strong and free.

150. By the mid-nineteenth century the doorway with the Neo-classic fan transom and the doorway with the Classical Revival square head had both been assimilated by the building trade. The door itself had fewer panels — four, two or one — and was of heavier construction. Verandah treillage, far removed from its Regency and Gothic sources, had likewise entered the idiom of the vernacular. Maclennan house, Williamstown, circa 1850.

184

6

My own, my native land

Consideration has been given to five attitudes toward domestic building prevalent in the eighteenth century and in the first half of the nineteenth, to the architectural styles resulting from them, and to the expression of these styles in Upper Canada. One has been immediately conscious of the diversity of composition possible within the definition of each style. One has been conscious to a lesser degree of the influence of social, economic and climatic conditions, both on the choice of the design and on the time required to complete the building. However, a number of houses were built in Upper Canada from the coming of the first settlers to the dawn of Confederation in whose design local conditions exercised rather more control. These are the vernacular adaptations, in which the style may be manifested with less clarity, but with undiminished charm. Lest the term "vernacular" may seem to imply the presence at all times of the common touch, common sense, the honest artisan, the worthy yeoman, good local building practice and no high-flown nonsense, it would be well to bear in mind that the term derives from a Latin word which means "a native of uncertain origin."

The architectural style which came into Upper Canada with the United Empire Loyalists was the Georgian and its earliest expression, with the possible exception of the manor at Wellington, was in log. Now, everyone who has at any time felt any interest in the buildings of Upper Canada has read discouraging contemporary accounts of life in the backwoods, of the frightful labour involved in building a house of round logs chinked with mud, and of the dismal life that was lived in the wretched place when it was finished. Unfortunately the accounts were true, but as a rule the descriptions were of the trials and tribulations of British Colonists and the letters were directed to their friends at home. Letters between the Loyalist settlers were concerned with fruit trees and garden seeds, newspapers, histories and bibles, hardware and whisky, fur trade and legislation. No one in Upper Canada would have felt the slightest interest in a description, however vivid the literary style, of the building of a

151. Necessity is the mother of vernacular building, and log as a medium was difficult to avoid in Upper Canada before 1800. The Ross House, Upper Canada Village.

log house, and as a news item, it would have elicited either acid or blasphemous comments. The origins might be uncertain in some cases, but the United Empire Loyalist was a native North American who knew to his sorrow a great deal about settlement. More than that, he was a military settler. The disbanded regiments had included pioneers in the military sense.

Very few of the Loyalist log houses have survived but the Ross House (151), now relocated in Upper Canada Village, seems to have been typical. This most elementary of Georgian houses, a single room with an overhead loft, achieved that harmony of proportion which the aesthetic sense of the late eighteenth century demanded of even its most humble dwellings. The planked log, or squared timber construction, of its walls, dovetailed securely at the corners, upholds to this day the cleancut military log tradition of the Loyalist settler. Behind it in serried ranks, broad axe in hand, stand the shades of the pioneer builders of the blockhouses which maintained the security of His Britannic Majesty's colony from Sandwich to the Quebec border. The Ross House originally stood very near to that border on the St. Lawrence and it is entirely probable that water access to the port of Montreal made possible, at such an early date, the ample use of window glass in this little house.

Fortunately for the success of the early settlement of Upper Canada, the United Empire Loyalists included representatives from every stratum of the social organization of the revolting colonies. There were potential governors and ranks to be directed; there were lawmakers and lawbreakers, there were artisans trained by the exacting school of the wilderness to be ingenious and self-reliant and there were potential clients, some of whom possessed either money or influence for immediate payment and many more who could barter one skill for another. These were settlers who already knew that the winters were going to be very cold, and the summers very hot, that only seasoned logs would stay straight and that only the best lime mortar would endure, that cellars and stone foundation walls were absolutely necessary to combat deep frost and that the only satisfactory chimney was one constructed out of brick or stone by an expert.

The Loyalists were settled by groups in areas assigned by military expediency within reach of water transportation. The land was heavily wooded and much of it given over to swamp and marsh. The high ground, naturally well drained, produced when cleared not only differing possibilities of crop production but also different materials for building. The vernacular house on a limestone ridge is unlikely to be of wood, and where deposits of heavy clay

187

abound, the ancient craft of the mud pie becomes the adult business of making brick. Occasionally the early settler discovered that he had cleared his land of trees only to find that it was still covered with stones. Such stones as were of suitable size and shape were used immediately for building foundations and chimneys. The bulk of the legacy of glacial boulders was removed to the perimeter of the field with the assistance of oxen, friends, gunpowder, and a stone machine. The stone machines were part of the Loyalist settler's military inheritance and were simply sling-wagons designed for transporting cannon, now converted to civilian use. The glacial boulder was to play its part in the vernacular building of Upper Canada at a later date when polychrome surfaces were admired and when stone masons were more numerous.

By a series of curious chances, another Loyalist vernacular Georgian building has come to rest in Upper Canada Village. Its much-travelled square timbers were first erected on Carleton Island at Fort Haldimand, and it was at this location that the new Governor of Upper Canada, John Graves Simcoe, and his Legislative Council first met in 1793 in the little weather-boarded house. The house was dismantled and moved to Kingston, where it gradually deteriorated. After many years it was again dismantled and stored against the time when interest in its history might re-awaken. In 1959 it was reconstructed in Upper Canada Village, resuming its original appearance. It shares, with the Ross House, Georgian proportion and a squat stone chimney, but it is an asymmetrical balance, a storey-and-a-half house with one off-centre dormer on its steep snow roof. The spare Georgian dormer passed into the vernacular tradition of Kingston, temporary resting-place of Simcoe House, and may be seen in row housing (152) in the older parts of that city.

Toronto saw fit to award a post-mortem ennoblement to Governor Simcoe, and well it might. For if Toronto made Simcoe a lord without his knowledge, Simcoe made Toronto the capital of Upper Canada without intention. Upper Canadians discovered in 1793 to their surprise that, although the bulk of the settlement was within easy reach of Kingston and the balance at Newark and Sandwich, the new seat of government was to be on Lake Ontario between the Don and the Humber and that the only military service that really mattered in the late revolution had been with the Queen's Rangers. Among the Loyalists who muttered but moved was William Jarvis. In the Jarvis papers in the Toronto Public Library are several estimates of costs for building a log house in York and one building con-

188

tract, dated at Newark, on August 26, 1794. In this document, Abner Miles promised to build for William Jarvis "a log house of square pine timber, at or near the town of York on Lake Ontario . . . the logs to be seven inches thick and squared on all sides, to be built fourteen feet high, sixty-eight feet long, built in three divisions." The house was to have four brick chimneys with two fireplaces to each chimney and a cellar seven feet deep, walled up with stone. Abner Miles promised to do the job for the sum of two hundred and fifty-six pounds, eight shillings, a very reasonable estimate, for York in 1794 was as short of good artisans as it was full of displaced legislators. It was also agreed "that the said Jarvis shall be at liberty to add or diminish the said building as occasion may require, at the same time increasing or diminishing the expense of the building in a fair and equitable proportion." One feels that the said Jarvis and Miles must have had previous transactions to their mutual satisfaction. Jarvis seems to have altered the original plan, by relocating the four fireplaces, doubling the number first indicated, and by adding two appendages, one storey in height with shed roofs, to the wings. The drawing (153) reconstructs this phase of the plan and if Mr. Secretary Jarvis did not in fact actually build a U-shaped weather-boarded house in York, others did so. Russell Abbey, the home of one of Simcoe's friends, was similar in plan.

152. Row houses, Kingston. In the halcyon days of its youth, Kingston was a trans-shipping point on the great fur-trade route. It maintained friendly rivalry with York and Newark but cultural ties were with Montreal.

William Jarvis was a Connecticut Loyalist who had held a commission in a Colonial regiment before the American Revolution. The little Government House from Carleton Island was a silent witness to Upper Canada's beginning. Ross had served in the King's Royal Regiment of New York and his wife and children had journeyed up the St. Lawrence from

153. A reconstruction of the Jarvis house, York, 1794.

189

the refugee camp at Sorel, partly by bateau and partly on foot. Mrs. Ross had, at one point, to retrace her weary steps through the swamp looking for the child who had fallen from his precarious perch on her back, as she led her other children, one on either hand. All in their several capacities were builders of Upper Canada. But it was neither the legislative ability of Jarvis, the endurance of Mrs. Ross, nor the brilliance of the Legislative Council which has brought their homes within the limits of this study. It was the architectural merit of the houses which they built, vernacular expressions of the Georgian style.

Once more it becomes evident that date of building, when that date can be ascertained, is of relative importance only. Vernacular Georgian houses were built in Upper Canada from its beginning right up to Confederation, if we consider as basically Georgian a Renaissance insistence on symmetrical balance, harmony of proportion and the persistence of the double-hung window of twenty-four, twenty or twelve panes, and the door of six panels with narrow architrave trim. There will be one noticeable difference in the later Georgian vernacular house — the roof pitch will not be that of the steep snow roof of early buildings in Upper Canada, but the lower, gentle pitch of the true English Georgian found in Upper Canada in the Neo-classic or Loyalist style.

It could be said with perfect truth that all Georgian architecture in Upper Canada was vernacular and it could even be said that all architecture of any description in Upper Canada was vernacular to a degree, an exercise in hair-splitting that could become endless as it is pointless. North American origin has not been claimed for any architectural style discussed and the term "vernacular" as applied in this study shall be understood to refer to a group of buildings in Upper Canada in which the personal or regional interpretation of specific architectural styles is most strongly marked.

In Upper Canada the vernacular Georgian was dependent for its quality on the retentive memory of the builder. Neo-classic vernacular was likely to be found eddying out, in diminishing excellence, from a fine house built locally in the Loyalist style. The Neo-classic or Loyalist house was the product of the combined skilled work of a number of master craftsmen under the direction of a good designer. The good vernacular Neo-classic house was built by a less inspired master craftsman with less skilled assistance for more modest requirements. The standard of craftsmanship was high in the early nineteenth century when a boy, apprenticed to a bricklayer or mason, and laying miles of common bond or dressing

190

154. Arcaded brickwork, the MacDougal-Harrison house, Niagara-on-the-Lake.

155. Ashlar wall with cut stone quoins, Cartwright house, Kingston.

rubble, could see in his mind's eye the warm brick beauty of the arcaded wall (154) of the MacDougal-Harrison house in Niagara-on-the-Lake, the enduring precision of the cut stone quoins (155) on the ashlar façade of the Cartwright town house in Kingston, and know that one day he could go and do likewise. The craftsmanship will be found to have been excellent, the structure sound, and the purpose sustained in the Loyalist vernacular and in all subsequent vernacular buildings, but the design quality will rise and fall like a fever chart from house to house and sometimes from room to room. An absolute eye is as rare in the visual arts as is absolute pitch in music. Nevertheless, everyone requires a house in which to live, so there are architects and there are builders, and Heaven help both, there are clients.

Unexceptionable, an eighteenth-century term of commendation now fallen into disuse, is the most apt description of the basic Loyalist vernacular house which enjoyed a wide range in Upper Canada. It is a balanced composition of good proportions, a long rectangle with centre hall in plan, rectangular of façade with a low-pitched roof whose gable ends have a moulded raking cornice and short returning cornices. This style of house was built as a storey and a half or in two storeys; it was of stone, brick, brick-filled frame, superimposed plank or, more rarely, of log. It was frequently stuccoed, as is the fine two-storey vernacular house at Dixie (156). So pleasing are its proportions that one scarcely regrets the

156. Neo-classic vernacular in two storeys at Dixie.

157. Neo-classic vernacular, a storey and a half near Prospect in Lanark.

158. A regional preference for the semi-circular fan transom without sidelights is evident in the Brockville area.

192

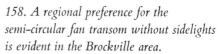

absence of the graceful elliptical fan transom of the true Loyalist doorway. In such Counties as Lincoln, Wentworth, Halton, Peel, York, Durham, Northumberland and Prince Edward, the square-headed transom in a Loyalist vernacular house is likely to be indicative of a later date, when elliptical fan transoms were becoming old-fashioned. However, sometimes it simply marks the evasion of a difficult building problem.

Eastern Ontario retained a longer affection for the elliptical fan transom. It appears in profusion along the St. Lawrence up to Kingston, and converges on the Ottawa area, along the Rideau and Ottawa water-ways. The illustrated storey-and-a-half house (157) of stout rubble stonework with well-cut lintels over door and windows is actually near Prospect in Lanark, but the form is typical of the Counties of Glengarry, Prescott, Stormont, Dundas, Grenville, Carleton, Leeds and Frontenac as well. An isolated pocket of semi-circular, fan-transomed doorways survives as a regional style of the Brockville area. Several houses on King Street East in Brockville have such entrance doorways (158). The panelling of the door reveals have retained the proportion designed to accompany a Loyalist door of six panels, although these houses have later doors of five panels, still fielded, but having rather heavy moulding.

Maplehurst (159) near Maitland, presumably a contemporary of the earliest Brockville houses, has a narrow fan-transomed door, but has the flanking detached windows of the Upper Canadian Georgian style and a six-panelled Loyalist door of great elegance. It may have been master masons fresh from building the Rideau Canal who gave to Maplehurst its shining morning face of ashlar, for this was the third of the houses built by George Longley in or near Maitland. An earlier Longley house in a simple Loyalist vernacular is illustrated in plan elsewhere. George Longley came to Upper Canada from Westmorland and rounded out a career of successful merchandising with a lumber contract for the Rideau Canal. Longley seems to have been happy

159. As George Longley's fortunes rose, he built more impressive houses. Maplehurst, near Maitland, was his final achievement.

193

in Upper Canada, for there are no nostalgic yearnings in the fabric of his houses. In style, Maplehurst was pure Loyalist internally and became vernacular only when viewed from out of doors. One finds a similar disparity between the skills used in many vernacular houses. The superior quality of the Neo-classic plaster cornice and of the panelled window reveals, of the elaborate type found in eastern Upper Canada, earned a place for the drawing-room of Maplehurst in the first study on the early architecture of Ontario published by the doyen of the field, Dr. Eric Ross Arthur.

Externally Maplehurst presents a somewhat contradictory collection of merits and absurdities: the ashlar façade of the central block is superb masonry work, the coarse rubble of the end walls, wings and the unbelievably long tail of domestic offices is well finished, the scored stuccoed faces of the wings shaded by the little porches create an illusion of ashlar, the graceful wrought-iron rails curve beautifully on either side of the porch steps. But how could all of these craftsmen, and most of them must have been masters of their trade, have turned a blind eye to the sheer ineptitude of composition present in the recessed porch? Was it perhaps completed when the stair was built at a later date, after the master craftsmen had departed? It may not always have worn its heavy architrave like a cold compress, for a decorative cornice may once have relieved the bad proportion, but the capitals of the columns can never have been any closer to the Ionic than they are now. Loudon remarked in his excellent work that exterior shutters "are the mark of an humble dwelling." The humbling of Maplehurst came late in its life, as it has to many another Loyalist house whose Edwardian owners chose to ignore the interior shutters installed in the window reveals.

Maplehurst, which was built over a great deal of ground, but which was not finished above stairs until a much later date, would in its prime have been classed for assessment as a one-storey house. For reasons such as this, assessment rolls are unintentionally misleading in the architectural story of Upper Canada.

There is a marked tendency in vernacular building to adhere to the "if a little is good, a lot is better" school and to attempt to enhance by multiplicity of detail. Emanating from Niagara-on-the-Lake in Lincoln County and in Frontenac around Kingston, repetition infected the fan transom; in York it seems to have been concentrated in the windows. The Georgian use of wooden muntins had imposed a salutary discipline on the fan transom, maintaining an armature of radiation from a visual centre. With the introduction of metal glazing bars, discretion was too often abandoned and an arbitrary pattern was set into the ellipse which bore no relation to it. A glimpse of such a pattern may be seen in the transom of the MacDougal-Harrison doorway in Niagara-on-the-Lake.

The Palladian triple window placed above the enriched entrance doorway was a beautiful functional member of the Georgian façade. It continued in popularity in the Neoclassic style and was present in many Loyalist houses in Upper Canada, sometimes in its Venetian form, that is without the round-headed raised centre, all the lights being of equal height. The Venetian window was popular in the Regency cottage as well but has seldom been installed with such a lavish hand as in the vernacular building of the County of York.

The Burr house from Woodbridge (160), now located in the Black Creek Museum complex at the intersection of Steeles Avenue and Jane Street in Toronto, is an excellent example of this regional style. In a storey-and-a-half house with gable or hip-roof the composition of Venetian windows with a transomed, sidelighted door has great charm. The concentration of trim occasioned by the reduction in height of the Venetian windows in the second storey of the Burr house becomes rather oppressive. The same

160. York County Venetian windows in abundance. The Burr house, Pioneer Village.

161. The barrel-vaulted porch usually rests on Classic columns in Lincoln County, but the unpretentious post has its own charm.

162. Walton Street, Port Hope. A slightly detached fan transom.

163. This floating fan transom is one of a pair which lights the upper hall of a Halton County farm-house.

164. *Cedar Lawn, Lyn, was built by Richard Coleman in the second quarter of the nineteenth century when Lyn was more prosperous than neighbouring Brockville.*

165. *Detail of the cast-iron treillage added to Cedar Lawn by the Cassels family in the 1860's.*

window composition may still be seen in the old Islington courthouse.

Vernacular building is fraught with unsolved mysteries. There is the minor riddle as to why the Loyalist porch, which retains the semi-elliptical vault designed to accommodate the fan transom, should, in a Lincoln County vernacular example (161), have been built to shelter a transom-less door. There is the major problem of the floating transom. Some people kept the fan transom, others liked the square-headed doorway, but some residents of Halton, Peel and Durham elected to have both. The fan, usually semi-circular, may be still visually attached to the doorway as it is in 286 Walton Street, Port Hope (162), or it may be designed to read with the windows of the second storey as was done in Halton (163), but in each instance where the severed transom appears, it has become a window to light the upper hall and rests, rather incongruously, on the floor of that apartment. This aberration, which dates to the 1850's, is often associated in Halton and Durham with patterned brick, a buff brick being used for the quoins and cornice mouldings.

In areas where stone was in common use, the vernacular house of dwindling Neo-classicism, built in the fifties, was likely to have cut stone quoins either in association with stone or with brick. Cedar Lawn (164) was built by Richard Coleman, mill-owner at Lyn. Lyn, at that time called Coleman's Corners, was a factory town of greater importance than its neighbour Brockville. The cast-iron verandah treillage (165), added in the 1860's by the Cassels family, was imported from France at the reputed cost of four thousand dollars and it is decidedly Classic in inspiration.

Vernacular building may imply a certain lack of architectural sophistication on the part of the builder but it has a closer affinity with accent than with income as a brief study of Public Works designs will demonstrate. Bytown was to afford some excellent examples of this fact in the sixties. Kingston was first in building what can be termed official vernacular in Canada West. Roselawn, built by David Smith in 1841, was one of the few Kingston houses to achieve and retain the patronage of a ruling caste. It has become the official residence of the Commandant of the Defence College.

The more impressive façade of Roselawn (166) is turned toward the garden, where its vernacular Palladianism can be savoured despite later intrusions. The floating fan transom, encountered before in smaller houses, succeeds at Roselawn because of the increased scale of the building. Internal alterations have impaired the symmetry of the façade. A window was inserted at the level of a new mezzanine when the kitchen was removed from the cellar to a new wing. But the dominant projecting bay is still strongly composed in triads, three arches, three windows. The central window might be called split Palladian, for here the fan transom has been raised to light the pediment, the Venetian section remaining to light the stair (167).

The stair of Roselawn winds gracefully in three easy flights with two landings across the end of a wide stair-hall. The light handrail of polished hardwood terminating in a scrolled newel cage was a legacy from the Loyalist style. The more pronounced turning of

166. Roselawn, 1841, is one of the few Kingston houses of that era which still enjoys official patronage.

167. The wide stair of Roselawn was an admirable expression of modified Neo-classicism.

168. The six-panel door of 1841 was sturdy Neo-classic. Roselawn.

the heavy banisters was a contribution of the forties. The signs of the times can be read in the trim also, in the increased depth of the skirting board and in the altered proportions of the door panels (168), the widest rail of which was set too low to meet the extra stress at the latch. Entrance doors of this kind will be found to have a bead run down the centre stile to reduce the apparent weight, a decorative device sometimes erroneously described as an unfinished door of two leaves, a strange misapprehension. Had the builders of the forties been given to hanging incomplete doors, they would scarcely have chosen the entrance as the spot for negligence.

In the meantime there had been a brisk interchange of influence between the British Colonists and the colony, neither of whom would ever be quite the same again. Highly individual Colonists might make noticeable inroads on the social and political life of Upper Canada, but it was the steady, quiet augmentation of the building trades by skilled craftsmen that made possible the rapid increase in the number of pleasant, comfortable houses being built in Canada West. The craftsmen had served their apprenticeships elsewhere, under settled social conditions, and in a continuous tradition of good building practice. When they had finished the construction of a Regency house for the half-pay officer, they were free to build houses for his near neighbours. Alert artisans were susceptible, then as now, to improvements in design and methods of construction and they acquired new skills and discarded obsolete practices as they went.

The simple, restrained phase of Regency building had much to offer to vernacular building and streams of influence can be detected. The Counties of Middlesex, Oxford, Perth, Huron, Norfolk (169), Waterloo, Wellington, Halton, Peel, York, Ontario,

169. Men of substance built houses like this all over Canada West and Tremaine happily enshrined them on the borders of the county maps.

Durham and Northumberland have or had vernacular Regency houses in quantity. The remaining portion of southern Ontario had fewer examples although they were present in every county.

Many of these houses were derived from the type which can be identified for purposes of study with The Briars on Lake Simcoe. The drawing (170) shows the original portion of the house as built by Captain Bourchier, R.N., and to which he subsequently retired in 1841. Captain Bourchier had once been stationed in St. Helena where the original Briars had been Napoleon's temporary house of exile. The Briars, York County, has led a much more peaceful existence. Its sole appearance in county history is as the house in which a meeting was held to organize local defence against the rebels in 1837. Captain Bourchier's house was a two-storey building of stuccoed rubble stone, the hip-roof decorated with little brackets. Its Regency characteristics were marked: pairs of tall chimneys with decorative caps, three square window openings on the second floor fitted with casement sash, and a square-transomed sidelighted door, flanked on either side by French doors with matching decorative transoms.

There had been large solid houses with hip-roofs in the reigns of good Queen Anne and all the Georges terminating with the Regent, who was not very good, but in the Regency examples the proportion of the openings and the height of the roof had changed and so had the trim. There was no small-scale detail to be found about a Regency house like The Briars, no roof balustrades, no belvedere, no dormers, but the austerity of such a design demanded the setting of a fine garden. In this The Briars has been exceedingly fortunate. Not only have its later owners, the Sibbalds, maintained the garden, added in reason to the house and built a carriage house with heraldic weather vane, they also gave to The Briars the only octagonal peacock-house in Ontario.

170. Below: The Briars, Lake Simcoe. Regency houses, like Captain Bourchier's, were objects for admiration and emulation.

171. Right: The Rideau Canal opened up a new area for settlement in the decades after Waterloo, and a new proportion of window opening, roughly square, appeared in the bedroom storey of many vernacular houses in the area.

Sometimes vernacular houses deriving from this Regency type retained the window composition seen in The Briars while abandoning the roof form. The smaller rubble-stone house of the Rideau area (171) does so with telling effect. Other houses which kept the hip-roof and massive chimney stacks are Regency vernacular only in that they eschew all but a functional minimum of exterior trim on doors and windows, only to increase the width of that seen indoors. A case in point is the Elliott house near Milton. A touch of ponderous fantasy was introduced on its façade in the neo-Tudor labels which crown the windows and door, but the true Regency character is discernible only within (172). The four-panelled door had arrived to stay as a part of vernacular building. It was not to be displaced in public favour until the present century had brought in another builder's vernacular, the slab door of fir plywood.

The interior door of the Elliott house has four panels, the two of greater length in the upper register of the door, the smaller rectangles below. The panels are moulded on both sides with a pleasant, simple profile. In houses as close in feeling to the Regency style as this one, rooms of lesser importance have a deep architrave trim of considerable projection on both door and window openings. The trim in the entrance hall, drawing-room and

172. The Elliott house, Milton, circa 1840. Regency taste was robust and in rural interiors found expression in plain, substantial joinery.

173. The mantelpiece received the same hearty treatment as the doors in the Elliott house.

perhaps dining-room is more strongly moulded and retains the corner-box. When the Elliott house was built, fireplaces were by no means the only source of heat. Stoves could be had for cooking, and stoves, riotously ornamented, for heating reception rooms were common. Franklin stoves were often used set against a pseudo-fireplace surrounded by a mantel-piece. The mantel of the Regency vernacular style was designed en suite with the door trim — a deeper architrave, a simple cornice, a straight-edged shelf to top off the whole, and one had a chimney-piece. In addition the Elliott drawing-room mantel (173) has a wide bolection moulding in dressed stone to replace the ubiquitous brick around the grate.

Builders of Regency vernacular houses treated the staircase simply as a means of communication between two storeys. Seldom imposing and frequently hidden from the reception area, the stair had ceased to hold the pride of place it enjoyed in the Loyalist vernacular. This may have been a statement of unconscious preference for the cottage, where the stair gave access to the cellar.

The importance which the cottage assumed in vernacular building of Upper Canada is not surprising. The wonder is that the plan was abandoned. The ancient enemy, boredom, was probably to blame, in spite of the logic of the design for an extreme climate and of the fascinating range of style found in surviving examples. Cottage building received its major impetus from the Colonists coming in to Upper Canada from Great Britain where the Regency was toying with the simple life. In a sense, they served to marshal Upper Canada in the way that it was going. The Butler house in Newark was a one-storey hip-roofed house. The real difference between such a house and the Regency cottage was a difference of philosophy and of social usage.

Vernacular cottages appeared in large numbers in the 1830's and forties. Few were being built in the twenties and sixties. One should also note that as early as 1836, J. G. Howard, architect, of Toronto, was designing a summer cottage, presumably on Lake Simcoe, for Joseph Ridout, a phase of the Ontario cottage that is still being built. The vernacular cottage, a permanent dwelling, was usually square or nearly so in plan, a storey and a half in height with a deep cellar frequently containing the kitchen. The roof was hipped, the windows were large, often of the Venetian style, or French casements. The vernacular cottage may be Georgian, Loyalist, Regency Picturesque, Greek, Gothic or Renaissance Revival in style, or may have little touches of several styles. A cottage deriving from the Georgian or Loyalist

202

174. The subtle charm of Regency vernacular in Peel County.

style will have comparatively narrow eaves in the Niagara area, where it is likely to be of brick or brick-filled frame, and eaves of greater projection in York and adjacent counties where mud or sun-dried brick was often used as a building medium. The eave reaches its maximum depth in the Counties of Durham and Northumberland, where the cottage appears to be wearing a large shady hat.

175. The Robinson-Adamson cottage, Erindale.

In York and Peel the half-storey is likely to be lighted by two dormers, set in the hip-roof just over, and equal in width to, the spaces which separate the entrance doorway and the windows on either side of it. In Prescott, Glengarry and Simcoe, there might be three dormers. The principal windows were usually Venetian in York and Peel, and one of the earliest cottages to have such windows survives. The Robinson-Adamson cottage, 1921 Dundas Street, Erindale (175), is Loyalist vernacular without and Regency vernacular within, in keeping with its history. John Beverley Robinson bought a parcel of land in the County of Peel from the Crown in 1828, when there was still salmon fishing to be had on the Credit River. The purchase price was two hundred dollars. A few years later he sold the property to Colonel Peter Adamson and his brother Dr. Joseph Adamson for three thousand dollars. In the interim the cottage had been built. John Beverley Robinson, Attorney-General of Upper Canada at the age of twenty-two, was of Loyalist stock and the protégé of Bishop Strachan. His father, Christopher Robinson, a Virginia Loyalist had served, luckily, in the Queen's Rangers and had accompanied Simcoe to Upper Canada. In 1830 John Beverley Robinson was appointed Chief Justice of Upper Canada and the little cottage on the Credit became the residence of Joseph Adamson, physician to the Missisauga Indians.

Remarkably elaborate late-Loyalist trim frames the windows (176) of the Robinson-Adamson cottage. It rises to meet an equally ornate cornice which encircles the cottage with a series of Loyalist ellipses. The knife-edged mouldings of the window frame are of the type one would normally expect to encounter on the drawing-room mantelpiece, but one does not do so here. The mantel in the cottage is of Regency vernacular persuasion. As an individual composition of space divisions, the glazing of the window and door sidelights in the Adamson cottage finds no peer until one reaches either Queenston or Kingston.

Surely the epitome of all the Regency vernacular cottage was meant to express is to be found by the stream in Odessa (177). The site, the square plan, the hip-roof of shallow pitch, the French doors, the verandah, the simplicity, are all in the best Regency tradition. It was also in the tradition to temper the austerity with the whimsy of a cast-iron roof coronet and a filigree verandah rail. Time passed, taste changed. The Picturesque became a serious thing, revivals were in the air. The Greek cottage, the Gothic cottage, the Bracketed cottage made their appearance. The Classical Revival made little external change in the vernacular cottage, save in the roofline. The half-storey, if lighted at all, received illumination from a belvedere or monitor. The cornice board, below a wide eave, would be wide and very simple in profile. The eave itself might be a cantilevered projection of sufficient depth to form a verandah.

The serious Picturesque, the Gothic and the Tuscan, did alter the basic shape of the vernacular cottage. The geometric purity of the square was broken by the addition of a central projecting bay on the principal façade. The bay terminated at roof level in a gable. If the Bracketed cottage had as great a claim to being a unified composition as the Bell cottage, situated at 57 James Street in Stratford (178), then the bay would be finished with a pediment. The brackets, the rusticated quoining, even the panels have a tenuous con-

176. The intricate pattern of glazing bars and knife-edged moulding of the windows is busy late-Loyalist and highly reminiscent of Kingston. The Robinson-Adamson cottage, 1828.

177. An Ontario cottage typical of the 1850's stands beside the stream in Odessa.

178. *The Ontario cottage with brackets, 57 James Street, Stratford.*

nection with the Renaissance. The trefoil window in the pediment and the Tudor labels over the windows were borrowed from the late Gothic, but it must be conceded that the whole composition, vernacular or not, reads very well. The design may have been found in a pattern-book or it may have originated with one of the increasing company of architects in Canada West, for the cottage had come full cycle. This is again a hip-roofed house of one storey. The identical design in two storeys is to be seen in Omemee, its patterned brick as yet unpainted.

In vernacular building, the Picturesque, as conceived by the Regency, becomes inextricably mingled with the full-blown Picturesque of the revivals. Vernacular builders, craftsmen and clients were usually eclectic in their choice of components for a design. Overall effect was paramount; purity of style meant very little. The net result over the settled area of an extensive province is very good, even if the few exceptions do exercise a horrid retentive fascination.

The dawning nineteenth century had discarded, along with other shibboleths of the past century, the well-bred harmony of muted colour and the long allegiance to contained form in the small house. In the vernacular house the new freedoms found expression in the dramatic silhouette and in the use of contrasting colour in brick and stonework. Drama in the

179. *Hurontario Street, Peel County. Patterned brick has been a medium for vernacular building from the dawn of human history. One may or may not like it: it is difficult to be indifferent.*

silhouette was achieved by placing decorative wings on both sides of the main house. The wings were one storey in height, might be flush with the house, or might project to frame the verandah, in each case exhibiting a roofline at considerable variance with the central block. More houses of this type were to be found in the Counties of Peel, Halton and West York than in any other area in Canada West. This was also the area dedicated to patterned brick, although colourful examples of this surface pattern range as far east as the Quebec border. Patterned stone makes its major appearance in Wentworth, Waterloo and Brant.

In the Renaissance patterned brickwork was common in some English counties and in parts of France, particularly in Normandy. Many people believe that the initial intention was to utilize all brick, sorting out the buff or grey from the red and working it in as string courses and quoins, and then in diaper, or lozenge, patterns. The making of patterned brickwork languished during the Georgian ascendancy, for it smacked too much of a craft to be fashionable. Whatever can be said for or against patterned brickwork, it must be admitted that it is both picturesque and unusual.

The county roads of Durham, Ontario, York and Peel afford excellent examples of the vernacular in patterned brick. Hurontario Street is, like Yonge, Dundas and King, a street in the Anglo-Saxon sense, that is to say, a lengthy highway, yet it appears to have been settlers of Irish extraction from the United States who built in patterned brick on either side of it (179). A charming legend attaches to these lozenge-patterned houses. One is earnestly assured that the brick was hauled to the building site by the faithful family oxen, one of which was called Diamond, and that his forehead star was the inspiration for the wall pattern and the gable. In 1844 there were three thousand, seven hundred and eighty-five oxen in Peel County and four thousand, one hundred and twenty-six in Durham and Northumberland, where the legend is also current. One wonders what the percentage of oxen named Diamond was and also what their yokemates were called. Perhaps they have been commemorated in some way in the unfortunate verge boards which all too frequently accompany the lozenge brick.

There were in Upper Canada in the mid-nineteenth century two strong currents in vernacular building. One was the conscious effort to follow the Romantic architectural revivals, the other the slow development of a provincial regional style. Much time, thought and hard-earned money were directed towards achieving the former, whereas the unsought indigenous style was built of the stones which the fashionable builder rejected—the aes-

180. *Left: The Mallory cottage, Kingston Road, Northumberland County. The scale of Greek trim presupposed the distant view. The six-foot hall does not allow for it.*

181. *Below: The Currie house, Iroquois, was an architectural collage of Loyalist door, Regency French windows and a Greek Revival cornice with grilles.*

182. *Below: The McKinley house, West Flamborough, 1855.*

183. *Right: Plan of the second floor of the Cronyn house, London.*

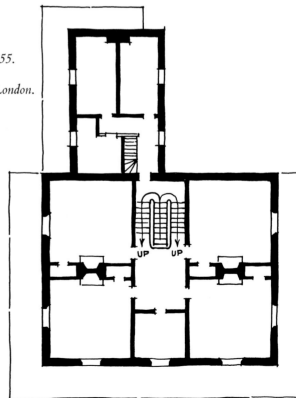

thetic needs of the people and the demands of the topography and climate of Upper Canada.

If it had proved difficult for experienced and convinced architects of the Classical Revival to convert the basic plan and form of a Greek temple to domestic use, surely it would be a labour of Hercules for a builder to reduce the whole concept to the dimensions of a small house for a lower income group, and hope to retain its Classic scale. When the builder freely adapted the style to his needs, little houses of great charm were built as has been seen, but this required a builder with immense self-confidence. The Classical Revival was a style of frightening pedantry and the poor builder was likely to be cowed into taking his detail directly from a pattern-book. The patterns were usually of details, noble, accurate, monumental; but unfortunately the relative distance from which they were meant to be viewed was seldom given and never followed. The congestion of architectural riches that ensued can be deduced by considering the hall of the Mallory cottage (180), a country house built by Justice Friend Mallory in Northumberland County. In this narrow apartment, the massive simplicity of the eared trim and the fine quality of the painted graining on the two-panelled door are submerged in a plethora of woodwork. The semi-columnar turned newel, just visible at the edge of the photograph, is typical of the Classical Revival stair-rail.

Major Greek Revival houses, such as Ruthven Park, had ornamental grilles set in the heavy frieze board below the roof cornice. The grilles of lyre or anthemion pattern made a pleasing break in the heavy board and helped to light the attic storey. Unfortunately this motif was adopted by builders of storey-and-a-half houses and employed to light the bedrooms. In the Currie house (181) on the St. Lawrence near Iroquois, the dismal effect was mitigated in the bedrooms by windows in the gable, but gloom hung over the hall, relieved only by a slot of light at floor level. The builder of this house wisely abandoned the Greek on the ground floor, and reverted to a mixture of the Neo-classic and the Regency styles, thereby ensuring maximum light in the area of principal use.

The McKinley house (182) in West Flamborough might almost be termed a Georgian revival in style, so lightly graceful are its Roman Doric columns, so handsome is its Palladian window. But the Palladianism of the window is tempered with Gothic and the door behind the Doric columns has a single panel, heavily framed. It is the vernacular Classical Revival door of American inspiration, highly appropriate for a house built in Upper Canada by a migrant member of a family which gave the neighbouring republic one of its presidents.

184. Verandah detail, Elora.

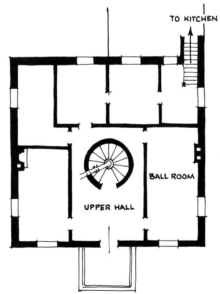

185. Hilltop Haven, Port Bruce. A concrete core containing the stair rises through the centre of this interesting house to the belvedere.

The McKinley house is a restrained member of a group. A more florid example of this type may be seen at Brougham.

Greek Revival and Greek vernacular houses were built in Upper Canada by both natives and immigrants, but a concentration of the style in its vernacular form indicates either the presence of a block of settlers from the United States or close local trade relations with that country. At this point one is tempted to inquire why there was continuous migration in the first half of the nineteenth century from the United States into a British North American colony. The whole frontier of settlement from Vermont to the Gulf of Mexico was advancing westward at the time and Upper Canada was, by a geographical oversight, untidily in the way, but that is hardly the answer. Governor Simcoe, desiring to augment the population of his infant colony by an influx of seasoned North American settlers, issued a tempting invitation which was speedily accepted. The younger sons were on the move again and if the immediate prospect pleased, they were not greatly concerned with the remoter forms of federal government.

The early land-hungry settlers were followed by groups who came into Upper Canada in pursuit of their various trades, the iron-founders to Wentworth and Norfolk, the plaster traders to Brant and the lumber traders to the Ottawa and the Rideau. Their major contributions to the domestic architecture of the province — the Classical Revival temple house, designed by an American architect, and the large, basically Classical, bracketed houses of Tuscan derivation built for clients of American antecedents — have been discussed in preceding chapters. The worthy, commodious, comfortable vernacular forms of these excellent houses, which abound in Waterloo, Wellington, Oxford, Norfolk, Haldimand, Welland, Elgin, Kent, Lambton, Perth and Huron and occur in pockets settled by industrialists in all other counties of southern Ontario, are so much an accepted part of the scene that they are in danger of being overlooked. One feels that each one of them must have been built by the Prodigal Son's elder brother (183). These houses may be of brick, stone, stucco, weather-board, imitation ashlar or even patterned stone, but it is only when one of them boasts the wildly fanciful verandah still to be seen in Elora, or contains a circular stair entirely encased in a concrete cylinder, that they excite remark (184).

Hilltop Haven, Port Bruce (185), the proud possessor of the concrete core, was designed with all the best features of its genre: two well-proportioned major façades, one to face the harbour, the other to overlook Lake Erie, a belvedere for a better view of both, pairs of gay brackets so located that the elevation might with equal ease have fitted an octagonal plan, large simple reception rooms on the ground floor, a goodly number of bedrooms and a ballroom on the floor above, fireplaces for aesthetic satisfaction and stoves for utility. A number of houses having this basic form may indicate nothing more or less than a burst of local prosperity in the forties and fifties. A clutch of belvederes, however, is likely to indicate the hand of Brother Jonathan.

The social historian sometimes dwells too long and too earnestly on the role of the newly arrived settler as the bringer of all innovations from abroad. The informed Upper Canadian was perfectly capable of going and finding out for himself and he did so. As early as 1811, Thomas Ridout, a student in England, was writing home to muddy little York an excited description of the incredible Gothicism of Fonthill which had just been built in Wiltshire. By 1851, when the whole Western world was dazzled by the marvels in the Crystal Palace, a first-hand account of the Great Exhibition was arriving in Dickinson's Landing, Canada West, from the pen of William Colquhoun, merchant of that hamlet, who was in England on a business trip. Ridout was to put his first-hand knowledge of the Gothic Revival

186. Above: *A Victorian recipe for house charm was to select a good two-inch plank and cut some verge boards. Stratford, circa 1845.*

187. Below: *The Preston area of Waterloo has a regional verge board in which tiny pairs of cherub-wings forever flit about the eaves.*

to use in partnership with F. W. Cumberland at St. James' Cathedral. Colquhoun came back to his pretty village on the St. Lawrence, apparently unshaken by the dramatic movement in architecture, for neither crockets nor brackets were added to his brick house, which retained its Loyalist vernacular charm until the whole village disappeared in the St. Lawrence Seaway power project. Ridout and Colquhoun may have represented the poles of architectural sense and sensibility of Upper Canadians abroad, and fortuitous circumstances have preserved their letters. But surely all the degrees of sensitivity were once expressed in the great volume of correspondence exchanged by their contemporaries and long since destroyed. One can be reasonably sure that the philosophy of Romanticism was flowing back and forth across the Atlantic without let or hindrance.

Humble and eager, the vernacular builders of Upper Canada were easily convinced that they must acquire a feeling for the picturesque. That they were already actually closer to the medieval than their exemplars were they could not know. The continuous building tradition of the people was not of interest to an architectural movement which was almost entirely literary in its origins. In an era when major paintings were not only required to tell a story but to point a moral as well, functionalism was bound to be at a very low ebb. Hence the vernacular builder, framing his house after either the Anglo-Saxon manner with queen-posts or the Norman method with a king-post to support the gable, wondered uneasily how he could give the resulting symmetrical box a Gothic look. The Italianate was much easier to achieve. Given the favourite building media of the Romans, brick, mud or a kind of concrete,

and a double handful of brackets, the vernacular villa grew almost of itself. The Italianate vernacular house in Upper Canada remained as Georgian in its proportions as did its would-be Gothic counterpart.

If collegiate Gothic was somewhat beyond the vernacular builder's capabilities, it was also mercifully beyond his requirements. Early Victorian propriety of taste and an inherent common sense alike directed both builder and client to consider the merits of Picturesque Gothic.

Picturesque Gothic was, of course, the pre-Pugin whimsical Romanticism, Regency Gothic — a stage setting

213

188. *The Eckhardt-MacKay house, Unionville, is vernacular Gothic in board and batten construction.*

in durable materials for the comedies and tragedies of life. It was a linear style, which made much use of the shadow patterns cast on plain wall surfaces by lacy treillage and the infinite variety of gay verge boards with which ingenious builders eased the rough edges of stern necessity. Unfortunately, since both treillage and verge board were executed in wood, it is these distinctive features of the Gothic vernacular style which suffer most from the depredations of time and alteration. One might without much difficulty match the pleasing rhythm of the verge boards and window trim of a charming stucco house in Stratford (186). It would be an onerous task indeed to find a carpenter who could replace the gay little cherub-wings that edge the roof of a fine Gothic stone house in Preston (187). Yet both houses are typical of the vernacular Gothic which existed in quantity and quality in Canada West.

The Preston house was designed on the asymmetrical L-plan which gave greater freedom of space arrangement to the builder than had the Georgian centre-hall plan. It also exposed a great area of wall surface to the extremes of both heat and cold. The winged verge board and the two little Gothic arched attic windows with their heavy dripstones seem to be found only in the County of Waterloo. The large window which centres the gable, a square-headed Palladian, with or without the Tudor label above it, is to be found in so many houses along the Ottawa River, in Prescott and Russell, that it becomes a recognizable regional type in those counties.

The Gothic disregard for symmetry led many a builder to change the pitch from gable to gable in the roofline. When a number of gables were involved, as in the Stratford house, the practice often produced a roofline of great charm, if some eccentricity. Where there are only two gables, eccentricity may predominate, but if the house is successfully

189. *The Kinloch house, near Martintown, was built in 1849 in the Quebec vernacular style by a Scottish stone mason who considered the New World romantic.*

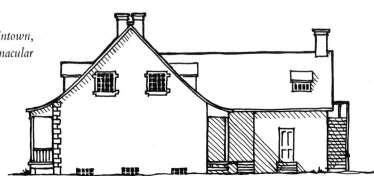

designed as a whole, such eccentricity may have a certain endearing appeal. One would hesitate to use this phrase in connection with a style other than the vernacular and even here it is applicable only to regional aspects in the Gothic period. But how else would one describe a house such as the Eckhardt-MacKay house in Unionville (188), which contrives to break so many rules of pedantic revival and is still such fun? The verge boards conjure up visions of many little buttered hands happily pulling molasses taffy. The little gable has the look of Hans Christian Andersen, but the exterior wall surface texture can be traced directly to the practical and sober pages of Andrew Jackson Downing's *Country Houses*. Downing expressed a preference for vertical boarding, "because it has an expression of strength and truthfulness . . . properly signifying to the eye a wooden house." It was to be "inch and a quarter pine boarding, tongued and grooved at the edges, nailed on in a vertical manner and covered by

190. Inge-Va is an early example of the evolving vernacular of Upper Canada. It was built in the Loyalist style in 1823 by Major Michael Harris. The Gothic gable was added later by the Radenhurst family.

neat battens." Board and batten helped to express the strength and truthfulness of Gothic designs far more academically exact than this one. Excellent examples of the medium are still to be found in areas as remote from each other as Canton and Sparta. Only in romantic Canada West could the Gothic style have been deemed suitable for either postal address.

In 1849 a unique expression of Romanticism was built near Martintown, Canada West, when a Scottish stone mason, Kinloch by name, once employed on the Lachine Canal, elected to build a French-Canadian house (189). Let canal magnates Merritt, Thompson and McKay build Classic villas if they liked, Kinloch's imagination was fired by the un-familiar, the vernacular of the new land, of the bell-cast roof and the verandah for the red rocking chairs, a style that had been maturing along the St. Lawrence, with very little outside influence, for two centuries.

Much less time in which to grow was given the Upper Canadian vernacular and its infancy was beset with clamorous interference from all sides, but eventually the form emerged, a true vernacular, shaped by the people and the climate from the land itself. As the climate and the topography did not differ greatly from the conditions prevalent in Lower Canada, the Upper Canadian house assumed the same basic shape up to the eaves. Since this was also the basic shape of the Iroquois longhouse, it may be considered to be the functional form of dwelling for the North American woodlands, where conservation of heat is the major con-sideration for nine months of the year, and the greatest nuisance for the other three.

The Upper Canadian began life in the colony as the last Georgian. The lineal ancestor of the Upper Canadian vernacular style is the smaller Georgian house, a storey and a half in height, in plan a long rectangle bisected by a centre hall. One of the finest examples surviving of this type of house, which has grown with alterations into the prototype of the Upper Canadian vernacular, is Inge-Va in Perth (190).

Inge-Va was built in 1823 by Major Michael Harris as a storey-and-a-half stone house in the late Georgian Neo-classic style. Inge-Va had four large, well-spaced windows of fine proportions on the ground floor. The vernacular descendant may have only two windows, but the fine proportions are usually retained. Not every vernacular house will rejoice in an entrance doorway of such elegance as this, but whether the transom be square-headed or elliptical, there will be two sidelights and a door of gracious width. In 1832 Inge-Va was purchased by Thomas Radenhurst. It was during the Radenhurst tenure that the house

216

was to know its most stirring days. The Radenhursts were progressive. They insulated the partitions with tan-bark. They ordered up-to-date furniture from Matthew Connel, cabinet-maker of Quebec City. They raised the roof, not the whole roof but just enough of it to serve two very useful purposes. A gable was introduced which broke the visually heavy line of the long low-pitched roof, and better still, it provided space for a fine round-headed window with casement sash to light the upper hall. The Radenhurst house had assumed the form which was to be used over and over again for houses of less historic interest throughout Upper Canada. The historic interest of Inge-Va has been commemorated by a plaque, for it was to this house that the body of the victim of the last fatal duel in Upper Canada was brought.

Although the Upper Canadian vernacular house is normally a storey and a half in height, there are instances of the style in two or two and a half storeys. When the house was planned with an increase in scale the central gable usually crowned a shallow projecting bay, which contained the entrance door and an ornamental window or windows above it. A pair of Italianate windows and pleasantly fanciful brackets grace a two-storey vernacular house in Halton County (191). Simple, spacious and dignified with its square-headed doorway and well-spaced twelve-paned double-hung windows, it was admirably constructed in an era when functionalism was tempered with grace. The little brackets break the severity of the façade but are not obtrusive. This was not always so; the brackets of a similar house in Carleton were meant to be noticed (192), for they are a repeat pattern of the double reversed scroll, the design motif of the house, which is seen again in the newel post (193). The reverse scroll newel is to be found in many houses of the Upper Canadian vernacular style, usually in close association with wide, simple, not to say dull, Greek trim.

Eastward from Toronto, Upper Canada was strewn with seemingly unfulfilled intentions, for one encounters again and again the vernacular house of a storey and a half which has a door set in the central gable over the entrance doorway (194) but which has not, and has never had, a balcony or porch to support the unwary. Perhaps the owners are still trying to choose a style for the missing verandah.

Should the house be in Northumberland or Durham, the verandah is likely to be in place, but the gable is very likely to be of the curious local style which reaches its peak in the Battel house in Cobourg (195). This remarkable structure has been likened to a nun's coif by Mr. Verschoyle Blake, the architectural historian most conversant with the area.

191. *Above left: On the old Dundas Road in Halton County.*

192. *Above centre: A house in Carleton County, bracketed with enthusiasm.*

193. *Above right: The S-scroll newel was an inheritance from the Greek Revival.*

194. *Below: Unfinished business, or the suicide door, was a regional lapse peculiar to eastern Ontario.*

195. *Above: The Battel house, Cobourg, has the nun's coif gable of Durham and Northumberland but its window treatment is native to Cobourg.*

196. *Bottom: Verandah posts might be united in composition either by a thin decorative line or by whimsical brackets.*

197. *Right: The vernacular Neo-classic stair in Prince Edward County. The Collier house, South Bay.*

Very few of the coiffed gables are as madly gay as the Battel, but the motif of three wine-bottle arches with stopper finials, the work surely of an individual builder, is to be seen elsewhere in Cobourg.

The normal verandah for the Upper Canadian vernacular house has a graceful roof of tent-awning sweep on curved rafters. It is supported either by treillage (150) or by strong posts, square or round in cross-section and lightly decorated by a simple curvilinear line below the eave (196). The photographs could have been taken in any part of the province. Actually the verandahs shown are near Odessa and Clairville.

Internally the Upper Canadian house was a Georgian division of space with later modifications in trim and major changes in its utilitarian facilities. The Georgian plan was a long rectangle bisected by a centre hall. The vernacular house may continue to have exactly this same division or it might have a shorter hall with a small room behind it. This was especially true when the kitchen had been placed in a wing at a right angle with the main body of the house. The small additional room behind the hall became an ante-room to the kitchen or a pantry. The shortened hall might be a small square room having three doors, one leading to the dining-room, one to the double parlours, and the third, directly opposite the entrance, giving access to an enclosed stair. This small hall was sometimes called a box-hall. If the stair were open, it might be a straight flight of steps with a simple rail and a turned vase-shaped newel, or if the builder were capable of producing it, the stair might be the vernacular expression of the Neo-classic spiral (197) found in the Collier house on South Bay in Prince Edward County.

As an architectural feature, the fireplace had been the focal centre of the principal reception rooms. It had established the character of interior design and exercised a restraining influence on the furniture selected for each apartment. It had been the builder's showpiece. Now, with the advent of the stove, the control of interior design passed to the quality of taste employed in selecting the furnishings. The stigma, frequently undeserved, which attaches in many minds to the term Victorian, was incurred by the overcrowding of furniture and the riotous patterns of conflicting movements in wallpaper, rugs, upholstery and curtains. The architectural features submerged in this welter of colour, if seriously examined, will be found to have been most pleasant.

More frequently called the parlour as the century advanced, the drawing-room

220

198. *A Victorian Parlour, Loucks farm, Upper Canada Village.*

199. *An 1828 summer kitchen and wood-shed in the Weller-Morrison house at the Carrying Place.*

of the Upper Canadian rural vernacular house was a well-proportioned room, provided by its builder with adequate light from two or more twelve-paned windows. If the house were constructed of brick or stone, the window reveals were still panelled as they were in the farm-house in Upper Canada Village (198). In this room can be seen the false fireplace, frequently encountered, which served as a decorative backdrop to an enclosed stove or could, with its panelled centre removed, house a Franklin stove in winter. A like simplicity of trim would be found in the dining-room, the sitting-room and the ground-floor bed-room, none of which was likely to have the false mantelpiece.

The major change produced by the stove was in the vernacular kitchen. The cooking fireplace had been a large installation, placed to ensure maximum efficiency combined with ease of operation. The kitchen stove was smaller and much easier to control. The kitchen could be decreased in size. More than that the little kitchen stove could be moved about and the kitchen rearranged for the housewife's convenience. In summer, it was customary to move the stove out of the kitchen altogether to the summer kitchen, a room which began its career of usefulness as a platform raised above the level of the wood-shed and separated from the piles of fuel by a row of vertical planks. An original summer kitchen of this type exists in the Weller-Morrison house at the Carrying Place (199). The double-hung window placed opposite the wood-shed door allowed free cross-ventilation in summer.

The working tail of the vernacular house sometimes grew to immense lengths when it contained a summer kitchen, a laundry, a smoke-house, a wood-shed, privies and ultimately a carriage-shed. One of the longest in existence must surely be the fine stone tail at Maplehurst, but it has been so altered internally over the years that its separate functions cannot be ascertained. A runner-up belonged to the Wismer house at Vineland but as the tail was detached it could scarcely be thought to count.

If one were an urban dweller, there was no question of having a summer kitchen. The new cooking-stove stayed where it was, firmly attached to the wall in the basement kitchen (200). Our Favorite is still with us, because the vernacular town house in which it resides was saved when the rest of the terrace row on the west side of Bond Street, Toronto, was destroyed. Number 82 Bond Street has been restored because it was once the home of the first mayor of Toronto, William Lyon Mackenzie, memorable but hardly a favourite.

200. The basement kitchen in the Mackenzie house, Bond Street, Toronto, has had its mid-nineteenth-century appearance restored to it.

201. *In the days when elevators were rare, much of the urban population inhabited terraced or row houses.*
Port Hope, circa 1850.

Row housing was in the European tradition, and it was practised extensively in Upper Canada. Toronto, Hamilton and Kingston had miles of it at one time. Many towns are still fortunate in possessing handsome terraces. The internal division of space and the room use of the row house is discussed in the following chapter with comparative plans. It should be noted in a consideration of the vernacular style that row houses were not planned by simply sticking one little vernacular house against the end wall of another little vernacular house *ad infinitum.* The vernacular builder usually contrived to treat repetition imaginatively so that the long wall became an interesting rhythm of void and solid. If it was not broken

202. *Official vernacular. The wing of Rideau Hall designed in 1865 by F. P. Rubidge of the Department of Public Works. The original plans are in the Public Archives of Canada.*

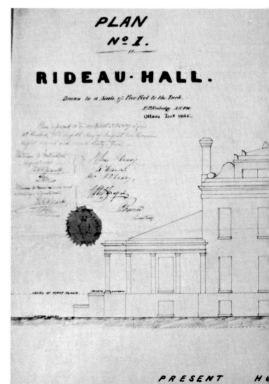

224

by the elliptical entrances of carriage-ways, then the wall surface itself might receive a low-relief pattern and galleries in the Regency style still to be seen in Port Hope (201).

Canada West was growing up and it was a complacent youth. The finger of fate had touched the map at Bytown and chosen it as the capital. The statesmen of the old colonies were busily shaping the federal organization of the new country — so busily that they had no time, if indeed they had the inclination or the training, to give mature consideration to the design for an official residence for the Governor General. Upper Canada was positively teeming with architects by 1865 but a self-satisfied bureaucracy was allowed to commission the Chief Engineer of the Department of Public Works, F. P. Rubidge, to design the addition which was to "improve" McKay's house, Rideau Hall, to a level commensurate with its new dignity as Government House.

Rubidge must have been inspired by patriotism (that can be conceded), for he designed the addition (202) in the Upper Canadian vernacular style. The Rubidge wing of Rideau Hall was undoubtedly "the old type of early Upper Canadian family residence of superior class combining the qualities of solidity and durability with those of snugness and comfort," and thus it was well within Dr. Scadding's definition. Rubidge should have remembered that patriotism is not enough. He may have been right in choosing the vernacular style. He may even have been under obligation to select the duller form of it, for he seems to have attempted to relieve the monotony of the long façade with cambered windows and an awning-roofed verandah.

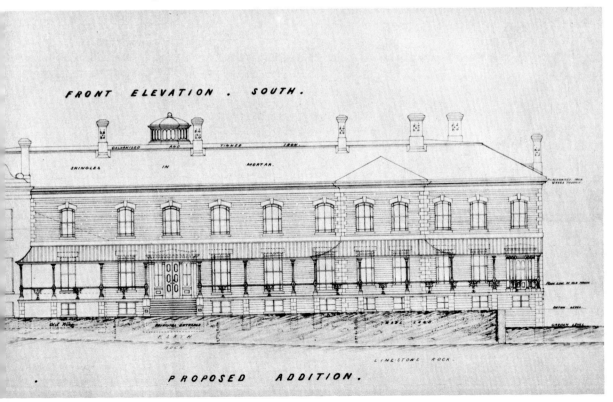

FRONT ELEVATION . SOUTH.

PROPOSED ADDITION.

It was the First of July 1867. Confederation was an accomplished fact. Upper Canada had been Canada West for a time, now it was to be called Ontario. The little vernacular house (203), still stubbornly Georgian in form and wearing its little gable with brave gaiety, became the abiding image of the province. It was to be the Ontario Classic style.

203. *The vernacular Classic wears a little peaked gable in Ontario and a bell-cast roof in Quebec but under both stands the ancestral small Renaissance house of western Europe.*

226

The last word

This concluding section attempts to tell the story of the house plan as it evolved under the influence of changes in architectural taste, in methods of heating, in the manufacture of building materials, and changes arising from a gradual improvement in living standards as the forests receded. It also attempts to show graphically with a minimum of text the details of the styles of Ontario architecture.

Plans of houses are shown as they were, in the opinions of the authors, when first built. The diagrams are taken mostly from field notes, and in transposition errors may have crept in. Dates are often conjectural. Plans, elevations and details of houses which are marked with an O are open to the public or are in public ownership; those marked with an X no longer stand. Perhaps there are no magnificent examples of superlative quality, but the citizen of Ontario need not decry the ancestry of his present architectural achievements.

227

The shanty

The typical shanty, or settler's first shelter, was of two kinds. The most primitive was composed of three log walls with one unenclosed side before which an open fire was built. The single-room shanty was enclosed on all sides. At one end it had an inverted funnel built of branches heavily daubed with clay to act as a chimney. Walls of horizontal logs were built to the height of the eaves, and a single opening was sawn out to contain both the door and a small window.

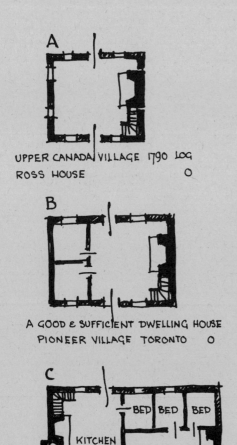

A
UPPER CANADA VILLAGE 1790 LOG
ROSS HOUSE   O

B
A GOOD & SUFFICIENT DWELLING HOUSE
PIONEER VILLAGE TORONTO   O

C
BED BED BED
KITCHEN
OSNABRUCK TWP. 1803 FRAME
STATA HOUSE

Simple plans without halls

The plan of the single-room house, common in all periods, is seen in Plan A. It has a masonry fireplace and chimney stack located at a gable end. The attic space in such a house, used as a sleeping loft, is reached either by a ladder or by a stair constructed against the projecting side of the chimney. The stair is enclosed by board walls, and there is a door at the foot to control heat loss. In the evolution of the simple house plan, the first additional ground-floor rooms were bedrooms. These were unheated and small, sometimes little more than closets. A common arrangement of two small bedrooms partitioned off the main room is shown in Plan B. To obtain a Crown land grant the settler was obliged to construct "a good and sufficient dwelling house." A house of such a plan was acceptable. The next step in the evolution of the simple house plan was the removal of the cooking process to a separate kitchen. Plan C shows a house with two main rooms. To the side of the cooking fire is a bake oven. These ovens were deeper than fireplaces and often projected outside the main wall.

Box-halls and central chimneys

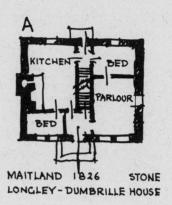

MAITLAND 1826 STONE
LONGLEY-DUMBRILLE HOUSE

An entrance hall added both comfort and grace to a house. The simplest form of entrance hall was a small box-like room off which doors opened to the main rooms. Such halls have come to be called box-halls. Plan A illustrates a box-hall with an enclosed stair between walls off it. This house appears to have had originally only one chimney to serve the kitchen cooking fire. A stove must therefore have been used in the living-room and was probably connected to the chimney stack by a stove-pipe through the hall and bedroom. Stoves were always available from Montreal or New York State. As transportation improved, their use became more common and by 1840 they were manufactured in various Upper Canadian towns. Many early houses which relied entirely on open fires for cooking and heating had single central chimney stacks. A single internal chimney saved money and conserved heat. Such houses usually had box-halls. After the introduction of furnaces most of these large central chimneys became unnecessary and were taken down to provide space. Plan C shows a house with five flues in a central stack serving three open fires downstairs and two upstairs. Open cooking fires and bake ovens added to winter comfort but in July and August they added to the summer heat. Plan C also shows one solution to this problem, the construction of a separate building for summer cooking and baking. Another solution was to house the kitchen in a single-storey projection and give the cooking fire a separate stack as seen in Plan B. In both plans B and C the room to the right of the hall would probably have been called the dining parlour or parlour — a living-room in which meals could be taken.

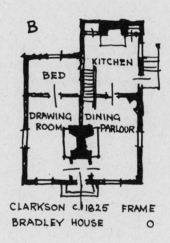

CLARKSON C. 1825 FRAME
BRADLEY HOUSE O

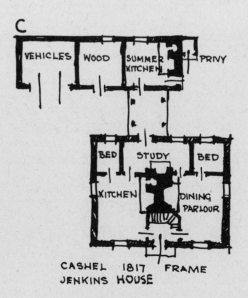

CASHEL 1817 FRAME
JENKINS HOUSE

229

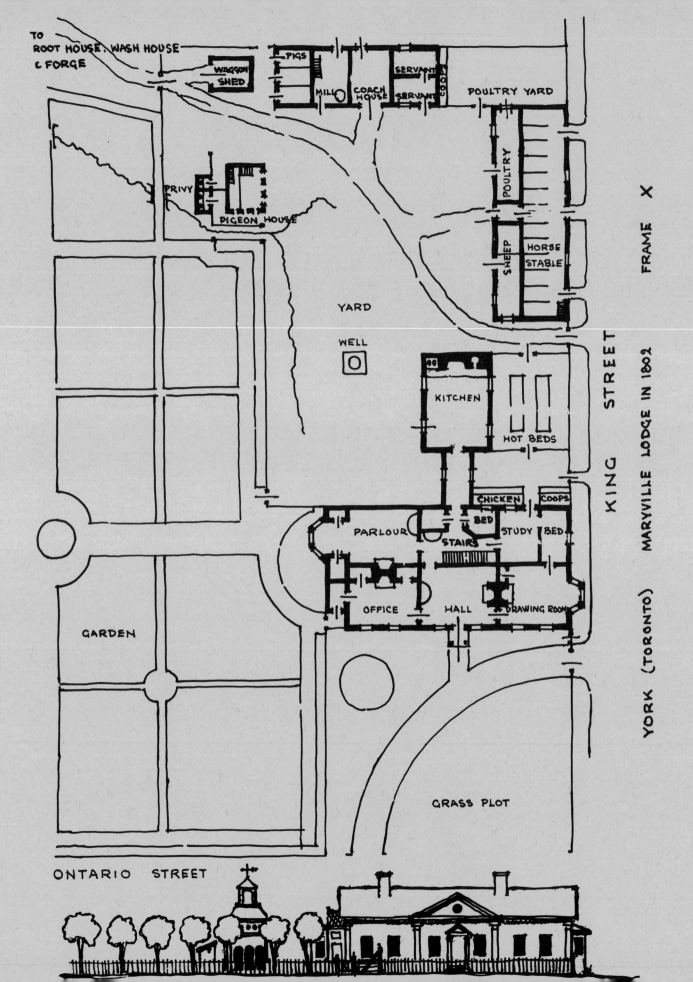

TO
ROOT HOUSE. WASH HOUSE
& FORGE

WAGGON
SHED

PIGS

MILL

COACH
HOUSE

SERVANTS

SERVANTS

COOPS

POULTRY YARD

POULTRY

PRIVY

PIGEON HOUSE

SHEEP

HORSE
STABLE

YARD

WELL

KITCHEN

HOT BEDS

CHICKEN

BED

COOPS

PARLOUR

STAIRS

STUDY

BED

OFFICE

HALL

DRAWING ROOM

GARDEN

GRASS PLOT

ONTARIO STREET

KING STREET

FRAME X

MARYVILLE LODGE IN 1802

YORK (TORONTO)

Mr. Smith's house in York, 1802

Reliance on the existing structural conditions of early houses for an understanding of their original plan and room use is misleading as so much has been altered. The Toronto Public Library has a book of water-colour drawings prepared in 1805 by the surveyor William Chewett, showing the house and estate of the Honourable D. W. Smith, Surveyor General of Upper Canada. One of these water-colours is redrawn and illustrated. The permanent kitchen is isolated from the house by a passage and is served by a cooking fire, bake oven and two stew holes. There is a large central room labelled hall entered directly by the front door. This hall has a bookcase. To the left is the office with a capacious recess on each side of the fireplace. The office has a separate outside entrance. To the right of the hall is the drawing-room equipped with a small closet beside the fireplace. Off this room is the ground-floor bedroom so popular throughout the nineteenth century and a study connects with it. Both these are without visible means of heat, although a stove in the study might have provided heat from its pipe to the rear passage. Behind the hall is a space containing the stairs leading to four bedchambers, a housekeeper's room and her bedchamber,

some fifty-five square feet in area. Off the stair passage and readily accessible to the kitchen is the parlour served by a large and small closet and devoid of windows in its long wall. In the parlour and the hall the water-colour drawing shows brown-tinted segmental shapes, one in each room, while the rear passage has two of them. No other furniture is shown. In this house the parlour was used for dining and against the long empty wall probably stood the sideboard. The segmental shapes are probably end tables used to enlarge rectangular tables for use as dining tables. Mr. Smith quite possibly ate casually in his hall but dined in the parlour.

Mr. Smith's house stood at the corner of present-day King and Ontario streets in downtown Toronto and its grounds ran up to Queen Street. The plan is additionally interesting as it shows the self-sufficiency of such a house at this date. Beside a great quantity of chickens and pigeons there were sheep and a vast vegetable garden. The blacksmith's forge may not have been entirely dependent on Mr. Smith's custom but the root-house and the wash-house were. Servants were presumably lodged above the coach-house as well as next to the coops for chickens.

Early centre-hall plans

House plans with a centre hall running the width of the house and containing within it an open stair were traditional in Europe and America before ever a house was erected in Upper Canada. The plan of two floors of an existing house reputed to have been built before the American Revolution by a fur trader on Lake Ontario is shown in Plan A. Settlers in the northern colonies soon found that foundations had to be laid below the frost line and the earliest settlers were vitally aware of the usefulness of basements. Basement kitchens, at least for town houses, were as traditional to Europe and America as the centre-hall plan. A kitchen here shares the basement with a storage

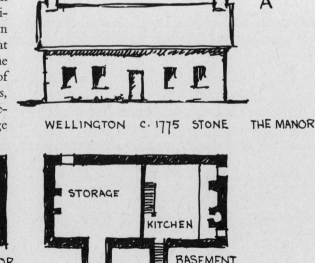

WELLINGTON C. 1775 STONE THE MANOR

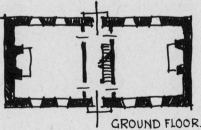

GROUND FLOOR.

STORAGE
KITCHEN
BASEMENT

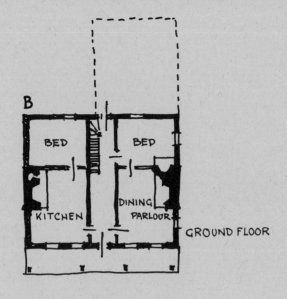

GROUND FLOOR

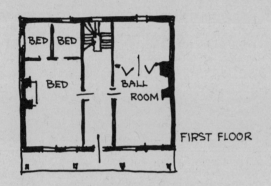

FIRST FLOOR

MILLHAVEN 1793 FRAME   THE WHITE HOUSE

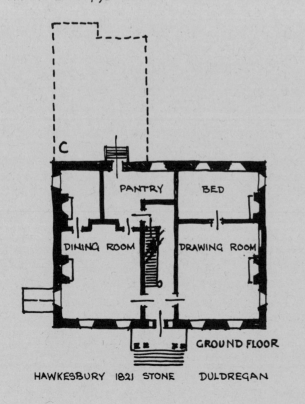

GROUND FLOOR

HAWKESBURY 1821 STONE   DULDREGAN

room, both of which have outside covered stair access. The ground floor shows the centre hall in its simplest form with a single room on each side and chimneys in the gables. The top floor was probably an open loft and is without fireplaces. Plan B shows the centre-hall plan of a Loyalist family who seem to have been able to draw funds from their relations left behind in the late colony of Vermont, as they built quite a large house in the American Georgian style not long after their arrival. There are single stacks in the gables but this house is wide enough to have more than one room on each side of the hall. The kitchen with its bake oven has a room partitioned off one end which was used probably as a housekeeper's room. On the right of the hall is the dining parlour with a heated bedroom off it. Upstairs is the typical arrangement of a large room with fireplace and two small rooms borrowing heat from it. This house has, however, the distinction of a large up-stairs room which can be converted into two rooms by folding doors. Upstairs living-rooms of this kind were not uncommon and were referred to as ballrooms. When not used for this purpose, they no doubt served as rooms for sleeping in, or for quilting-bees and on other community occasions. The large centre halls upstairs were used for spinning, sewing and the performance of other domestic chores not related to the kitchen. The house of Plan B is unusual in that, unlike most early houses, it has a two-storey gallery which faces south on Lake Ontario. Such galleries were far more common on inns. Plan C shows the ground floor of a larger and later house with a centre hall and four chimney stacks, two on each gable to serve two full rooms on each side of the hall. This house was built in the new Loyalist or Neo-classic style of architec-ture, and typical of this style, it has a room especially set aside for use as a dining-room with an elliptical arched recess for a sideboard. The kitchen was originally in the basement and food was brought up the back stairs to a pantry. To the right of the hall is the drawing-room and at least one of the two back rooms on the ground floor is a bedroom. At later dates both the houses of plans B and C had their original kitchens relocated in an extension at the back of the houses as shown by the dotted lines.

MAITLAND

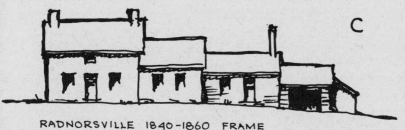

RADNORSVILLE 1840–1860 FRAME

C

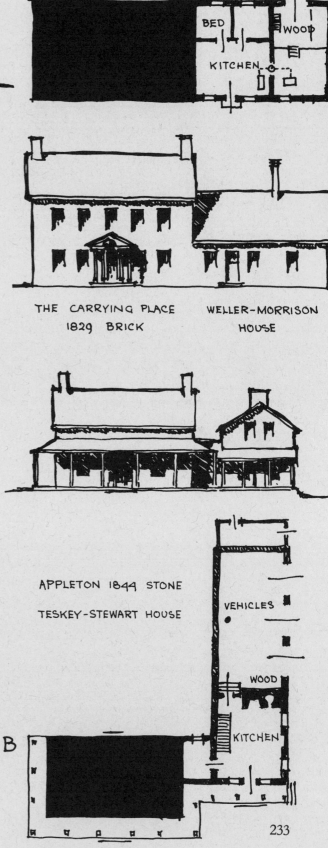

A

BED WOOD

KITCHEN

THE CARRYING PLACE   WELLER–MORRISON
1829 BRICK   HOUSE

APPLETON 1844 STONE

TESKEY–STEWART HOUSE

VEHICLES

WOOD

KITCHEN

B

Kitchen wings and tails

There is some evidence that Southern Loyalists brought the tradition of permanent separate kitchen dependencies to Ontario. By the 1820's, however, preference was being expressed for the permanent kitchen to be located in a side wing or tail such as those added to Duldregan and the White House at Millhaven. Plan A shows a house built in the 1820's with a contemporary one-storey wing containing a kitchen with the usual two little rooms off it. Beyond this kitchen is a high open wood-shed into which has been built a platform illustrated on page 221. Cooking in this house is done on a cook-stove in the kitchen and not in a cooking fireplace. In the summer the cook-stove is placed on the platform in the airy wood-shed. This arrangement gained very wide acceptance. Pipes from stoves could be carried to a single-flue brick stack set on brackets in the attic. Such stove chimneys on brackets were of far smaller dimension and cost much less than a multiflued stack carried to the ground to serve open fires. Two-storey service wings, or tails, were also common when there were servants' bedrooms above the kitchen, less interest being taken in keeping servants cool in summer. An example of this is shown in the elevation and plan of Diagram B. Diagrams C and D show the elevations of typical wings, that of C still attached to a small farm-house and giving a quaint air of a family of little buildings or even of a railway train, as summer kitchens, wood-sheds, carriage-houses, etc. begin to attach themselves to the main house.

D

840 STONE   THE TAIL OF MAPLEHURST

Mr. Jones' house in Toronto, 1833

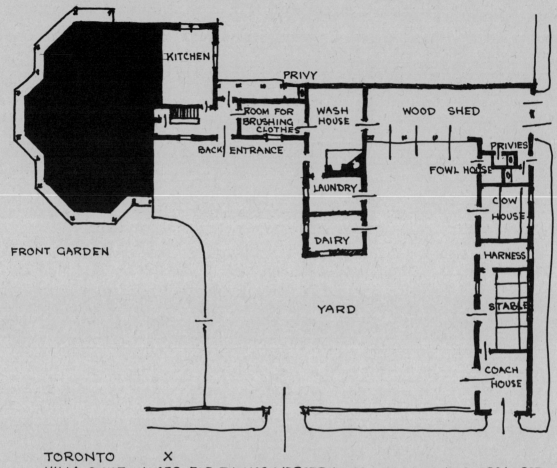

KITCHEN

PRIVY

ROOM FOR BRUSHING CLOTHES

WASH HOUSE

WOOD SHED

PRIVIES

BACK ENTRANCE

FOWL HOUSE

LAUNDRY

COW HOUSE

DAIRY

HARNESS

FRONT GARDEN

STABLE

YARD

COACH HOUSE

TORONTO   X
VILLA BUILT IN 1833 FOR THOMAS MERCER JONES . JOHN HOWARD ARCHITECT.

The social and technical changes which have taken place since Confederation have eroded the tails, wings and attached outbuildings of houses, so that it is difficult today to determine their original state. An example of their extent may be gleaned from a plan of the outbuildings of a house built for Mr. and Mrs. Thomas Mercer Jones in Toronto in 1833, the plans of which may be found among the papers of John Howard, architect, in the Toronto Reference Library. Self-sufficiency is still as much in evidence in 1833 as it was in Maryville Lodge in the 1790's.

Mr. Jones' servants are, however, accommodated within the house and not, like Mr. Smith's, next to the chickens. The uses of the spaces are indicated in the drawing as they were written in by the architect on the original plan. The privies were drawn by the architect but not named, and there is no space set aside in either the wing or the house for bathing. Probably many of the household used the wash-house for this purpose, others a portable tub. The house and estate eventually became part of the first Bishop Strachan School for girls.

Below stairs with the Governor, 1841

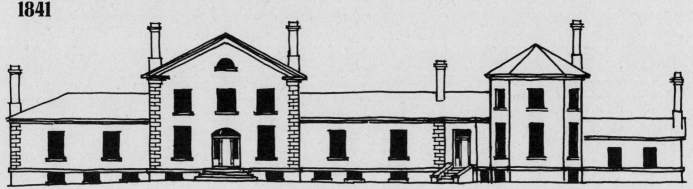

NORTH FRONT GOVERNMENT HOUSE ALWINGTON KINGSTON IN 1841

The domestic offices accommodated in the tails of small houses were located in the basements of greater houses. The plan shows the basement floor of Alwington at Kingston, destroyed by fire in 1959. The plan is taken from the Archives of Canada and shows the house as it was altered in 1841 to be the first Government House of the United Canadas. The portion with thick walls was the basement of the house of Charles Grant, Baron de Longueuil. The central block of the old house with its own stair contained the wine cellar, the men servants' bedrooms and a water-closet, carefully isolated. The still room was "where the more delicate dishes are prepared and where liquors, preserves and the like are kept." (Webster) The 1841 addition was dominated by the kitchen which measured twenty-four feet by twenty-seven feet and was fifteen feet high. It was entered by way of a stair-hall. Since there was no furnace, the Archives plan shows locations for two stoves, one in the passage outside the cooks' bedrooms and one in the servants' hall, the pipes of which brought some heat to other places. These same stove-pipes also set fire to the house during construction.

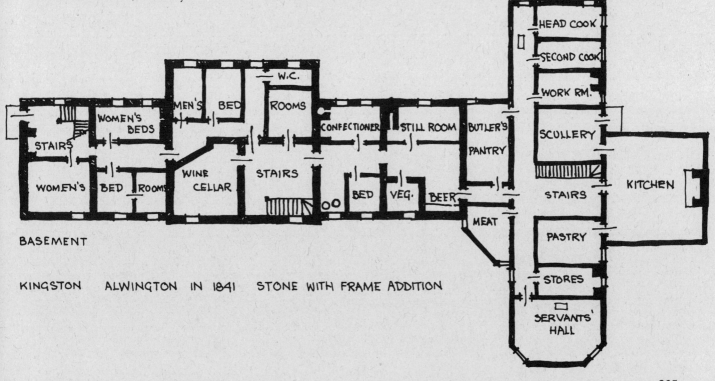

BASEMENT

KINGSTON   ALWINGTON   IN 1841   STONE WITH FRAME ADDITION

235

Side-hall plans

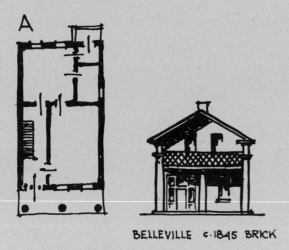

BELLEVILLE c·1845 BRICK

By 1820 Upper Canadians were beginning to build their houses on an axis similar to that of a Classical temple, so that the gable end was towards the front, and the front door was therefore on the shorter side of the rectangular house. The side-hall plan which resulted from this narrower façade had been used in terraced houses in cities because the narrow side had of necessity to face the street. This plan became very common in the Greek Revival houses of the 1840's. The simplest form of side-hall plan in an individual house is shown in Plan A. This house was heated entirely by stoves with pipes running to a bracketed stove chimney, so that no chimney stack shows on the ground-floor plan.

Plan B shows a side-hall plan with a kitchen wing. The designer intended to have a side hall with a stair in it but the Lutheran pastor for whom it was built preferred to have a study and the stair was relocated off the dining parlour. In the 1840's the isolated kitchen, in its own wing with sink room off it and a trap door to the cellar, still had an open cooking fire but by this time the rest of the house was being heated by stoves. A single central stove chimney stack with one flue serving two floors and several stoves may be seen here taking up far less space than the central chimneys of earlier houses heated by fireplaces. The disappearance of fireplaces and the introduction of stoves necessitated room ventilation. At first small ventilation holes were cut high in the partition walls but these did not prove satisfactory nor did they help in the circulation of heat. Therefore heat holes with doors or removable panels the width of a normal door and about three

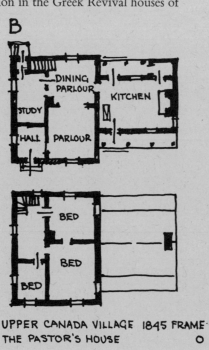

UPPER CANADA VILLAGE 1845 FRAME
THE PASTOR'S HOUSE

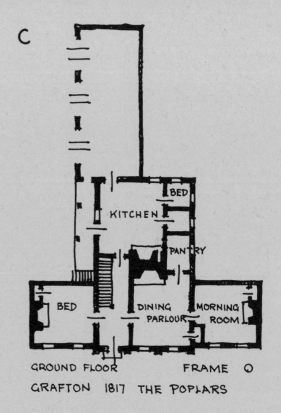

GROUND FLOOR   FRAME O
GRAFTON 1817 THE POPLARS

236

feet high became common. Two heat holes show in this plan, one between the study and the dining parlour and one between two of the bedrooms upstairs.

Plan C shows the very beautiful Barnum house of about 1820 illustrated on page 45. It has a two-storey Neo-classic centre block with its narrow gabled end to the front, and two symmetrical wings and a tail of one storey in height. This house is considered as having a side-hall plan since the room to the left of the hall, which may have been a bedroom or an office, is in a one-storey wing. Heating and cooking is still by open fire, and there is a large central chimney. The kitchen has its usual little rooms off it, one of which, a pantry, gives access to the dining parlour. A room off this, the most elegant in the house, may have been the usual ground-floor bedroom but its elegance indicates it is more likely to have been a morning-room. The drawing-room is upstairs across the front of the house, and its ceiling is higher than that of the rooms below. The tail of this house has vanished but there was one originally. It may have contained servants' rooms and undoubtedly housed a wood-shed and a carriage-house facing onto a yard.

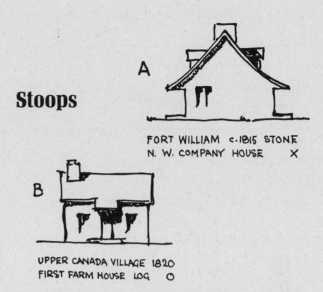

FORT WILLIAM c.1815 STONE
N. W. COMPANY HOUSE   X

Stoops

UPPER CANADA VILLAGE 1820
FIRST FARM HOUSE LOG   O

In primitive houses eaves were occasionally extended to give protection to platforms in front of the door or alongside the house. These platforms were common in Lower Canada. They are rare in Upper Canada and the Dutch name "stoop" (step) is used for them. Drawing A shows a typical French-Canadian house with bell-cast roof taken from an early photograph of Fort William. Elevation B is a cabin with a roof over a door stoop. The curious house with two stoops in C is that of the Dutch immigrant from New York. Elevation D is a small house with the stoop along one side.

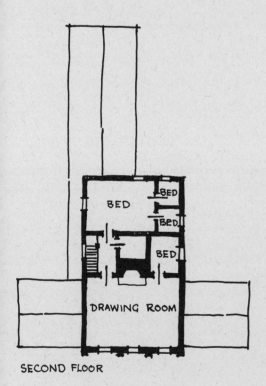

SECOND FLOOR

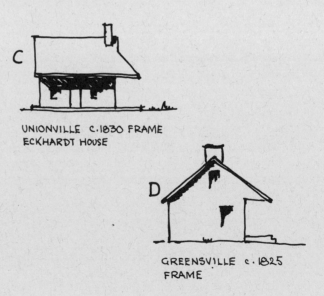

UNIONVILLE C.1830 FRAME
ECKHARDT HOUSE

GREENSVILLE c.1825
FRAME

237

Porches

Porches were always common, and varied with the style of architecture. Some in the Classical, Gothic and Italianate styles are shown. Many houses had doors at the second-storey level which were meant to open onto the flat roofs of porches. Failure to build these porches or their rotting off and removal has left the suicide doors common in Ontario.

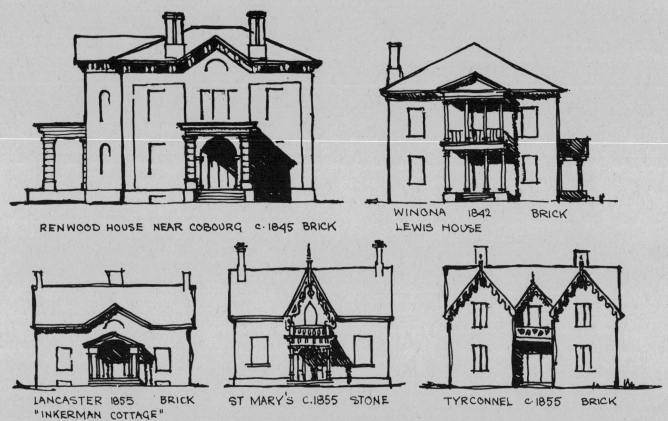

RENWOOD HOUSE NEAR COBOURG c·1845 BRICK

WINONA 1842 BRICK
LEWIS HOUSE

LANCASTER 1855 BRICK
"INKERMAN COTTAGE"

ST MARY'S c·1855 STONE

TYRCONNEL c·1855 BRICK

Umbrages

Umbrages, or areas recessed in plan and protected by the roof or by the floor above, were never very popular but they were used before the verandah became common. Two examples are shown, one in the Loyalist style and the other a Regency cottage with both a porch and an umbrage.

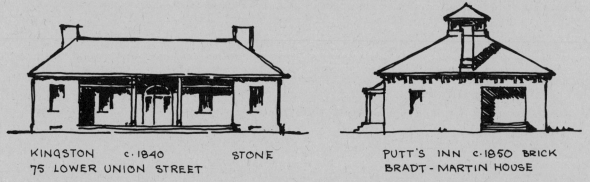

KINGSTON c·1840 STONE
75 LOWER UNION STREET

PUTT'S INN c·1850 BRICK
BRADT·MARTIN HOUSE

Verandahs and galleries

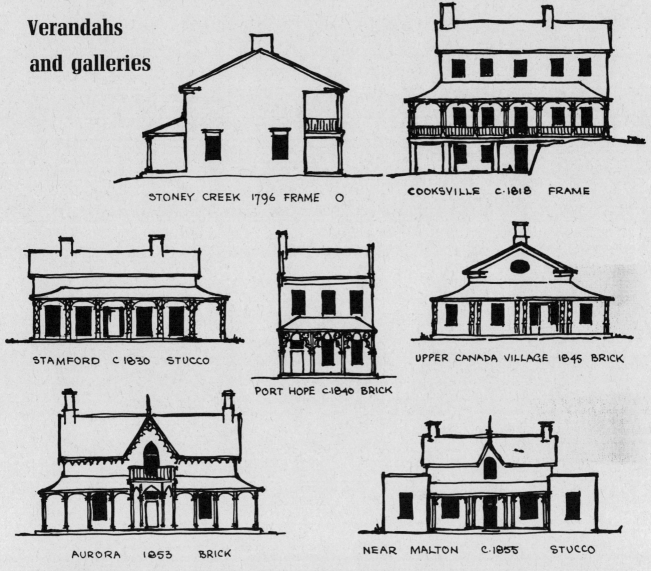

STONEY CREEK 1796 FRAME O

COOKSVILLE C·1818 FRAME

STAMFORD C 1830 STUCCO

PORT HOPE C·1840 BRICK

UPPER CANADA VILLAGE 1845 BRICK

AURORA 1853 BRICK

NEAR MALTON C·1855 STUCCO

OTTAWA 1863 STONE

One-storey verandahs became an almost universal addition to houses in Upper Canada and Canada West from 1830 to 1855. Earlier houses also had them but less commonly. They were added across the whole of the front of the long rectangular-shaped houses with the centre-hall plan and to the kitchen tails. In houses which had a main block with a side-hall plan the verandahs were frequently limited to the kitchen wings or tails. The Ontario Cottage in the Regency style favoured verandahs around three sides. The roofs of the earliest verandahs were supported by simple posts or Classical columns. Verandahs from 1835 to 1860 often had elaborate treillage. From 1860 on treillage was replaced in fashion by posts with brackets. A selection of verandahs in various styles is shown.

239

The Ontario Cottage

The one-and-a-half-storey house with a cottage roof, or hip-roof, has always been built. Owing to the popularity of the Regency style with encircling verandahs, this one-and-a-half-storey house, rare in the northeastern United States but very common in Ontario, has been termed here the Ontario Cottage. Its evolution and types are shown. Elevation A shows the earliest long rectangular form with heavy internal chimneys. B is an example with external chimneys and a Neo-classic porch. C is an example of the form with encircling verandah supported by posts. D is an example, square in plan, with simple Regency treillage in wood supporting a tent-shaped roof. E, F and G ex-

A

TORONTO 1800 UNBURNED BRICK
POTTERY ROAD

B

GRIMSBY C.1822 BRICK

C

MARTINTOWN C.1830 BRICK
MC MARTIN HOUSE

D

MILLBROOK C.1835 FRAME

E

BOND HEAD C.1835 STUCCO
WILLIAMS-ADAMS HOUSE

F

DESIGN FOR A SUMMER COTTAGE BY
JOHN HOWARD 1840

G

CHUTE AU BLONDEAU
ROSE COTTAGE

emplify the full Regency cottage, square or almost square in plan with a single slope roof covering both house and verandah. H shows a "house with a hat" with verandah posts, a form common in Northumberland and Durham counties. This example also shows the regional nun's coif dormer. I shows the Ontario Cottage with a belvedere on the roof lighting two family bedrooms and a hall in the attic space. J and K show the Ontario Cottage form without verandahs. K has a Gothic gable and window to light the attic, whereas J has a belvedere in the latest vogue of the day but with an elliptical arched doorway of the earlier Loyalist or Neoclassic style.

K

TORONTO C.1855 STUCCO
CHARLES STREET EAST

H

COBOURG C.1838 STUCCO
KING STREET

I

WOODSTOCK c. 1833 STUCCO
DREW COTTAGE

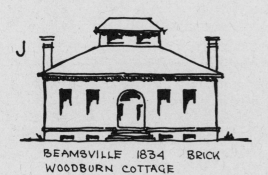

J

BEAMSVILLE 1834 BRICK
WOODBURN COTTAGE

Octagons

Buildings have been erected on octagonal plans in every age. They were made popular in the nineteenth century by a well-to-do phrenologist, Orson Fowler, in his book *A Home for All*. The centre of their popularity was New York State where well over one hundred still stand. Most are from the 1850's. Many are built in grout. A number of octagonal houses were built in Ontario, of which two are illustrated. The octagonal-plan house had the reputed benefits of having less wall for the space contained and of being able to be heated centrally by a furnace. Nearly all had belvederes or skylights.

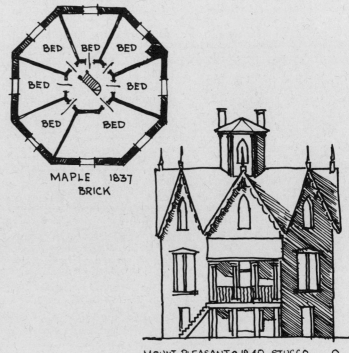

MAPLE 1837
BRICK

MOUNT PLEASANT C.1840 STUCCO   O

Treillage

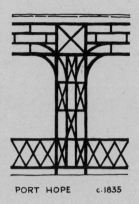

PORT HOPE   c·1835

STAMFORD   c·1835

MALTON   c·1845

The Regency desire for cottage simplicity and for bringing the garden and house closer together resulted in the replacement of the Classic column to support verandah roofs by wooden posts and trellis-work on which vines could grow. Ontario is rich in treillage. The example from Stamford shows a common and elegant type reminiscent of the early ironwork of Britain. Early trellis posts were composed of an arrangement of straight wooden bars connected by some form of arch, usually elliptical. At Port Hope we see a very extensive development of treillage with possible Chinese influence. This, if covered with vines, would have blocked out light to the glazed French doors behind. At Malton the treillage has a studied rustic look. Ontario treillage blossoms into full Victorian bloom at Kleinburg. The fret saw

has come into common use and curved elements have replaced the straight wooden bars. There is a Gothic panel in the main body of the treillage and a cut-out above the cap mould of Greek derivation. In front of the solid fascia board which upholds the verandah roof wooden derivatives of the upholsterer's art are suspended. The tassel-like decorations hang freely on hooks. The Westport example shows the fret saw in complete command. All elements of the composition are cut from boards. Even the fascia board behind the eaves board is pierced with diamond-shaped holes. Eventually treillage lapsed in popularity and the post came back, not in Classical form but with ornamental brackets as at Whitby. Iron treillage is rare. An example is shown on page 196.

WESTPORT   c·1855

KLEINBURG   1856

WHITBY   c·1867

Belvederes and roof walks

The space immediately below a sloping roof can be lit by windows in gables, by dormers or by belvederes on the crown of the roof. Buildings with hip-roofs and no gables need either dormers or belvederes. Diagram A shows the section and plan of an Ontario Cottage in Northumberland County with a belvedere which provides light to four bedrooms and a hall, none of which, therefore, has a complete ceiling. Diagram B shows the section through a Greek Revival house in Paris in which the wall between bedrooms and hall rises to the roof of the belvedere thereby providing greater privacy than would be available in the house of Diagram A. Light to these rooms, however, comes in either above the level of the ceiling through the belvedere or below the level of the knee through little windows inserted in the deep architrave below the exterior cornice. Diagram C gives a section through a four-storey house in the Greek Revival style also in Paris. It is illustrated on

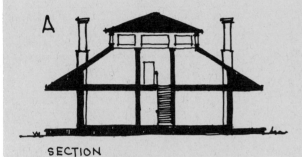

SECTION

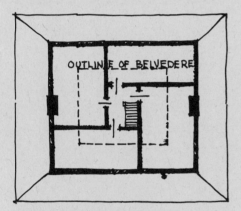

PLAN OF BEDROOM FLOOR

HALDIMAND TWP NEAR GRAFTON 1845
MALLORY HOUSE   BRICK

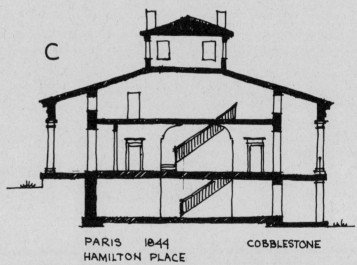

PARIS   1844   COBBLESTONE
HAMILTON PLACE

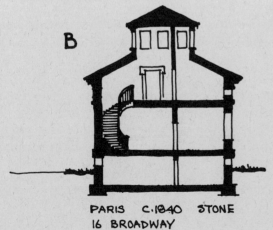

PARIS C.1840 STONE
16 BROADWAY

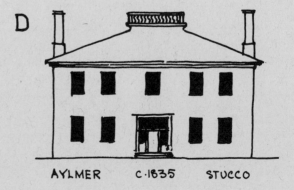

AYLMER   C.1835   STUCCO

243

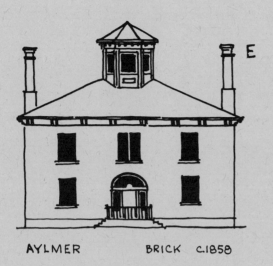

AYLMER   BRICK   C.1858

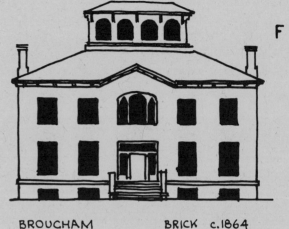

BROUGHAM   BRICK   c.1864

page 140. In plan it has a central hall with a stair in a recess off it. The section is taken through this hall. Built on the sloping bank of the Grand River, it has a kitchen and dining-room at the lowest level. At the third level is the bedroom floor where on three sides windows look out under the roof of the surrounding colonnade onto the back of the deep Doric architrave, so that no hint of this floor is visible from the outside. The belvedere, on the other hand, provides a room thirteen by twenty-four feet brilliantly lit by ten windows. This room is reached by an enclosed stair and a trap door.

Large bracketed houses in the Italianate style with all main rooms comfortably lit often had belvederes on their roofs to give interest rather than illumination to an attic floor. Two such, E and F, are shown above, E. has a hexagonal belvedere.

Roof walks were in occasional use in the Neo-classic style, which also favoured decorative balustrades and small domed cupolas on the roof. One is illustrated on page 65. These walks were occasionally combined with belvederes as illustrated on page 210. D is an example of a roof walk without a belvedere.

Picturesque plans

The popularity of Picturesque styles in detached houses was largely due to the flexibility which they allowed in planning and in making additions and alterations. Dormers and steep gables, scarcely permitted in any styles of a Classical Revival nature, became essential to the Picturesque silhouette and to the Gothic Revival style building. Plans and elevations of studied irregularity came into vogue with architects, although many of the vernacular Gothic houses maintained the old rectangular plans with centre or side halls and altered only their silhouettes and roof pitch. An example of how the ordinary centre-hall plan with a kitchen wing could be manipulated to provide a house in the new

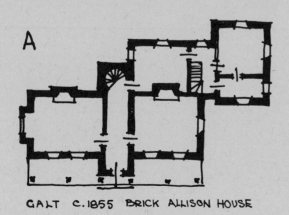

GALT C.1855 BRICK ALLISON HOUSE

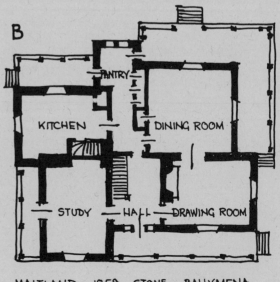

MAITLAND 1858 STONE BALLYMENA

style is shown in Plan A. This house, though much altered, has seven gables. Plan B shows the Gothic Revival house built by the rector who succeeded the Reverend Mr. Blaikie at Maitland whose Loyalist style house is illustrated on page 32. This later house also shows the change that had come to be wrought in the old centre-hall plan. It has five gables and half a dozen large pinnacled dormers. In both plans A and B there are separate dining-rooms, the drawing-rooms have descended to the ground floor to stay, and the kitchens no longer have to content themselves with a sink room or closet but now have full pantries. Both houses are now heated by hot air furnaces and the fireplaces serve only for the enjoyment of casual heating. Even the box-hall and central chimney plan could be manipulated into the Picturesque. Among the drawings of John Howard, architect, found at Colborne Lodge recently, is the cottage shown in C. It gives evidence of an architect pioneering in the development of the Picturesque for a summer cottage in 1836, but in effect using a plan not too dissimilar from the rectangular plan used with central chimney and box-hall. The parlour here is a dining parlour. The over-manipulation of plan and excessive dexterity in the provision of silhouette was not popular with Ontario farmers. During the 1850's the most popular plan was the L-plan. This allowed for a choice of gable and roof pitch, a piece of verandah with the front door entered off it, a kitchen tail — an asymmetrical house which could be extended in every direction, and which obviated the necessity to balance room sizes about a centre hall in order to give Classical order to a façade. An example of this plan is seen in D. It is the house in which W. L. Mackenzie King spent a great deal of his boyhood. The parlour here is a drawing-room. E shows a labourer's cottage with the "good and sufficient dwelling house" plan dressed in Picturesque garb to amuse the landlord.

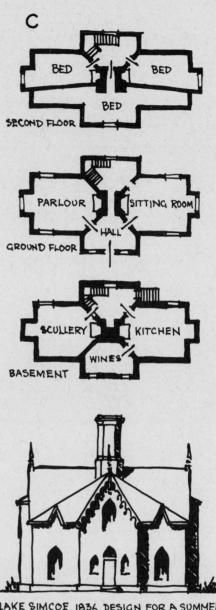

LAKE SIMCOE 1836 DESIGN FOR A SUMMER COTTAGE FOR JOSEPH RIDOUT.

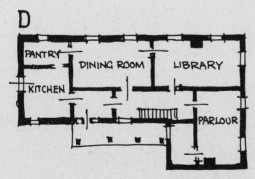

KITCHENER 1853 BRICK WOODSIDE ○

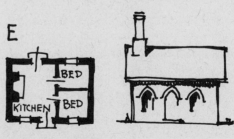

TORONTO C. 1840   X
DESIGN FOR A LABOURER'S COTTAGE.

245

Double houses

Double houses, or semi-detached houses, were always common. There are a number of fine ones of various types built in Kingston, and every little mill village had mill-workers' houses which were most often semi-detached. Large houses required private stabling and as lanes are notably absent in Ontario towns, access to stables and other service buildings was often by an arched opening. Eleva-

KINGSTON C·1845 STONE
EDGEWATER HOUSE EMILY STREET

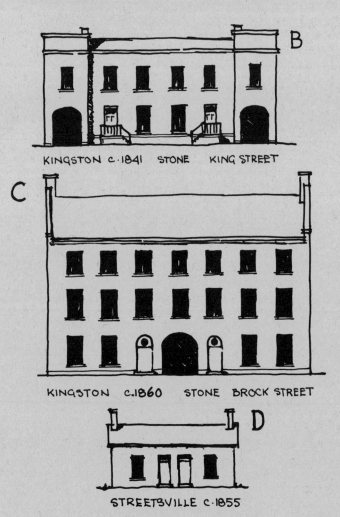

KINGSTON C·1841 STONE KING STREET

KINGSTON C·1860 STONE BROCK STREET

STREETSVILLE C·1855

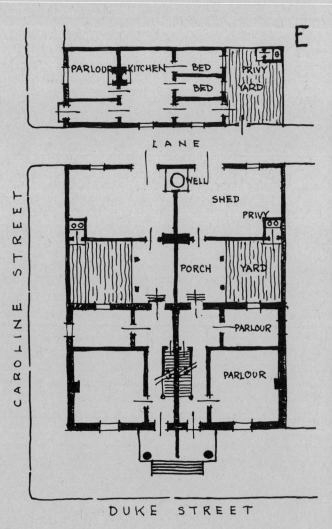

tions A, B and C show three double houses in Kingston. A is a beautifully sited house built for a brother and sister on a spacious lot overlooking Lake Ontario and has side access to its stables. B is a house built speculatively and has individual arches giving access to the rear yards. C is a large severe double house for two Horsey families. It was built on the same lot on which their father had built the Gothic fantasy, Elizabeth Cottage, illustrated on page 165, and may have been an architectural reaction to his whimsy.

D shows the elevation of mill-workers' houses in board and batten. E shows plans by John Howard for Mr. Harris for the sweating of a corner lot in Toronto. A ten-foot lane ran across the parcel. Between it and Duke Street stood a double house for two tradesmen's families. To the north of the lane was a labourer's house. The sheds on the lane could serve as stables or as work-shops. The only water supply is a joint well equidistant from the privies and within the shelter of the sheds.

Row houses

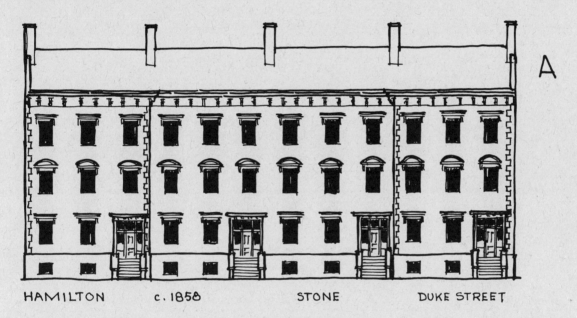

HAMILTON   c.1858   STONE   DUKE STREET

Neither terraces of fine aristocratic houses nor tall rows of tenements came to be built in Upper Canadian cities. Some terraces of moderate size were to be seen in Toronto and one or two remain in Hamilton. Cities were small up to 1867: there was ample space for expansion and the problems of transportation were minor. The well-to-do preferred to escape from the centres of the little towns and from developments like that of Mr. Harris to the fringes rather than live in the terraced majesty of town houses as in the greater and earlier cities of Europe and America. Diagrams A and B show rows still standing on Duke Street in Hamilton and Duke Street in Toronto. An entirely typical example, which has a severely plain façade in

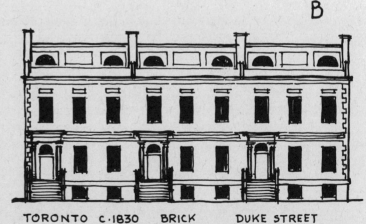

TORONTO c.1830   BRICK   DUKE STREET

247

C

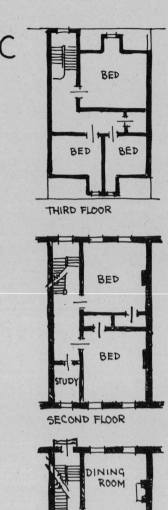

THIRD FLOOR

SECOND FLOOR

DINING ROOM

HALL PARLOUR

GROUND FLOOR

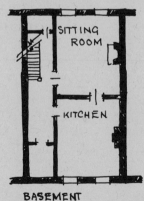

SITTING ROOM

KITCHEN

BASEMENT

TORONTO C. 1855 BRICK
82 BOND STREET   O

brick, is shown in Plan C. It was presented to William Lyon Mackenzie by his admirers in 1859 and he died there in 1861. It has the side-hall plan of most terrace houses. There was no furnace and the house is now restored with stoves throughout except in the basement sitting-room. Owners

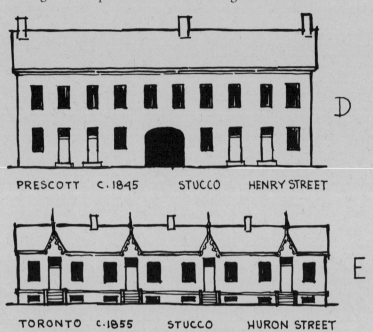

PRESCOTT   C. 1845   STUCCO   HENRY STREET

E

TORONTO   C. 1855   STUCCO   HURON STREET

of other houses in his terrace might have called this sitting-room a servants' hall but Mackenzie was in straitened circumstances and his family probably found this the most pleasant and usable room in the house. Sliding doors separate dining-room and parlour. The parlour has now ceased to be a room for dining in and has become the formal living-room for those who do not aspire to drawing-rooms and morning-rooms. Elevation D shows an early form of multiple dwelling common in towns of all sizes. The central archway allowed horse-drawn vehicles into the rear yards of all houses. Kitchens and wood-sheds were in the usual one-storey attached tails projecting into rear yards. Many miles of one-, two- and three-storey row houses still stand. Some of the earliest type are shown on page 189. A single, small late Toronto example is shown in E. An example of substandard housing which stood in Toronto until the 1950's is shown in Plan F. It was sandwiched between others. The unlit centre room had a trap door to the cellar.

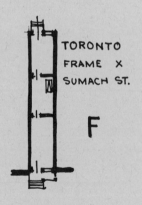

TORONTO
FRAME X
SUMACH ST.

F

Privies, water-closets and bathrooms

The earth privy was located in a concealed position at a reasonable distance from the house. Some were built in brick or masonry and had architectural elegance and rose arbours. When the house had a long tail of outbuildings, a privy was often incorporated in the wood-shed. Diagram A shows an impressive privy placed over a water cistern draining into a French drain. There is a panelled foyer. The privy itself has five holes, three for adults and two small ones with a foot step for children. A curious multiplicity of holes even over cisterns was common. Few householders braved the objectionableness of the medieval *garde-robe* on the bedroom floor, but at Horaceville in the house of Mr. Pinhey on the Ottawa River, there is a small second-storey one-hole necessary. It was flushed manually and had a flue in the thickness of the wall falling to a cistern with a French drain. This is shown in Diagram B. A remarkable two-storey privy exists in Rock Castle, Hamilton, as shown in Diagram C and illustrated on page 169. The upper floor is accessible by a bridge from a bedroom passage. It also has a flue.

The idea of piping water to a closet and so keeping a privy place sanitary is older than Upper Canada. In 1818 Sir John Soane inquired why water-closets were not asked for in the proposed Government House in York. But the early iron hoppers, primitively trapped and usually home-made, as well as the mechanically inefficient Brahmah patent water-closets were usually found objectionable inside a house. After 1875 patented water-closet design improved but the best water-closet that Andrew Jackson Downing could recommend in 1852 in his *Cottage Residences* he had taken from Loudon's *Encyclopaedia* of 1836, and this was

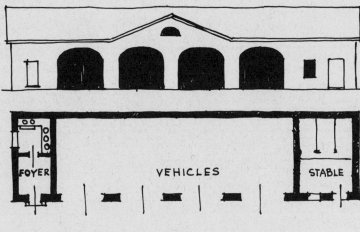

PRESCOTT ALPHAEUS JONES HOUSE
STONE 1835

presumably what Lord Sydenham found at Alwington when he became Governor. The only water-closets shown in a plan of Dundurn of the 1860's are two off a passage by the back door, but the Rideau Hall plans in the Archives, illustrated on page 102, show the existence of several.

Plans in handbooks begin to show bathrooms on bedroom floors after Thomas McKay supplied water to his house, Rideau Hall, with a hydraulic ram. It had two bathrooms, a laundry and two water-closets in 1838, all supplied with water. Houses began acquiring bathrooms in small bedrooms or off one end of the upstairs hall built earlier. The plan of Dundurn, mentioned above, shows two baths seven feet long, one installed in a bedroom, the other in a sitting-room. Loudon shows a bath sunk in the library floor. In 1865, Earnscliffe, Ottawa, had an "Ablution Room" with a bath in it in the basement. Colborne Lodge still contains a complete bathroom installed in the late 1850's and illustrated on page 93.

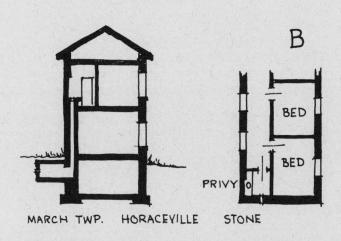

MARCH TWP. HORACEVILLE STONE

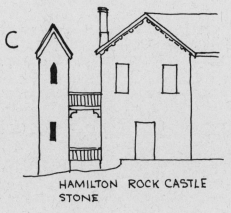

HAMILTON ROCK CASTLE
STONE

Door and window trim

IONIC ARCHITRAVE   DORIC ARCHITRAVE

1 — c.1805	2 — c.1810	
3 — c.1815	4 — c.1820	
5 — c.1820	6 — c.1822	
7 — c.1827	8 — c.1829	
9 — c.1830	10 — c.1830	
11 — c.1831	12 — c.1835	
13 — c.1836	14 — c.1838	
15 — c.1838	16 — c.1839	
17 — c.1840	18 — c.1844	

If the traveller, the historian or the antiquarian wishes to be able to date buildings or alterations with some degree of accuracy, the surest method is by understanding the evolution of the profiles of mouldings on trim around doors and windows and on mantels. As their evolution was quite regular, mouldings, properly interpreted, are often more certain sources for dates of buildings than registry offices or assessment rolls. Mouldings in trim derived at first from the Ionic architrave. Greek Doric architrave mouldings did not become popular until the late 1830's. The late eighteenth-century designer sought to achieve a sense of repose and of stability in his old-fashioned Georgian house. It was the proportion of the opening rather than its fancy trimming which appealed. The glazing bars were strong and heavy and the mouldings on trim blunt and severely Classical (1 and 2). Trim seldom exceeded five and a half inches in width. Classical mouldings were limited in number but the variations in their profile were limitless.

As the colony became established, the taste of the second generation of Loyalists favoured elegance. Trim in the fine white pine of the country became wider. Mouldings multiplied in number and decreased in size (3 and 4). Simple enrichments run by plane became popular. The British Colonist of the 1820's deplored such "Yankee pretensions" in the bush. The mitring of the corners of wide trim with small-scale moulding presented difficulties. To overcome these the boxed corner, seen in the door trim illustrated on page 54, was developed. Architrave trim, when run to a flat square, or box, at the corners of door and window openings, did not look well. Architrave trim, therefore, went out of fashion and flat trim with moulded centres came in (5 to 17). Infinite variety exists in this trim in Ontario. As the Loyalists' Neo-classic style progressed, the twiddles in trim and detail became excessive (8 and 9) and a reaction set in. Mouldings either became plainer again (14) or else used ancient Greek derivatives which were often rectangular in section (11 and 12). Some houses with late Neo-classic façades were trimmed in Greek internally, as in the MacMartin house, Perth (21), but some early Greek Revival houses kept on with the twiddles inside and made them heavier, as in the Bluestone House, Port Hope (15).

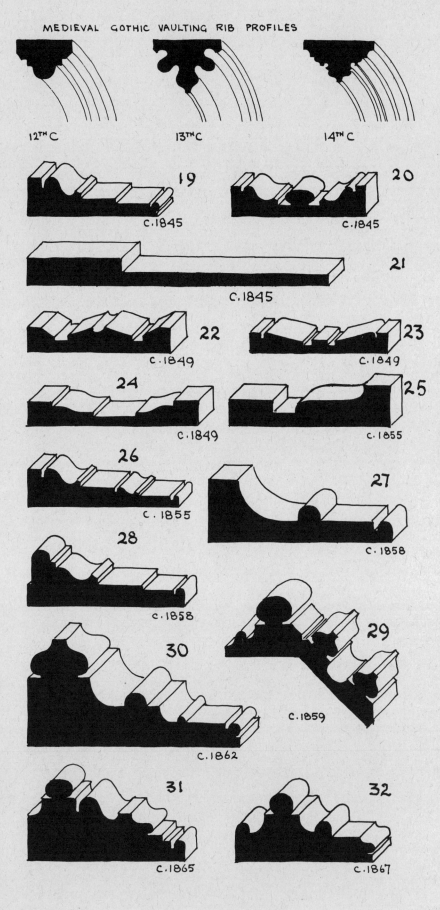

12TH C

13TH C

14TH C

19
C.1845

20
C.1845

21
C.1845

22
C.1849

23
C.1849

24
C.1849

25
C.1855

26
C.1855

27
C.1858

28
C.1858

29
C.1859

30
C.1862

31
C.1865

32
C.1867

The Regency designer was not interested in looking at windows. His interest was beyond the window. When possible, his windows were glazed doors. The Regency style developed no trim of its own but used Greek mouldings as at Dundurn, Hamilton, illustrated on page 101, or simpler profiles (13, 16 and 18) or profiles of larger detail, as at Rideau Hall (20). In Canada West Greek style detail was far more popular inside than outside the house. Greek trim was at first extremely severe (11, 12 and 22) and simple and very wide (21). Baseboards two feet high are not uncommon. The Greek Doric architrave became the inspiration of much trim. The parabolic profile in the capital of the Greek Doric Order, seen at the head of the page opposite, was adapted as a moulding profile (23). The books of Asher Benjamin offered numerous suggestions. The corner-box had no Greek or Classical antecedents, and was not used where the Greek style was fully favoured and Classical forms replaced the boxed corners.

As interest in the Picturesque began to influence taste, houses in the Gothic and the Italianate styles increased in number. Medieval Gothic was a rich mine of inspiration for mouldings. Created in the less sunny climates of western and northern Europe, the mouldings were bolder and fuller than Classical mouldings, and to achieve the required shadow lines, the undercutting was deeper. The profiles around the Gothic doors and windows of Canada West derived chiefly from the mouldings on the stone vaulting ribs built to support the stone ceilings of English churches of the twelfth to the fifteenth centuries. There were no "orders" of medieval architecture and the Canadian had full rein. The deep shadows on the trim were, however, inhibited by the dark green or chocolate-brown paint with which the trim was usually covered. Diagrams show the evolution of the medieval rib moulding and Canadian derivatives (29, 30, 31 and 32). The most obviously Gothic profile was composed of two reverse curves coming to a flat fillet (29 and 30). Many Gothic style houses designed by architects and most vernacular Gothic houses did not use bulky medieval mouldings. Their designers kept to Classical profiles for inspiration (24 and 26). The Italianate style used Classical profiles in its mouldings but they were full and round and the trim large (25, 26 and 28).

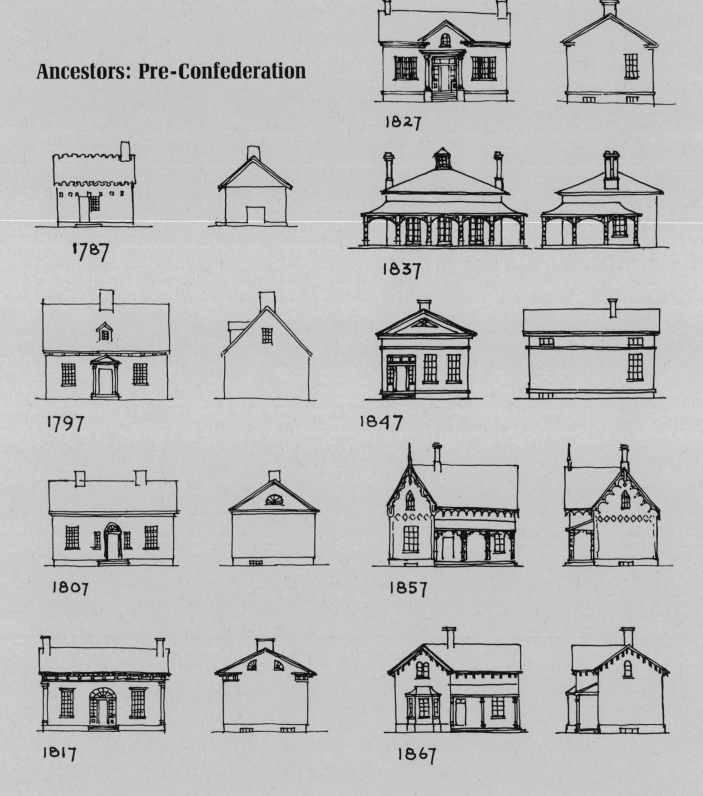

Ancestors: Pre-Confederation

1827

1787

1837

1797

1847

1807

1857

1817

1867

Ancestors: Post-Confederation

1917

1877

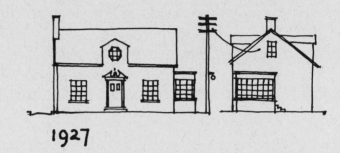

1927

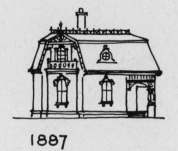
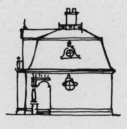

1887

1937

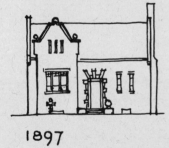
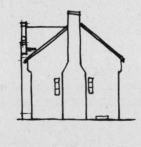

1897

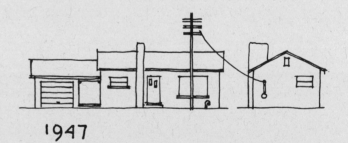

1947

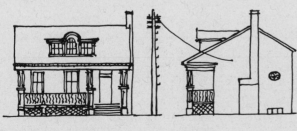

1907

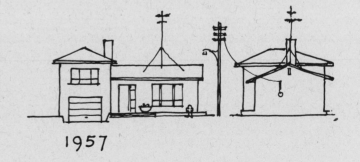

1957

Entrance doorways

WILDERNESS GEORGIAN

GRIMSBY 1789

STONEY CREEK 1792

LOYALIST NEO-CLASSIC

MOULINETTE 1821

NIAGARA ON THE LAKE 1820

REGENCY

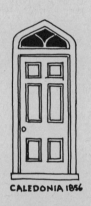

CALEDONIA 1856

SUTTON 1835

GREEK REVIVAL

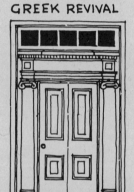

HAMILTON 1845

QUEENSTON 1840

GOTHIC REVIVAL

ST MARY'S 1840

COBOURG 1830

ITALIANATE

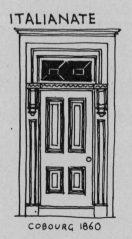

COBOURG 1860

TORONTO 1865

Glossary

ACANTHUS LEAVES: leaves of a common Mediterranean plant used in Classical ornament.

ACROTERION: Classical ornament at the peak of a gable.

ANTA: pilaster standing behind a free-standing column.

ANTHEMION, or PALMETTE: a honeysuckle or palm leaf ornament.

ASHLAR: squared stonework.

BASE COURSE: the lowest layer of masonry in a wall.

BATTEN: a vertical piece of wood covering a joint.

BEAD: a semi-circular moulding.

BELL-CAST ROOF: a curved roof profile flaring out at the bottom.

BLIND ARCADE: a line of arches projecting slightly from a solid wall.

BOLECTION MOULDING: a raised moulding of ogee profile around a panel or opening.

CAMBER: a flattened arch, usually segmental.

CAP (CHIMNEY): a protective top.

CHAMFER: a bevelled corner.

CORBEL: masonry built out from a wall to support weight.

CORONA: the greatest projection in a cornice designed primarily to throw off rain from a roof.

CROCKET: a decorative carved floral ornament applied to steep gables in Gothic architecture.

CUSP: a projecting point in Gothic window tracery.

DADO: the lower defined band on an interior wall.

DRIPSTONE, or LABEL: a moulded wall projection to throw off rain.

EARS: lateral projections of the trim around the top of a Classical opening.

FASCIA BOARD: a horizontal wooden board below the eaves, or one of the faces of an Ionic architrave.

FIELD: a raised centre of a door panel.

FINIAL: a pointed ornament at a peak.

FLASHING: metal used to prevent rain entering a building at a roof intersection.

FRET: a cut-out ornament of geometrical composition.

GABLE: the enclosing lines of a sloping roof.

GLAZING BARS: narrow pieces of wood, stone or metal which hold panes of glass in a door or window sash.

GOUGED MOULDING: moulding decorated with shallow ornaments made with a gouge.

GROUT: primitive concrete.

HUSK MOULDING: moulding decorated with a pattern of carved wheat husks.

KEYSTONE: the central stone of a masonry arch.

KING-POST: a vertical post supporting a tie beam in a roof.

LANCET ARCH: a sharply pointed Gothic arch.

LANTERN: an erection with glazed sides on top of a dome or roof.

LINTEL: the top supporting member of a door or window opening.

MEDALLION: a circular decorative panel.

MITRED MOULDING: moulding cut diagonally to form a right-angled joint.

MODILLION: a bracket which carries the upper member of a cornice.

MONITOR: see lantern.

MULLION: a vertical member dividing window lights.

NEWEL CAGE: balusters surrounding the terminal newel of a curved stair-rail.

OGEE: a line made up of a convex and a concave curve.

ORIEL WINDOW: a window which projects from the wall.

PEDIMENT: a triangular section of wall in a Classical gable.

PIER: a mass of supporting masonry.

PILASTER: a rectangular feature of pillar shape which projects slightly from the wall surface.

PLASTRON: an applied ornament not an integral part of the architectural composition.

PLINTH: the projecting base of a building or statue.

PODIA: piers supporting columns.

QUATREFOIL: a panel divided by cusps into four sections.

QUEEN-POST: one of two vertical posts which support a tie beam in a roof.

QUOIN: a projecting corner-stone at the angle of a building.

RAKING: inclined.

REEDING: convex raised ornament, the reverse of fluting.

REVEAL: the side of an opening cut through a wall.

SKIRTING BOARD: a board along the bottom of room walls.

SOFFIT: the underside of any architectural member.

SPLAY: the sloping surface of a wall opening.

STILE: a vertical section of framing.

STRING COURSE: a projecting course running horizontally on a building surface.

SWAG: a festoon of flowers, fruit or drapery.

TABLET FLOWER: a stylized flower of square, circular or polygonal shape used in Gothic architecture.

TORUS MOULDING: a large convex moulding.

TRABEATED: beamed.

TYMPANUM: a flat wall surface within either a pediment or an arch.

VOLUTE: a scroll or spiral.

WEATHER-BOARDS: boards arranged to overlap on an exterior surface.

WINDER: a tapered tread of a curving stair.

Index

Note: Italicized figures indicate pages on which the reference is found in the caption. Addresses are alphabeted according to the name of the street.